Political Life in Cairo's New Quarters

Political Life in Cairo's New Quarters

Encountering the Everyday State

Salwa Ismail

University of Minnesota Press | Minneapolis | London

Photographs in the book were taken by the author.

Published by the University of Minnesota Press
111 Third Avenue South, Suite 290
Minneapolis, MN 55401-2520
http://www.upress.umn.edu

Printed in the United States of America on acid-free paper

Library of Congress Cataloging-in-Publication Data
Ismail, Salwa.
    Political life in Cairo's new quarters : encountering the everyday state / Salwa Ismail.
        p. cm.
    Includes bibliographical references and index.
    ISBN-13: 978-0-8166-4911-2 (hardcover : alk. paper)
    ISBN-10: 0-8166-4911-1 (hardcover : alk. paper)
    ISBN-13: 978-0-8166-4912-9 (pbk. : alk. paper)
    ISBN-10: 0-8166-4912-X (pbk. : alk. paper)
    1. Cairo (Egypt)—Politics and government. 2. Political participation—Egypt—Cairo. 3. Islam and politics—Egypt—Cairo. 4. City planning—Political aspects—Egypt—Cairo. I. Title.
    JS7763.A2I76 2006
    306.20962′16—dc22   2006015464

The University of Minnesota is an equal-opportunity educator and employer.

12 11 10 09 08 07 06   10 9 8 7 6 5 4 3 2 1

Contents

Acknowledgments

THE FIELD RESEARCH for this book would not have been accomplished without the kindness and generosity of the residents of Bulaq al-Dakrur who admitted me into their everyday communities, letting me into their sociability circles, giving me a seat at the coffee shop, or just talking to me while they went about their daily work and activities—fixing a car or repairing an electrical fan. Through their narratives, they allowed me to grasp something of what goes on in their quotidian encounters with state agents and agencies. I have kept their identities anonymous by changing names in the text, and I hope that I have been faithful to the spirit of their narratives. I am particularly indebted to Manal, my main informant. She was tireless in helping me set up interviews and gain entry into many spaces—homes, workshops, and street corners—and her support and humor were invaluable.

During the different periods of my research in Egypt, many individuals provided me with material, ideas, and suggestions. I owe special thanks to Nadia Farah, Mahmoud Abd Al-Fadil, Alia al-Mahdi, Iman Bibars, Amal Abd al-Hady, Ahmad Seif, Hafez Abu Si'da, Baha' Taher, Gasser Abd al-Raziq, Huwwayda Adly, Wahid al-Dissouqi, Sarah BenNefissa, Agnes de Boulet, and Patrick Haenni. I am grateful to Imad Mubarak, who assisted me in pursuing some lines of inquiry and setting up interviews, and to Adel al-Itriby, who facilitated introductions and helped with data collection. Marwa Bayoumi, Dalia Bayoumi, Nadia Abd al-Hadi, and Muhammad Hakim were willing and wonderful interlocutors. As always, Mona Sharaf's friendship and advice were invaluable.

The help and support of a number of colleagues and friends in the United Kingdom is greatly appreciated. I thank Jim Piscatori, Nelida Fuccaro, Kamil Mahdi, Dario Castiglione, and Gabrielle vom Bruck. I also thank Marsha Pripstein Posusney and Jillian Schwedler, in the United States, for their encouragement. Through her inspiring friendship and her enchanted view of the world, Zuleikha Abu Risha made my travel and research much more enjoyable than it would otherwise have been.

I presented parts of this research at conferences, workshops, and seminar series. I thank Jennifer Olmsted and Tarik Yousef for inviting me to "The Social Contract in the Middle East," a workshop organized within the framework of the Mediterranean Meeting in 2001. I also thank the participants in that workshop for their comments. The members of the Middle East Studies Group in the United Kingdom were generous with their comments and feedback on two presentations I made in 2000 and 2002; in particular, I wish to acknowledge Sami Zubaida. I thank the participants in the MESA Thematic Conversations on Cairo in 1999 and 2000, especially Diane Singerman, who had the idea to hold the conversations and took the initiative to organize them. I benefited from the feedback I received from presentations at the CEDEJ in Cairo in 2000 and at CDAS, McGill University, 2003. For inviting me to the seminar series in 2003 at Edinburgh University, I thank Yasir Suleiman as well as the participants for their feedback and comments. I also appreciate Nezar AlSayyad's invitation to present at the CMES series at the University of California–Berkeley in 2003.

The progress of this work and my confidence in it were helped a great deal by Nezar AlSayyad. At a crucial moment in its development, his endorsement of my research provided much needed reassurance. As one of the two manuscript readers for the University of Minnesota Press, he provided thoughtful and critical comments for revisions. Paul Lubeck was also a manuscript reader, and he encouraged me to develop my thinking on the different sites of governmentality and on regimes of discipline. His advice, critical reading, and comments improved the manuscript significantly.

I should like to acknowledge the institutional help I received from the Centre d'études et de documentation économique, juridique et sociale (CEDEJ) in Cairo. I am particularly grateful for access to documentary resources and for the help of the library staff. The fieldwork and writing of the research were supported by a research grant from the Economic and Social Research Council (ESRC) of Great Britain (R000-22-2970) and by an ESRC research fellowship (RES-000-27-0007). I thank the four ESRC anonymous reviewers of an early research and fieldwork report for their comments and suggestions. My department at the University of Exeter provided additional travel support, for which I am grateful.

In preparing the maps, I benefited from the expert help of Paul Martin, which is well appreciated. I thank Carrie Mullen, former editor at the University of Minnesota Press, for her initial interest in the manuscript, and I thank my editor Jason Weidemann for his support and for the care he took to see the manuscript through the editing and publication processes.

I extend my sincere appreciation to my family for ongoing support throughout the years, especially to Nadia El-Maraghy and Gilan Allam, my mother and sister respectively.

My deepest gratitude, felt with wonderment and joy, is for Brian Aboud. His unbounded capacity to share has sustained me throughout this work and much else. I am grateful for his patient readings of numerous drafts and for his comments and suggestions.

A Note on Transliteration

I have used the system of transliteration for Arabic set by the *International Journal of Middle East Studies*, except for the diacritics. In reported speech I have used the "g" to transliterate the hard "g" sound particular to the Egyptian Arabic dialect. For example, the word *jara* (neighbor) in classical Arabic and in other local Arabic dialects appears as *gara* in reported speech segments in this text.

Glossary of Arabic Terms

'ashwa'iyyat	haphazard in conception and planning; a term referring to quarters and areas of the city not planned by the government
awlad al-balad	sons of the country; denotes cultural authenticity
baltaga	thuggery
baltagi	a thug (*baltagiyya*, plural)
bango	a kind of hashish
biytkabarluh	someone to whom one defers (colloquial)
dawla	state (as in "the Egyptian state")
futuwwa	tough, manly; invokes qualities of chivalry and bravery
hajj	honorific title and form of address; designates an individual who performed the pilgrimage to Mecca; also a sign of respect for the individual's devoutness
hajja	feminine noun of *hajj*
hara	alley; historically refers to a district of the city
hirafiyyin	tradesmen, craftsmen (*hirafi*, singular); used interchangeably with the colloquial *sanayy'iyya* (plural) and *sanayy'i* (singular)
hitta	colloquial for neighborhood, also meaning area
hukuma	government, rule
ibn al-balad	son of the country

isthtibah wa tahari literally, "suspicion and investigation"; involving the administration of certain police practices of stopping, questioning, investigating, and reporting on individuals

kibar al-mantiqa elders of the area or neighborhood

mahdar police report

majlis tahkim arbitration council (*majalis tahkim,* plural)

majlis 'urfi customary council (*majalis 'urfiyya,* plural)

mantiqa area (*manatiq,* plural)

multazim observant (of religious rules, for example)

muraba' square; refers to a set of contiguous streets

musalaha reconciliation

raqi prosperous and of high standard (*raqiyya,* feminine)

sha'bi popular; designates someone or something close to the people (*sha'biyya,* feminine)

shari'a conventionally refers to laws derived on the basis of Islamic jurisprudence and having the Quran and the Prophetic Tradition as authoritative foundation

sulh conciliation

sunni Muslim majority sect; used in everyday speech to designate an individual exhibiting devoutness and having an Islamist orientation

sunniyya belonging to the Sunni sect; followers of the Tradition (*Sunna*) of the Prophet; in everyday speech, designates groups with an Islamist orientation

tahajjud refers to engagement in prolonged night-prayers

tajir   merchant (*tujjar,* plural)

um   title used to address married women in
            popular city quarters and in villages, meaning
            "mother of" and usually, but not always,
            followed by name of eldest son

zakat   alms-giving, one of the five pillars of Islamic
            beliefs and practices; as a religious obligation,
            zakat is the subject of Islamic jurisprudence,
            which stipulates percentages and proportions
            owed in alms in relation to annual
            accumulation in capital, goods, or harvest

zakat al-mal   alms given in relation to annual capital savings

Introduction

Space, Politics, and the Everyday State in Cairo

THIS STUDY investigates everyday practices of government in Cairo's new popular quarters. Its research problem centers on the role of sociospatial variables in shaping quarter residents' relations with the state and with the wider urban setting. The motivating interest behind this inquiry emerged, in part, from my earlier work on Islamist activism, in which I came to see the Islamist movement as a protest movement that had a particular spatial grounding (Ismail 2000, 2003). Indeed, I found that in various urban settings of Cairo, support for the movement, as well as the movement's mobilization of activists, was anchored in the sociospatial organization of these settings. Hence, as a student of urban activism and politics, I was faced with the need to inquire into the sociospatial arrangements that undergird collective action and opposition.

The research questions posed in this work are formulated against the backdrop of the retreat of the state in the economic sphere and the emergence of spaces of societal autonomy that accompany the growth of informality in the labor market and in housing. Egypt's changing political economy, marked by a shift to neoliberalism, introduces new variables for understanding forms of governance as well as strategies of negotiating or opposing them. These variables must be brought to bear on any inquiry into social and political activism. In this context, it becomes imperative to take a closer look at the nature of exchanges and interactions between citizens and apparatuses, agencies, and agents of state power and control. In broad terms, this inquiry engages with the theoretical and empirical literature on the nature of government and the definition of the political. One of my main concerns is to draw out the terms through which the sociality of space gives shape to forms of governance in everyday life. In this Introduction, I outline the key analytical problems with which this inquiry deals.

Informality, Resistance, and the State

Cairo's new popular quarters emerged in the 1970s and have since then expanded in size and number as a result of citizens' communal efforts to acquire housing and create residential space. These quarters are commonly referred to as the *informal housing communities* due to the unregulated nature of their establishment. They constitute a distinctive element of the contemporary urban landscape by virtue of their physical organization and spatial relationship to the rest of the city. There are seventy-nine such communities in the Cairo area alone, their populations representing about one-third of the city's total inhabitants—approximately three million people.[1] To gain an understanding of the dynamics of state–society interactions as they pertain to the new urban quarters, the study explores everyday practices of government and the forms of social and political organization that have emerged in them. One of my central research questions is how the specific physical, social, economic, symbolic, and cultural characteristics of the new quarters influence the overall web of power relations between the residents and the state.

The study focuses on the case of Bulaq al-Dakrur, a new quarter located in the governorate of Giza, one of three governorates making up the Greater Cairo region. Bulaq is situated on the northwestern edge of Cairo and was originally an agricultural area on the city's urban fringe. It was converted into a residential area through the illegal construction of private housing, in a context of wider urban and sociopolitical change in Egypt. The case study approach allows for a detailed examination of the terms of the quarter's autonomy, its everyday forms of social and political organization, and its patterns of interaction with state authorities.

The process of unregulated urban expansion began on a large scale in Egypt in the 1970s and lasted through the 1980s and into the early 1990s. This was a context of decline in state provision of subsidized housing and of rising prices for real estate in planned areas of the city—prices that contractors and proprietors ratcheted up beyond the means of most citizens. Unregulated housing became the solution for millions in the Greater Cairo region, especially residents of Old Cairo, migrants from rural areas, and newly married couples who were all trying to meet a basic and essential need. Land invasion through squatting and the illegal subdivision of agricultural land into plots for construction were the means by which this need was met. Some of the early phases of construction took place after squatters had settled on public land, usually on Cairo's northeastern desert edge. Unplanned construction was also localized in the agricultural urban fringe where contractors parceled lots and sold them to families in search of shelter. During most of this period of increasing and expanding construction, the state ignored the phenomenon of "informal housing."

This neglect and the relative autonomy gained by the communities in their processes of implantation and establishment meant that most of them escaped state regulatory control in the areas of housing and urban planning. In the late 1980s and early 1990s, however, state indifference and tolerance of informal settlements was replaced by hostility, as a number of these areas became sites of Islamist oppositional activities and confrontation with the government. Hence, state authorities began to see these communities not only as an urban management challenge but also as a security threat. In dealing with the Islamists and with the informal housing communities, the state—in particular, its security apparatus and urban planning directorates—constructed the challenge in terms of an urban pathology. The communities and their residents were represented as problematic, marginal, unintegrated elements of the urban setting (Ismail 1996). A security approach was therefore deployed to deal with the problems presented by the informal communities.

This security approach should be situated in relation to the operation of neoliberal principles of governing the social. The shift to neoliberalism is particularly evident in the new popular quarters. For instance, they have seen a greater degree of labor market informalization than have older districts of the city. Indeed, Bulaq's labor force is predominantly in the informal sector with a significant percentage of economic activities located within the bounds of its territory. In addition, its share of public social services is comparatively low. For example, there is not a single public high school in Bulaq, yet its population numbers more than one-half million people. If we compare these conditions with those of Maadi or Zamalek, two affluent city quarters, we come to realize the enormity of the widening social gaps and the extent of entrenchment of social distinctions to which the marketization of education contributes. While residents of rich quarters enjoy the benefits of the liberalization of educational services, such as the opening of new private schools, masked and unmasked fees have been introduced into the public school system, negating the principle of education as a free and universal right.

In the new popular quarters, the lack of public investment in social service provision extends to health care as well. With the transition to a market economy, the residents of these quarters have had to rely on their own initiative to provide for basic services. Indeed, they have done just that in resorting to illegal construction to acquire shelter or in pooling resources to build and establish clinics, extend sewage lines, or set up tutoring classes in mosques and community development centers.

With the introduction of neoliberal policies, we also find that discussion of public issues has been framed in the language of neoclassical economics (Mitchell 2002). Economic health, for instance, is explained in reference to adjusted financial and monetary policies. Thus, the international financial organizations—the overseers of economic health—direct recipient-countries to rationalize their economies by cutting social spending and trimming state ownership. The guiding idea is "less state and more market." This approach evacuates the social from the economic equation, ignoring the question of the social costs of marketization and saying little about the ever-expanding range of private services and exchanges. Instead, individual responsibility, personal initiative, and entrepreneurship are promoted as the ultimate economic values and principles that should guide the newly fashioned selves tantalized and bedazzled by global consumerism. Neoliberal programs seek a destatization of government (relocation of programs of government from state institutions to nonstate sites). Toward this end, they deploy a variety of social technologies that act on the population and are detached from political government. Thus, we witness the entry and expansion of nongovernmental organizations (NGOs) and community organizations as new actors in this form of government. Linked to this is a process of individualization whereby the subject is constructed as a responsible and self-reliant member of a self-governing community, not a "social citizen in a common society" (Rose 1996, 56).

The movement away from welfarism along with the articulation of a neoliberal ethos of government shapes the patterns of relations between the state and the new popular quarters. The framing of the informal communities "problem" as something akin to a pathology or disease is a discursive construction that articulates with conventional ideas of urban planning and that supports state objectives of establishing social and spatial control. This perspective on the new quarters ignores the question of the bases of urban activism. Indeed, it is my contention that Islamism has found a home in these communities because their spatial, social, cultural, and economic characteristics have contributed to their emergence as spheres of dissidence (Ismail 2000). Islamist activism in these areas builds on existing social, economic, and cultural networks, which afford the residents varying degrees of autonomy from the state and serve as the foundations for collective urban action.

Official representations of the informal communities as carriers of a social disease are challenged by studies that focus on the survival strategies that members of the urban lower classes develop to meet their economic needs (Hoodfar 1997; Tekce, Oldham, and Shorter 1996). Also, recent research on the politics of everyday life, inspired by James Scott's work (1990), has drawn our attention to the various ways in which the "urban poor" have dealt with their socioeconomic circumstances. These studies argue that many of the strategies and tactics of low-income households are not merely coping mechanisms but forms of resistance against the state and the dominant classes that aim at a redistribution of goods and services (Singerman 1995). Further, these efforts serve to reshape social and political relations and are part of these groups' and individuals' action in creating new living conditions.[2]

As the state has withdrawn from its role as welfare provider and main employer, employment networks and mutual aid societies have risen in its place to deal with the people's social and economic needs. The impact of this substitution must be taken into account in studying the political positions of the residents of the new quarters in relation to the state. Recent scholarship and census data point to the association of informal housing with the informal economy (Kharoufi 1991; Tekce, Oldham, and Shorter 1996). An increasing number of the new quarters' residents are engaged in informal economic activities as shop owners, self-employed artisans, peddlers, and so on. The question that arises is whether economic disengagement leads to political disengagement and, ultimately, resistance.

This last question links with the wider problematic of how we define the political when dealing with informal communities that, by definition, exist outside the presumed formal boundaries of the state.

For some, the political is manifest in the shift from distance and invisibility to contact and confrontation vis-à-vis the state. In other words, those communities characterized by informality in their social, economic, and housing conditions become political when state intervention in their residents' lives threatens community gains and achievements (Bayat 1998, 14). It is my contention, however, that structures of collective action and contestation develop in the spaces of autonomy and in social networks that may be mobilized against the state even when no state intervention has taken place. Does it follow from this contention that all aspects of the everyday life of "the informal communities" are political? Can we draw clear distinctions between coping mechanisms that are not necessarily political and resistance strategies that are? While there is strong inclination to answer the first question in the negative and the second in the affirmative, it should be recalled that it is not possible to determine a priori which aspects of everyday life are political and which are not. Further, the distinctions between survival and contestation must be drawn in relation to the context of the practices under study. My argument here links up with Sherry Ortner's (1995, 175) proposition that we need not decide once and for all that a given act fits or does not fit into a box called resistance. Ortner raises doubts about arguments that the actors' intentions determine whether their acts constitute resistance. She points out that intentions evolve through practice. As such, the meanings ascribed to an act, rather than being fixed, are of a dynamic nature.

This said, I want to draw now on de Certeau's insights into practices and strategies of action pursued by the subjects of domination. For de Certeau (1984, 26), tricking the order of things is what characterizes popular tactics of resistance. Through the art of trickery, "popular" tactics turn the order of things to their own ends: "styles of action intervene in a field which regulates them at a first level . . . but they introduce into it a way of turning it to their advantage, that obeys other rules and constitutes something like a second level interwoven into the first" (ibid., 30). In other words, trickery or popular tactics insinuate a mode of using and, by extension, subverting the existing order to the needs and desires of the subordinates.

In de Certeau's conception of tactics we can locate the crux of the argument about everyday-life practices of resistance. De Certeau identifies resistance with subversion of the order of domination in a manner that serves the interests of subordinates. He does not view a reversal of the order as a condition necessary for an act of subversion to qualify as resistance. In critical reviews of research on everyday life, some scholars have argued that in working around the foundations of domination rather than shaking them, subordinates are merely engaging in survival strategies and are not challenging their domination.[3] Their acts, in such instances, would not qualify as resistance. Indeed, subordinates may be complicit in their own subordination. In response to this view, it may be argued that subversion entails chipping away at the edifice of domination. It is an incremental process of causing small cracks that would eventually bring down the structures of control. Without wishing to displace the issue of the distinction between survival and resistance, I want to suggest that what needs to be thought out is the potential of everyday-life practices to become infrastructures of action—foundations upon which resistance in the form of collective action can be built. Social movement theorists have long recognized this potential (see McCarthy 1996). They have also noted other conditions that are required to actualize the potential of these infrastructures. One such condition is the existence of social movement organization, serving to consecrate into an encompassing movement the microspaces of everyday action.

Another dimension of the argument about the limited potential for survival tactics to transform into resistance emerges in the discussion of the complicity and accommodation that such tactics involve. Timothy Mitchell's propositions on the "everyday metaphors of power" shed light on the issue of subordinates' implication in their own domination. The implication of subordinate subjects in the disguise and euphemizing of power relations necessary to maintain regimes of domination could not be simply explained away as belonging to the order of appearance or the public performance that hides the truth of resistance (a truth that can only be seen in the hidden performance behind the scenes as suggested by Scott). Mitchell (1990) rightly contends that the so-called obstacles and inhibitions to resistance are the effects of hegemonic practices, which may include the material/symbolic inducement of fear leading to inaction and perhaps paralysis.

I think it is imperative that in examining everyday-life practices in terms of the forms of resistance they represent, we also consider the nature of the edifice of domination, the structures of control and their hegemonic effects. Much of this edifice comes under what is conventionally referred to as *the state*, but, as will be elaborated in this Introduction and in the rest of the study, would be better viewed in terms of practices and rationalities of government. The concept of government defined by Michel Foucault as "the conduct of conduct" allows us to broaden our inquiry into power relations and forms of domination to include the governing of conduct in relation to a range of objects, from society or a population to the individual (conduct of the self). My calling on the ideas of government and governmentality—understood as the rationalities that guide practices of rule—came about as I reflected on the nature of practices of control undertaken in the name of the state and ascribed to it by differently situated subjects, in particular those on the margins of power. Needless to say *the state* remains a contentious concept in the study of politics and my use of the term refracts, at once, the fuzziness of the social sciences' attempts to grapple with the idea as well as the contradictory impulses, feelings, and understandings that mark the ordinary citizen's experience of the state. In the next section, I turn to some dimensions of the contentions surrounding conceptualizations of the state, and I present my case for the relevance of the concept of governmentality to the investigation of the everyday state in a non-Western context.

Projects of State: Governmentality and Control of Space

In examining definitions of the state, we realize that control of space is central to the operation of state power. In the Weberian definition, the state's ability to impose its laws over all its territory is part of what defines it as a state. Also, within this optic, the key defining feature of state—its monopoly over legitimate violence—is territorially grounded. It is in the territorial centralization of the state that Michael Mann (1986) locates the autonomy of state power. Of all forms of social power, he contends, only the power of the state is centralized and administered throughout a specific territory. In a critical reading of Mann's account of the problematic of state power, Mitchell Dean (1994) crystallizes some important issues regarding government in space. Dean (ibid., 146) points out that Mann's conceptualization of state power casts a revealing light on the mechanisms of rule. Mann sets despotic power, which is nonroutine and unpredictable, in opposition to the infrastructural power of the modern state. This latter form of power allows the state to infiltrate civil society and put into use capacities that frame the daily lives of the population. Such capacities include taxation, enforcement of laws, and collection of information.

This account is an advance on the idea of the state as a set of institutions and on analyses that are concerned in large measure with bureaucratic processes and policies that organize the relations between state and society in terms of externality. Thus, Mann's notion of the infrastructural power of the state brings into discussions and analyses of the state a concern with the techniques of power. However, there is a need for nuance and for recognition of what this notion leaves out, namely the question of the political nature of the techniques of power and control (Dean 1994, 147). In Foucault's (1991) concept of governmentality, we find that this question is addressed from the perspective of the practices and rationalities that compose rule and the exercise of governmental power (ibid., 153).

Foucault's concepts of government and governmentality rest on his explication of power. Power, as delineated by Foucault, is about the management of conduct, a way of acting on the conduct of one or more active subjects (Foucault 2003a, 138). Power, in this sense, is seen to undergird government in its multiple forms. These forms are socially diffuse, crossing over in some cases and in others annulling or reinforcing one another (ibid., 141). Power is dispersed and in a sense has no center. It is inscribed in social relations and operates by means of techniques and instruments that penetrate the social body. In analytical terms, the focus on microprocesses of power is designed to crystallize the dispersion and penetration of mechanisms of power into the nooks and crannies of the social body (Dean 1994, 156). At the same time, these mechanisms and techniques are deployed in a coordinated manner to produce macroarrangements of control (ibid., 157). Foucault acknowledges that in contemporary times, all forms of power must refer to the state. This corresponds to the idea of the governmentalization of the state—the investment of techniques of government in state institutions.

Foucault's genealogy of the rationalities of government is relevant to an analysis of the production and control of space. Along with time, space is seen by Foucault as a constitutive element of the techniques of power and the practices of governance (ibid., 172). Indeed, practices of power and rule work to manage human activities in time and space. Put differently, the exercise of power has temporal and spatial dimensions (ibid., 173). Through the various spatial forms of management and control, institutions, practices, and social relations are organized, and means and techniques of government and rule are deployed. The government of populations in space is a problem addressed by various projects of state Foucault discusses, namely the police and liberal projects. The particular approach to governing in space depends on the rationality of government at work.

In his genealogy of governmental rationality, Foucault contrasts the police project of government, dating to the seventeenth century, and the liberal project of government, whose origins lay in a critique of the police project. I think that paying attention to the concerns, conceptions, and techniques particular to these rationalities allows us to ask different types of questions regarding the nature of state power in both Western and non-Western contexts. Indeed, in exploring the assumptions about society and the individual that each of these rationalities embodies, we may arrive at cogent explanations of the techniques of power and control deployed in various forms of power. For this reason, I will dwell, in what follows, on the substance and on the underlying assumptions of these rationalities, and I will address their relevance to this study's purposes.

In the police project of government, society is thought of as the "meticulously subordinated cogs of a machine" achieved through the "permanent coercions" and training of bodies whose docility is the ultimate objective (Foucault 1995, 169). The police project was a detailed system of governmental regulation.[4] "'[P]olice' . . . embrac[ed] all the agencies and activities in a society that had as their aim the production and maintenance of good order in a territorial community" (Hindess 2000, 123). As Barry Hindess (ibid.) observes, government by police required two kinds of knowledge: a theoretical and applied science of disciplinary control over the conduct of the individual and detailed data about the population. Police administration related to hygiene, roads, morality, food supply, health, and more. It was concerned with extending government and acting on society, conducting the conduct of all. This sense of *police* should be understood as the practice of totalizing interventionist government and not merely as the institution of public security apparatus that the modern sense of "the police" evokes.

In contrast to police, the liberal project proceeds from the premise that society has norms that should be worked into government (Osborne 1996, 101; Burchell 1991). It also relies on a different type of knowledge—a theoretical knowledge of the population of the kind found in the social sciences. This knowledge relates to the practices of self-government that traverse society. The assumption here is that individuals are self-regulating and that this capacity for self-regulation is essential for rational government (Hindess, 2000). In other words, in the liberal project, government operates at a distance with the knowledge that it can rely on individuals to regulate themselves by, for instance, behaving in an "orderly fashion" or in a "civilized manner." The self-regulating domains of social life are harnessed to the objectives of state (ibid., 123–24). Owing to these different assumptions about society, the liberal project breaks with many of the methods of the police project of government, although, as Hindess (ibid.) points out, this is not an absolute or complete break. Key elements of continuity in the two projects are the ideas that governmental ends are immanent to the population of a state and that this population can be regarded as a self-contained unit that is also a self-contained society (ibid., 126). In a similar vein, Paul Brass (2000, 317) notes that in interrogating the *how* of government, Foucault wants to show that all modern states operate as police states in the older, pre-nineteenth-century sense of the term *police*. What this refers to is the penetration of technologies of government into all the nooks and crannies of society.

My excursus on Foucault's genealogy of governmentality confronts us with the question of relevance—in what way this genealogy of rationalities of government particular to the West can be relevant to non-Western contexts.[5] Hindess's (ibid., 122, 126) contention that the idea of society as a self-contained unit is a fiction (although perhaps, one may argue, a necessary one) suggests the terms through which we should be able to see the workings of disciplinary regimes, processes of population control, and practices of government as operative in spaces that cannot be delimited by the boundaries of the nation-state and its presumed corresponding society. If we consider the dispersal of practices of government from the standpoint of their travel and integration across space and time, the workings of Western rationalities in non-Western settings may appear as the result of borrowing, copying, or parodying on the part of non-Western states. Yet, something more is at work. As Hindess (2004) notes, the idea of the government of the state as immanent to a self-contained population has been exported to contexts where the Western, and particularly liberal, version of state is absent. In other words, the techniques of power and the practices of government that emerged in Europe were seen as adaptable and applicable to other territories and populations.

The point about adaptability and transferability is evident in the workings of colonialism: in setting up administrative structures and legal systems, in devising boundaries and the like to delimit populations and territories, and in formulating policies in relation to specific populations. It is also undeniable that many non-Western states have embarked on similar governmental projects and have, of their own volition, adopted these processes and practices in what has come to be termed *defensive modernization*. However, something else is at play in this dual process of export and volitional copying of technologies of power. The technologies of power have a global import and cannot be localized in the nation-state. They are also necessary for disciplinary regimes whose logic is global. A good example of this global character of technologies of power concerns the control of population movement. Regimes of entry control in Western and non-Western countries rely on a wide range of shared technologies, from the passport, to medical tests, to data banks containing personal information, travel histories, and the like.

The question that appears to follow from the preceding discussion of the relevance of Foucault's genealogy of governmentality is: What kind of political rationality guides the government of non-Western societies/populations, in particular those of the "global South"? On the face of it, the answer is simple. With the apparent absence in these countries of an assumption about individual liberty at the core of ideas and understandings of the individual and society, there could not be anything other than a police project that has as one of its objectives the breakdown of traditional forms of authority and regulation. Once again, however, the simplicity of this formulation provides many reasons for suspicion. Primary among these reasons is the invocation, implicit in the answer, of the tradition–modernity dichotomy. This dichotomy, it should be noted, is postulated by Foucault in his conceptualization of resistance, whereby he saw that opposition to technologies of power may emerge from traditional forms of authority. Notions of modern and traditional occlude the fact that there are no pure essences in the social world. So-called traditional practices can and do incorporate modern techniques of self, which are integral to bio-power practices of government. They may be harnessed to seemingly traditional concerns, but, ultimately, they are cultivated through modern techniques.[6] Indeed, Foucault's methodological notes on the analysis of power relations recognize that forms of institutionalization may mix "traditional conditions" with legal structures (Foucault 2003a, 141). In my examination of how power relations structure modes of organization in the quarter, I found that "traditional" sources of authority linked up with "modern" practices of government. For example, local figures of power and individuals in positions of influence derived their power, in part, from their visible links to state authorities, although the basis of their authority was constructed in relation to conventional norms of goodness (notables as being *men of good*). At the same time, their traditional role as community mediators and arbiters was co-opted by modern institutions for the purposes of "better" governance (notables as being "men of power").

In reflecting on Foucault's genealogy of disciplinary regimes in the context of historical practices of control in non-Western societies and specifically in Muslim settings, I find it difficult to draw a definite line separating the modern and the traditional. Many practices of government and techniques of self-regulation that were present in premodern times clearly arise out of what is taken today to be a modern logic of population control. For example, throughout much of Islamic history and across many Muslim societies, we know that the ruler made use of inspectors in the marketplace and in public space to oversee prices and the observance of the codes of morality. In some sense, we can say that these practices prefigure the modern techniques of surveillance, monitoring, and collection of information applied to the populations of states as a whole.[7]

My concern with governmentality in space emphasizes the importance of the spatial inscription of practices of control and also underlines the fact that the deployment of techniques of rule is spatially grounded. How does this concern figure in my account of the politics of the new popular quarters? In explicating this, it is important to note, first, the limitation of the view that sees the emergence of the quarters and their modes of organization as having been solely driven by or shaped by the restructuring of labor markets, speculative real estate, and class exclusion. Indeed, what this account leaves out is the inscription of governmentality in space, not through territorial control but through the control and regulation of sociospatial practices. As Foucault demonstrates, the liberal project of state counts on the governed to govern themselves in space—to conform to the exigencies of orderly conduct. In other words, the governed must conform to ideals of civilized movement such as keeping their places in queues and not blocking the flow of traffic. The subject's internalization of rules of conduct in space allows for government at a distance (Hindess 1997). This internalization is achieved through disciplinary practices and techniques, backed up by the discursive articulations about civilized order. The government of individual practices in space is continuous with the government of the state.

In the case of the new popular quarters, the state cannot exercise its control of space through the self-government of the governed. This is so because of its assumptions about the individuals and the society that inhabit these quarters and because the processes of the quarters' emergence precluded the spatial inscription of bio-power techniques.[8] This break in governmental practice (i.e., being unable to govern at a distance) must be mended through the enactment of the police project involving the monitoring and patrolling of streets along with a range of other strategies designed to allow for state infiltration into everyday-life spaces. To this end, state agents carry out their inspections of markets and food supplies, implement hygiene regulations, and engage in practices aimed at disciplining recalcitrant subjects. These power practices are not merely concerned with control of population but also with its welfare. It should be noted that even in a police project of state, a minimum of welfare provision is required to prevent the collapse or failure of the state.[9] Famines and uncontrolled epidemics are the hallmarks of failed states.

The state practices of power and control that I examine in reference to the new popular quarters extend a police project of state that originated in the early modern period, sometime around the middle of the nineteenth century. However, this extension of the police project into the present, in a manner of reenactment, corresponds to the contemporary security objectives of the state. These objectives, part of an overall politics of security, articulate with neoliberal principles of government. My argument here in some sense builds on Hindess's (2001; 2004, 28–29) proposition that the liberal project incorporates authoritarian practices in the governing of subject populations whose members are thought of as incapable of improving or governing themselves. It follows that we need to avoid adopting a deterministic, sequential, or linear view of state development, one that proceeds from the view that the liberal project of state and the police project are mutually exclusive. Rather, an articulation of the two projects may obtain. For example, a population of a given state may be categorized into groups that are capable of autonomous action and those that are not (ibid.). We may also find the market serving as the model for a range of social and economic relations while being sustained by authoritarian practices associated with the police project. I suggest that with a shift away from welfarism, those who govern perceive a greater need for the expansion of security politics.

The Everyday State and Practices of Government

In exploring the politics of everyday life in Bulaq al-Dakrur, I have focused my investigation at the microlevel of governmental practice. This entails an examination of spaces of encounter and actual instances of encounter between citizens and the state. I looked at quarter spaces such as the outdoor market and the street, where citizens and state would sometimes meet, and at government spaces, like offices of the municipal administration or of various local authorities, where citizen–state encounters also occur. In these encounters, citizens come face-to-face with representatives of state authority in charge of implementing a variety of policies relating to public order, hygiene, supply regulation, service provision, and the like. The analysis of these encounters allows us to grasp something of the everyday state that, in the Egyptian context, is to some extent encapsulated in the politics of discipline and security—the increased monitoring, surveillance, and disciplining practices of population control. Although this study was not conceived with the question of government and state at its core, the investigation and field research led me to address the question of the state in everyday life and, in the process, to reflect on the ethnographic study of the state (e.g., Gupta 1995; Taussig 1992; Navaro-Yashin 2002; Hansen and Steputtat 2001; Coronil 1997; Anagnost 1997; Joseph and Nugent 1994).

In both its approach and the questions it poses, the research follows on Akhil Gupta's (1995) proposition that the idea of the rational state, of the Weberian type, is not relevant or useful for understanding politics and governance in many settings. Significantly, this view resonates in recent work on the state in comparative politics. Joel Migdal's *State in Society* (2001) represents one of the more daring attempts in the field of comparative politics to transcend the impasse to which conceptions of the rational state have led. The work also highlights the tensions familiar to students of comparative politics who were taught to look for the state in formal structures and institutions of government. Migdal acknowledges that in theorizations and representations the state has been both elevated above society and separated from it (ibid., 17). In the process, it was invested with metaphysical qualities, "mythicized" in Foucault's terms. There is much to be commended in Migdal's propositions to bring the state down to earth. He suggests that we look in the trenches, the dispersed field offices, and the like to understand the workings of state in society. More importantly, in dialogue with Foucault, he suggests that we examine the practices that pit themselves against the mythicized images of the state, those that give the Godlike state a good battering. He alerts us to the importance of counterpractices and contradictory practices that destabilize the unitary construct of the state. In other words, we should pay attention not only to the practices that produce the image of the state as an all-powerful agent, but also to those that undermine this image. In this sense, I suggest that while certain rituals of state power bring citizens up to the state's majesty others bring them around to see its broken nature. As such, I analyze the citizens' encounters with the everyday state as rituals of power that bring the state down to the people and, in so doing, may occasion ridicule, contempt, and derision.

The fuzziness of the construct of the state and its elusive and slippery character have been discussed in some recent and insightful conceptual work on the state.[10] Michael Taussig's (1992) view that the state is the greatest fetish in contemporary society decries the reification produced in both state theory and practice. For Taussig, the Godlike, metaphysical entity of the state is a product of practices of government deployed by administrators, governors, army, and police. The Godlike state is also a projection of the imaginary of those on the margins of state power who are actively reifying it. In a similar vein, Timothy Mitchell (1991) proposes that this reification is a product of "the state as effect"—more precisely, the state as effect of structure. Does the state exist then? Navaro-Yashin (2002), drawing on Žižek (1989), calls it a fantasy that survives its own death. It is the Lacanian *objet petit a*—a fantasy, a fetish, a myth, an effect of structure. These various descriptors underscore the elusive character of the social sciences' construct of the state.[11] It is indeed elusive, appearing and disappearing like magic. Now you see it, now you don't. However, social scientists are not in the business of pulling rabbits out of hats. Or are they?

In raising these questions and concerns about the concept of the state, I am not proposing that we abandon it as an analytical category. Rather, my purpose is to echo the cautions that advise against using a term that contributes to myth making and reification. To this end, I suggest we need to look at the everyday state—that is, the practices of government and rule that are deployed at the microlevel of everyday life. This, in some sense, corresponds to Migdal's (2001) notion of "the state in the trenches" and to Derek Sayer's (1994) emphasis on "the materiality of everyday forms of state formation." Indeed, I propose in similar fashion that by looking at the quotidian practices of officials and agents of the state and at the ways in which citizens negotiate their relations to these representatives of the state, we get a sense of the concrete forms of government and control, a sense of what is done in the name of the state and what is experienced by individuals in relation to the state as effect, as fetish, as *objet petit a.*

The ethnographic data discussed in the forthcoming chapters allow us to see the contradictory impulses that guide citizens' relations with and views of government. On one hand, there is a sense that government is illegitimate, something that citizens can do without. As one of my informants put it, "Things were better when there was no government." Many of my informants ventured to say that there was no state *(mafish dawla),* but they also almost always added that they existed "in a state other than the state" *(ayshin fi dawla ghayr al-dawla).* The state in which the citizens of Bulaq existed was the one they constructed in comparing the state of affairs in their quarter with that in other quarters. "The state that is other than the state" is run by police officers, municipality agents, and figures of power. The analysis of their actions and activities serves to undermine the idea of the state as a unitary entity. Yet the citizens, as subjects of disciplinary power, recognize that there *is* government understood as a system of rule that is both pervasive and dominating. Through various accounts of their experiences in dealing with state agencies and their encounters with "the everyday state," citizens grapple with the elusive construct of the state. Looking at the strategies they deploy in their encounters with the state and at their representations of their experiences, we can, as Gupta suggests (1995, 393), come to understand how the state is constructed, at a specific historical moment, out of the practices and representations of government and its subjects.

This brings us to the question "What of society?" I realize that the order of questions appears to oppose two entities: *the state* on one side and *society* on the other. However, this conception of state and society as opposites is undermined when we shift the focus from state as an entity to state as sites of coordinated practices of government that are not exhausted in structures ascribed to it (Rose and Miller 1992). In other words, the governmentalization of the state is a long-term effect of the dispersal of techniques of rule and power and practices of government that cannot be said to reside in the state alone. Rather, these techniques and practices are inscriptions on the population that involve the work of nonstate actors as well. Where then does that leave politics and resistance? Chattergee (2004, 40–41) argues that political society emerges out of popular groups' maneuvers and negotiations with the interventionist social and political projects of government. That is, the efforts of the governed to convert projects of subjection into entitlements such as housing rights and access to social services are constitutive of political society. I think this formulation captures the paradox of claim making vis-à-vis the state: in seeking to gain entitlements, "the governed" become subjects of technologies of power that they may have escaped in their position of marginality. Therefore, we need to look closely at what goes on in this process of claim making and negotiation.

By the same token, the techniques of power and rule are not inscribed on pliant bodies or empty receptacles and hence could not be said to have uniform effects and results. Studies of the implementation of programs of government show that their existence, backed up as they may be by centers of power/knowledge, is not in itself a guarantee of their success.[12] In resisting processes of subjection, individuals and groups bring much to bear on these processes. For example, as members of communities, they bring their shared values, their social relations, and their own projects to bear on the projects of government. Furthermore, as noted previously, tactics of trickery and subversion are deployed in everyday-life practices to invert the purposes of the interventions introduced by those in power. At the same time, it is imperative that we do not map out the relations between rulers and ruled as dichotomous instances of domination and resistance. Rather, as demonstrated by Achille Mbembe (1992, 2001), the relationship between ruler and ruled encompasses much equivocation, improvisation, and bargaining. There is also predictability and indetermination (Mbembe 1992, 132). Conviviality and intimacy at times characterize the exchanges between rulers and ruled. Through practices of government, the state descends to the level of people's everyday lives. However, as Mbembe notes, it may take them to the heights of its *majesté* as spectators in the theater of violence, albeit not as neutral spectators.

It is here that the range of performances by the ruled may attest to complicity or to contempt. The ruled may laugh at and applaud the tragicomic expressions of power and its farcical and obscene manifestations. By thinking outside the box of dichotomies of domination and resistance, we may be able to reflect on their entanglement—the mutual ensnarement of rulers and ruled. As I try to discern the elements of intimacy, conviviality, and promiscuity in the relations between rulers and ruled, many examples of citizens' encounters with the everyday state come to mind. We see these elements in the episodes of encounter discussed in chapter 5 (for example, when citizens share their knowledge of the corrupt workings of local government for the purpose of getting water services or when they avoid police raids in the markets by organizing countermonitoring systems). In the next section of this Introduction, I turn to the question of the spatial grounding of practices of power and contestation and their mutual entanglement.

Space and Modes of Social Organization: Everyday-Life Practices of Government

An important analytical premise guiding this investigation is the idea that space is social. It is so in the sense of de Certeau's (1984) assertion that

> [a] space exists when one takes into consideration vectors of direction, velocities and time variables. . . . It is in a sense actuated by the ensemble of movements deployed within it. Space occurs as the effect produced by the operations that orient it, situate it, temporalize, and make it function in a polyvalent unity of conflictual programs or contractual proximities. (117)

De Certeau captures the sociality of space in terms of the likeness of space and discourse. Like discourse, space acquires its meaning and actualizes itself in practice. The relationship space has with place is like that of discourse with language. Place is the order of things without movement or action, similar to the unspoken words of the dictionary prior to their investment in speech and their articulation according not only to linguistic rules (which, in the order they provide, serve to confirm power relations) but also to the rules of discourse—rules that are first and foremost social. As de Certeau points out, the sociality of space means that "space is a practiced place."[13] Practices, action, and movement make space lived and, as such, social. Through practices, place is attributed meaning, is rendered social, and at the same time becomes inhabited by power relations. Also, in this sense, space is used to obscure power relations in the appearance of the neutrality of order and design (see Low and Laurence-Zuniga 2003; Mitchell 1989; Soja 1989; Keith and Pile 1993).[14] De Certeau's attention to individual practices in everyday life aims to show how users of space appropriate it in ways that contest spatial domination. Social movement theories and studies of urban collective action draw our attention to the spatial grounding of popular action. Tactics of mobilization and repertoires of protest entail reappropriation of space and contest over its uses.[15]

Control over space is a dynamic process embodying relations of power and resistance. Modes of social organization and social practices invested in space inform us of the forms and techniques of power that undergird state and societal modes of government and control. The question of spatial arrangements has been integral to the study of societal modes of achieving a level of autonomy from centralized political power. This is evident in the case of Cairo's old quarters. Historical and sociological studies have depicted these quarters as discrete entities usually composed of *hara*s (alley-based units) with clear physical boundaries (Abu-Lughod 1987; Raymond 1968). They are characterized by hierarchical street systems and markers signaling the transition from public space to semiprivate and private spaces (e.g., moving from the main street and public arteries into side streets that branch into alleyways with further smaller streets and ending in a cul-de-sac) (Abu-Lughod 1987; al-Messiri-Nadim 1979). Embedded in this hierarchy are social mechanisms of control governing gender relations, norms of neighborliness, and systems of exchange (Stauth

1991). The physical, cultural, economic, and moral arrangements at this level serve to demarcate the quarter from the outside world run by public authorities where social and cultural changes are managed by the central state (Abu-Lughod 1987).

Cairo's new popular quarters, on the other hand, appear to be lacking physical boundaries. However, certain conditions have allowed them to reproduce the physical autonomy of the old quarters of the city. These have to do with their semi-peripheral location on the outskirts of the city, as well as their ecological characteristics such as unpaved roads and a hilly environment, which render the spaces less accessible to outsiders (Ismail 1996). Thus, a first step in considering the question of autonomy is to apprehend the physical characteristics of the space itself—the degree of integration into the municipal road system, the street layout of the area, and the terms of division between public and private space.

The organization and control of space is intimately linked as much to the normative outlook of the community inhabiting it as to the legal regulations affecting the public and private spheres. A particular community's normative frame may be invested in the public space in a manner not necessarily sanctioned by public regulations but reflecting social relations of power and modes of control. In the old quarters, community mechanisms of social control are inscribed in the spatial organization, making it possible to monitor gender relations and to preserve a wide range of social practices. There are indications that the Islamists have tried to reenact these mechanisms within the new quarters of Cairo and in both old and new quarters in Algerian cities (Davis 1992; Ismail 2000, 2003; Slymovics 1995). The fundamental point that the investigation of these questions helps crystallize is that space is social. By this I mean that the physical and symbolic characteristics of a given space embody social relations that are ultimately relations of power. Space is also the site of practices in the everyday life. Practices are temporally and spatially marked; that is, they are governed by rules in which space and time considerations are essential to any normative assessment. In other words, temporal and spatial rules determine the appropriateness of conduct or practice. These rules are socially produced and subject to negotiation. An important dimension of the analysis, therefore, is to sketch out the normative framework that guides the residents' actions and activities and, in conjunction, to grasp the ways in which cultural norms are invested in both public and private spaces of the quarters.

This raises the issue of the ways in which the spatial organization of the new quarters diverge from that of the older ones and how these differences serve to sustain or undermine the normative outlook invested in space. In certain ways, the new spaces undermine the rules of morality in both public and private. For instance, the practice of sharing a single dwelling among more than one family makes it impossible to maintain gender segregation in private space due to the presence of men and women from different families. In the public spaces, male domination, without the benefit of arrangements and enforcers of the rules of propriety, have made it difficult to guard the modesty of women; women in public are subject not only to the male gaze but to antagonistic practices. In this instance, the adoption of the veil may be a strategy designed to shield women from such practices. Islamism, whether militant, moderate, or conservative, is only one of the forms of collective action aiming at the control of space and at the investment of space with a particular moral outlook. Other forms of collective and individual activities are yet to be examined.

The production and control of social space is one dimension of societal practices of government. This is particularly the case in relation to social rules aimed at the management of gender relations. As noted previously, with the ongoing urban transformations, it is no longer possible to maintain gender segregation in space by designating rooms within the house that are only for females or by limiting women's public presence and mobility. Techniques of enforcing moral rule in space include the monitoring and surveillance of gender mixing, of women's comings and goings, of women's attire, and of their conduct in public. Social devices such as gossip, exclusion, and threats of eviction are all used to ensure compliance with the moral code.

The management of gender relations in space emerges as an important arena of societal governance that interacts with state practices of government. In my examination of youth discourse on gender relations and interaction, I found that young Islamist and non-Islamist men held similar views about women's public presence. For instance, both objected to gender mixing and women's immodest dress. Yet, youth with an Islamist orientation, such as members of the Ansar al-Sunna al-Muhammadiyya or al-Tabligh wa al-Da'wa, or simply those who cultivate an Islamic lifestyle, were developing techniques of self and were fashioning themselves in conformity with an ideal Muslim self. As such, the young men refrained from "chatting idly with women," and some preached the veil to their female neighbors and reproached them for transgressions. These youths reconstructed the image of the ideal marriage partner and the code for selecting her: veiled, modest, and conforming to interdictions on gender mixing. Techniques of self developed through practices of humbling oneself before God (*tahajjud*, for instance) contribute to the production of self-disciplining and self-disciplined Muslims. Can we speak, then, of an Islamist governmentality or a regime of Islamist government that counters state practices? Perhaps, but the question should be posed in a way that leads us to inquire into the ways in which state practices of government interact with other practices of government found in the sphere of gender relations. My discussion of these issues in chapter 4 shows that state practices of government have a direct bearing on men and women's positioning from each other. In responding to abusive public authority and practices of discipline, women intervene as mediators with state authorities. This introduces a new dimension to power relations that invokes the idea of male honor and constructions of masculinity and that allows for the fluidity and instability in the codes of gender interaction to become evident. Young men's practices of self and their discourses on gender relations cannot be understood outside the sociopolitical context in which women have emerged as mediators with the state or without reference to the ongoing processes of renegotiating masculinity and femininity.

In the face of state practices of discipline, young men articulate an ethic of self that emphasizes self-dignity and is expressed in instances of refusal in the face of police tactics of intimidation (see chapters 4 and 5). Thus, we may concur with Foucault that resistance to disciplinary techniques may possibly be located in traditional relations or communal practices. In the case of the youths in Bulaq, we find an ethic of self that reworks existing discursive traditions and anchors opposition. At the same time, the social field is traversed by power relations that do not obey a single logic or principle. Thus, in asserting their masculinity in the face of disciplinary practices, young men may also be reproducing terms of masculine domination.[16]

Both societal practices of government and self-disciplining practices shape positioning vis-à-vis state practices of rule and government. In looking at the experience of militant Islamists in new

popular quarters in the 1980s and early 1990s, we find that their engagement in societal practices of government entered into their constitution as oppositional forces enjoying a degree of popular support.
In this respect, one question that has emerged in relation to the study
of the rise of Islamist movements concerns the nature of their spatial
implantation and the terms defining their activism. The Islamists'
ability to invest themselves in spaces of the new quarters was determined by a number of sociospatial factors.[17] Many of the Islamist
practices were inscribed in the communities' modes of social organization and practices of government. For example, Islamist activists
were engaged in arbitration practices. In Imbaba Sheikh Gaber, the
leader of the al-Jama'a al-Islamiyya, settled disputes within families
and between neighbors. Al-Jama'a activists operated through a network of mosques that served as sites of charitable activities, mobilization, and education. The al-Jama'a's insertion into Imbaba was
facilitated by the social and political positioning of the residents of
the quarters. As many of their social and economic activities were informal, the residents' position vis-à-vis the state was potentially confrontational. For instance, informal markets were the sites of conflicts
with the police authorities whenever they attempted to impose the
state's rules of law and order in space. This positioning brought about
a merger of sorts between al-Jama'a activists and some of the residents. In confrontations with the police involving the vendors, the al-
Jama'a intervened. Likewise, when the police pursued al-Jama'a
members, vendors and residents supported them.

The militant Islamists' modes of action were inscribed in micro-
practices of the everyday life in popular neighborhoods, in particular
in societal practices of government. For example, Islamists monitored
gender interaction and women's comings and goings and, on the
whole, oversaw that public morality codes were observed. They undertook action to warn violators and at times instituted penalties on
whatever conduct they deemed to be a serious violation. In many of
their interventions, the practices of al-Jama'a members reworked historical modes of action of old popular quarters. As such, their interventions in neighborhood brawls, their monitoring of social mores,
and their engagement in social welfare activities recall the roles associated with actors of the *futuwwa-baltagi* type (see El-Messiri 1977). The
militants' success in mobilizing popular support during confronta-

tions with the state owed much to their ability to ground their ideological practices in the social antagonisms that are part of the urban landscape (Ismail 2000).

In drawing a composite picture of the new popular quarters, I have highlighted certain sociospatial characteristics that have contributed to their emergence as spheres of dissidence (Ismail 1996, 2000). The new quarters can be characterized as having achieved a level of disengagement from the state in areas such as employment, welfare assistance, and services provision. Further, they occupy oppositional positionings associated with rights to land title, the legality of construction, and access to public services. In this context, marked by dynamics of disengagement and contention, the research questions that guide the study are as follows:

1. What is the impact of sociospatial arrangements on the patterns of interaction among the residents of the quarter and between them and the wider society?

2. What forms of social and political organization develop in the everyday life of new popular quarters? In particular, what forms of social and political organization have emerged and developed in the quarters to deal with issues of governance and to address residents' concerns and needs?

3. How and to what extent do the forms of internal governance and the material conditions of the space allow for the development of alternative forms of political organization? Do these alternative forms constitute modes of resistance and opposition to domination and the exercise of authoritarian governmental power?

4. What are the techniques and practices of government deployed by state authorities to effect control of the lived space in the new popular quarters? How do quarter residents negotiate, challenge, and/or comply with these techniques and practices?

These points of interrogation zero in on the relations between everyday forms of governance and the apparatuses of power and rule. At issue is the extent to which these forms provide a degree of autonomy in the management of quarter affairs and the extent to which they imbricate the quarter residents in practices of power and domination involving state structures and agents. Further, the questions proceed from the premise that practices of government are multiple and do not reside in the state alone. However, as noted previously, these state and nonstate practices may overlap with, annul, or reinforce each other. The actual configuration of practices of government within the quarter and their interrelations are the subjects of the chapters that follow.

Chapter 1 locates Bulaq al-Dakrur in the Cairo urban setting. In this chapter, I argue that the production of the new popular areas in public discourse as *'ashwa'iyyat* (haphazard communities) is part of a dominant system of representation that coheres with the Egyptian state's security objectives of discipline and control. In contrast, the representation of space as *lived* allows us to see it as it becomes practiced and invested with meanings by those who inhabit it. To get a sense of the spatial location of Bulaq as a new popular quarter, I outline its location in macro and micro terms, describing the physical layout of the quarter and its relationship to the rest of the city. I also situate the emergence of the quarter in relation to historical modes of sociospatial organization, in particular the evolution of the *hara* (alley) as an important component of the urban form. My analysis of Bulaq spaces sketches the inhabitants' sense of their quarter spaces, and their articulation of an identity that derives from their experience of these spaces. The analysis highlights the notions of "inside" and "outside" as they structure discursive practices relating to lived space. In its final section, the chapter situates the rise of the new popular quarters in the context of the withdrawal of welfarist arrangements in favor of neoliberal government. The discussion traces the contours of the ongoing process of reconfiguring Cairo, a process that is guided by neoliberal principles.

Chapter 2 addresses the following interrelated questions: (1) What forms of internal governance have been developed by the residents of popular quarters to deal with collective needs such as security and the preservation of morality? (2) How do social hierarchies shape residents' relations with each other and with the state? (3) Are the local forms of governance autonomous with respect to state institutions? The inquiry into spheres of sociability and modalities of interaction among the residents shows the existence of forms of organization that deal with everyday-life concerns and provide the basis for internal governance. Through informal gatherings of elders and customary councils, the residents have furnished their communities with structures of internal governance that are designed to deal with conflicts and disputes without resorting to state authorities, in particular the police and the courts. Further, social hierarchies of power emerge as a factor shaping a wide set of relations, including relations with the everyday state. Through locally developed institutions, figures of authority known as someone *biytkabarluh* (to whom one defers) have risen to positions of mediators among the residents and between them and the government. The analysis underscores the constitution of mediators as a class of "lesser notables." It raises salient questions on the politics of the lesser notables: their political agency and the modalities of their engagement in practices of government. My investigation of state strategies of co-optation and infiltration into societal spaces is undertaken in comparison with the Islamist experience of activism in Imbaba, where parallel everyday forms of organization served as infrastructures of action. In conjunction with my inquiry into processes of co-optation and infiltration, I take a closer look at the workings of government at the local level. This reveals the blurred boundaries between state and society. Here, the examination of episodes from the life of local government helps to demonstrate the shifting sites of government and the informality of its mode of operation. The chapter concludes that political government in the new popular quarters takes the forms of mediation, but not representation.

In chapter 3, I argue that with the movement away from a welfarist rationality to a neoliberal rationality of government, the notion of the social contract can no longer provide an explanatory frame for understanding state–society relations in Egypt. Before outlining the terms of the shift to neoliberalism, I provide a background overview of the welfarist rationality of government and its links to the system of rule, especially to a corporatist style of political government. I then trace the contours of the emergence of a neoliberal rationality in governing the social. This form of government is actualized through a number of moves, including the relocation of public welfare to the private sector, in NGOs and other civil associations. The chapter investigates the existence and operation in Bulaq al-Dakrur of an expansive network of charity, run primarily by religious organizations such as al-Gam'iyya al-Shar'iyya and al-Gam'iyya al-Khayriyya. I survey the workings of these organizations in the area of poverty relief and social welfare and point to the techniques of discipline they inscribe, in particular the inscription of the category of "the deserving poor" as the targeted subjects of charity. I also discuss the grounding of the move to private welfare in a discourse of philanthropy that mixes two registers: religious conservatism and Western philanthropic traditions. Finally, I examine the relocation of welfare to the "private sector" as a process that articulates with a wide range of technologies of discipline such as those involved in the engendering of the entrepreneurial, self-sufficient, and self-providing subject as the ideal citizen. To illustrate my argument, I discuss the programs of microcredit promoted by foreign aid organizations through local NGOs as a case study of the production of new subjectivities.

Chapter 4 examines the interplay between young men's interaction with the state, their constructions of masculinities, and gender relations. Underlying this line of inquiry is the view that gender is a social category that mediates interaction between citizens and the state, especially between young men and the state. The chapter explores the role of fraternities in the shaping of masculine identity and young men's social engagement and political activism. Fraternal relations reinforce a spatial identity that is quarter based and linked to a lifestyle and a particular set of social norms. Against this background we can comprehend the constructions of masculinity, gender relations, and interaction with the state. My examination of young men's encounters with the everyday state shows how these encounters disrupt the dominant masculine construct while also instituting young men in oppositional positions to the state. This disruption helps explain the ongoing process of renegotiating gender relations in the family and in public. Thus the positions that young men adopt in their everyday encounters with the state—defiance, challenge, and refusal—may be understood, in part, as expressions of particular social constructions of gender and as particular enactments of masculinity. I argue that by virtue of their class position and their experience of subordination, young men locate themselves in the power hierarchy through constructions of masculinity that not only express their marginalized position but seek to reproduce hegemonic masculinity. These constructions are contextually shaped and take the expression of "injured masculinities" that youths negotiate through acts designed to reproduce their dominance at home and in their circumscribed public space. These constructs of masculine selves are also negotiated through narratives of leveling that aim to achieve vindication of their injured manhood. Meanwhile, the spectacle of injured masculinities combines with ongoing changes in gender relations in the family and in public to open up a space for women to question hegemonic masculinities. The disruption in gender relations and the experience of injured masculinities also, inevitably, shape young men's meditations on relations with the state. The terms in which they incorporate this experience may be read as ranging from submission to rebellion.

Chapter 5 outlines the workings of the security state, paying particular attention to the politics of discipline and control. The chapter identifies an intensification of encounters between the residents of popular quarters and the everyday state in the spheres of control, surveillance, and discipline. The analysis focuses on the sites and dynamics of interaction with the state authorities over such matters as the use of public space, building and construction codes, misuse of public utilities, and disorderly conduct in public. Accounts of these encounters can be characterized as narratives of oppression and resistance in which images of government are conveyed and positions vis-à-vis the state are articulated. The chapter traces the reinvention of "thuggery" *(baltaga)* in public discourse and the adoption, in 1998, of the law on thuggery as part of the ongoing expansion of the politics of security. It points out that these discursive developments underwrite official violence targeting young men. Also, they are integral to the construction of the new popular quarters as *'ashwa'iyyat* that thus should be subject to policies of order and discipline. Finally, the chapter examines practices of policing. In particular, attention is paid to the workings of procedures of "suspicion and investigation" *(isthtibah wa tahari)* and the construction of "suspect" subjects. Various police authorities are deployed in the quarter for the purposes of monitoring and regulating activities in a range of areas, from public morality to juvenile delinquency. Based on police and court documents, interview data gathered, and personal field observations, I present the growing evidence that the politics of security has come increasingly to structure interaction between the state and quarter residents.

The Postscript reflects on citizens' relations with state authorities. It begins with a brief overview of the politics of contention that have marked citizens' expressions of dissatisfaction with government. Looking at a range of contentious actions that have taken place over the past decade, I assess the terms in which opposition to government is expressed and try to draw insights into the potential for transformative action. In conclusion, I take a recent incident in the life of the Egyptian state—the confrontation that took place between the Interior Ministry and drug lords in Upper Egypt in February 2004—to reflect on the ways in which the state exists for the people and the ways in which it does not.

Chapter 1

Reconfiguring Cairo: New Popular Quarters between the Local and the Global

IN THE AFTERMATH of the 1992 confrontation between the state and the al-Jama'a al-Islamiyya activists in Imbaba, the term *'ashwa'iyyat* gained prominence in public discourse.[1] The term, literally meaning "haphazard," was used to refer to varied urban forms thought to have escaped state control and regulation. It designated entire quarters of the city as well as markets and areas with concentrations of huts and kiosks. In public discourse, *'ashwa'iyyat* identified what went wrong with the city, evoking motifs of social deviance, crime, and the like. Unplanned by the state, the *'ashwa'iyyat* came to be viewed as problematic places and as sites of potential unrest. Proposed solutions ranged from demolition and removal, to integration into the existing urban infrastructure. The monolithic, undifferentiated view of informality and informal sectors, including housing, obscures the fact that the development of the new urban popular quarters was a result of citizens' initiative. In appropriating space and living it, whole segments of the population engaged in creating an alternative set of living conditions and a new urban environment that in some ways reproduced, but also modified, older forms of sociospatial organization. In this respect, neither the category of "informal housing" nor the descriptor *'ashwa'iyyat* capture the specificity of space and how it is lived and experienced. Indeed, not only does the label *haphazard* privilege, in an overgeneralized way, conditions of marginalization and uprootedness, but it also fails to take into account how opportunities and constraints of urban living are actively negotiated. In problematizing the construct of *'ashwa'iyyat* and adopting a different optic on the new popular quarters, I draw on Henri Lefebvre's

1

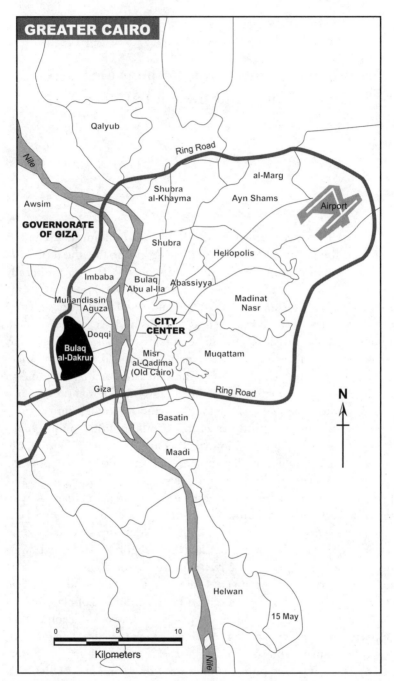

Map 1. Map of Greater Cairo.

distinction between "representation of space" (the conceived) and "spaces of representation" (the lived). The official discourse of 'ash-wa'iyyat can be better scrutinized when situated within the wider cognitive representation of space found in the discourse of urban planners and state authorities. Against this representation of Bulaq space, and spaces like it, we should consider the new popular quarters as lived space—lived through the experience of their inhabitants. For Lefebvre (2001) "space is directly lived through its associated images and symbols, and hence the space of 'inhabitants' and 'users', . . . who *describe* and aspire to do no more than describe. This is the dominated—and hence passively experienced—space which the imagination seeks to change and appropriate" (italics in the original) (p. 39).

In approaching Bulaq space as a space represented by its inhabitants, I hope to explore how the new urban spaces are lived. I also propose that these lived spaces represent Cairo's new popular quarters. Rather than being haphazard, the new quarters demonstrate a utilitarian approach to space, using forms of spatial organization that reproduce and modify historical urban forms. As quarters, they are not external to the city but of it. Their history is interwoven with the history of Cairo, its urban growth, the planning and housing policies that have been put into effect since the 1950s and the latest reconfiguration of Cairo as a global city. In reference to these factors, the new popular quarters are a development of the modern city, the global city. They are part of historical Cairo, not only because a significant portion of their populations come from older sections of the city, but also because the city's history is shared. Its memory is claimed even in difference.

To apprehend the specificity of space in Bulaq al-Dakrur, I begin by locating the quarter, in physical and symbolic terms, within the Greater Cairo urban setting. In the first instance, I inquire into the quarter's relations to the rest of the city, considering contiguity, separation, transport, and spatial mobility. I also analyze the terms of integration and forms of interaction between Bulaq residents and the wider urban setting. At the symbolic level, I draw out the image of Bulaq and the rest of the city as depicted in interviews and other narratives, such as the media discourse on unregulated housing. This portrays the divisions within the city, the crisscrossing worlds that coexist in Cairo, and the process of othering that these narratives effectuate. Bulaq's rise as a new popular quarter cannot be separated from macroeconomic and political developments, in particular the growing informalization of the labor force and the ongoing reconfiguration of the city. Bulaq's location in a reconfigured Cairo is shaped by state urban planning policies and the desires of metropolitan elites to fashion an urban environment that is in tune with globalized lifestyles.

'Ashwa'iyyat in the Representation of Space

Government and media discourse projects a negative representation of Bulaq space and spaces like it. This projection arises in relation to a wider system of representation in which the conceptualization of urban planning projects is based on modern visions of order, progress, and civilization. The same system that relegated the old city to the past because of its narrow, winding alleys and hierarchical street arrangement is now reproduced with modifications, but with the same effect and objectives of control. In the modern representation of space, the valorization of the grid format is associated with making space more visible through wide boulevards. A guiding principle here is that there should be no secrets or mysteries. Everything should be public, unambiguous, and wide open for inspection. Within this frame of representation, the 'ashwa'iyyat are produced as the city's internal other. They are the sites of crime, drugs, illness, degradation, immorality, decay, and decline.[2]

In the discourse of 'ashwa'iyyat, we find echoes of some of the tenets articulated in the exercises of spatial ordering that took place in Cairo in the second half of the nineteenth century. During this period of constructing the modern city, order and discipline were the key objectives of urban planning and were consonant with modern aesthetics. In the words of one planner responsible for the remake of Cairo, "[t]he transformation of the city of Cairo from an aesthetic point of view [required] the opening up of main streets and new arteries . . . the surfacing of roads, the construction of drains, and regular cleaning and watering" (quoted in Mitchell 1989, 65). As Mitchell notes,

> [t]he disorder and narrowness of the streets that open boulevards eliminated were considered a principal cause of physical disease and of crime, just as the indiscipline and lack of schooling among their inhabitants was the principal cause of the country's backwardness. (65, 67)

The spatial ordering of Cairo was guided by policing imperatives as well as the needs of capital accumulation. Once again, we find historical parallels between the earlier phase of reordering Cairo and the current one. Following the 1992 confrontation with the Islamists, the policing imperatives became paramount in the government's approach to the "unplanned" quarters. The discipline and control objectives took on the sudden urgency noted by Mitchell (1989) in reference to the earlier phase of reordering:

> The 'disorder' of Cairo and other cities had suddenly become visible. The urban space in which Egyptians moved had become a political matter, material to be 'organised' by the construction of great thoroughfares radiating out from the geographical and political centre. At the same moment Egyptians themselves, as they moved through this space, became similarly material, their minds and bodies thought to need discipline and training. The space, the minds, and the bodies all materialised at the same moment, in a common economy of order and discipline. (68)

I think it is safe to argue that contemporary Cairo and its inhabitants are going through a new phase of ordering in which the "economy of order and discipline" is being put into effect. This reordering and disciplining can be found in policies that aim at the control of public space. We have only to look at the systematic removal of markets to the outskirts of the city or to the new planned cities and at the establishment of walled markets and plazas enclosed for the purpose of better surveillance. Artisans and their workshops have also been targets, as evidenced by the setting up of new artisanal quarters in places that are out of the way and out of sight, such as the Dewiqa district of Manshiyyat Nasser or the Fifteenth-of-May district of Helwan in the south of Cairo. Vendors, craftsmen, and residents in the informal sector use metaphors of exile, banishment, and entombment to describe their condition of subjection to formalization and ordering. Against the systematic dislocation that the ordering strategies bring about, we should consider these spaces from the point of view of their inhabitants.

The Location of Bulaq: Spatial Practices and Representation

The location and patterns of development of the new popular quarters are shaped by a number of factors. Primary among these are the exigencies of the real estate markets, which express trends of residential mobility determined by people's economic means and by policies of urban planning and housing. The configuration of these factors

contributed to the emergence of Cairo's eastern, western, and northern fringes as new settlements for low-income households. Two main
types of settlement were actualized through popular initiatives of urbanization: squatting on state-owned desert land in the eastern and
northern periphery of Cairo and construction on agricultural land in
the west of the city, mainly in the Giza governorate.[3] These new settlements in time developed into full-fledged urban neighborhoods with
marked patterns of territorialization as well as a sense of locality. In
this section, I focus on the particularities of sociospatial arrangements
that define Bulaq al-Dakrur's position in the city and on some of the
spatial practices that shape everyday life in the quarters. In subsequent
chapters, I will explore in greater depth the sociospatial practices that
are constitutive of power relations in the quarter and that are at work
in modes of community organization and state–citizen relations. My
present purpose is to provide a broad description of the spatial characteristics of Bulaq.

The spatial arrangements in Bulaq should be analyzed on two levels. First, there is Bulaq's location within the macro urban setting—
that is, its geographical position within the urban agglomeration, its
position in relation to other quarters of the city (particularly those it
borders), and the terms of its integration into the overall urban infrastructure of services and utilities provision. Second, there is the micro
level of spatial organization within the neighborhood. Micro-spaces of
the quarter, in particular the *hara* (alleyway), structure the everyday
life of the inhabitants and provide terms of reference for the construction of territorially based identities.

The Quarter in Relationship to the City

Bulaq is located in the northern part of the Giza governorate, one of
three governorates making up the Greater Cairo metropolitan region.
Immediately adjacent, along its eastern border, are the upper-middle-
class suburbs of Doqqi and, to the north, Muhandissin. Bulaq's core
area, known as Bulaq al-Qadima (Old Bulaq), traces its beginnings to
the 1930s. Old Bulaq is delimited by Hamfirst Street on the north,
Tir'at Zanayn Street on the south, Tir'at al-Zumor Street on the east,
and Street Ten on the west. Today, only one plot of land is still undeveloped in Old Bulaq: the Basili Garden on Tir'at Zanayn Street. The
area surrounding Old Bulaq is known as Bulaq Central and includes
the subdistricts of Nahya to the north and Zanayn to the south, both

of which have been built up substantially with little vacant space remaining. In recent years, construction in Nahya's northwestern zone has been advancing into the Six of October subdistrict.[4]

Bulaq was built on agricultural land. Until the early 1950s, when the first phase of modern urban construction began, there were fewer than one hundred farm dwellings in what today is the old section of Bulaq. Migrants from Upper Egypt and residents of older sections of Cairo were attracted to the area because it offered cheaper housing. The Upper Egypt railroad, which transits through Bulaq, contributed to the arrival and settlement of rural migrants. The earliest of the migrant settlers came to work in the nearby factories and industries, in particular in the Coca-Cola plant, in a cigarette manufacturing firm, and on the railroad. Meanwhile, residents of old quarters of Cairo, such as Bulaq Abu al-'Ila, Bab al-Shi'riyya, and Al-Azhar, moved to Bulaq al-Dakrur when their old homes collapsed or became too small for their growing families.

Between the 1950s and 1970s, residential and commercial construction progressed gradually. It was in the 1970s, however, that the transformation of agricultural land into residential real estate began in earnest. It is important to note that earlier construction was "illegal," and even in later phases, a good deal of construction transgressed some public regulation. Long-time landowners and new proprietors began subdividing the land and selling small plots to newcomers. Proprietors also built small homes that they sold or rented.[5] Most of this construction was unauthorized and was not integrated into the public amenities system (water, electricity, and sewage). In time, proprietors and tenants engaged in a process of regularization and of obtaining services. In the newer areas of Bulaq, the residents themselves connected their homes to the main sewage lines. Yet, in 2002, some areas, such as the Six of October subdistrict, were still not integrated into the public sewage system. In addition, water and electricity remain unevenly supplied to homes in various subdistricts of Bulaq.[6]

In terms of physical location and distance to the city center, Bulaq al-Dakrur is not peripheral to the city. Yet certain spatial and social characteristics of the quarter, as well as their symbolic investment, produce the effects of separation and division. Physically, the railroad tracks separate Bulaq from the neighboring communities of Doqqi and Muhandissin. An additional element of separation is al-Zumor canal, which runs parallel to the tracks and constitutes the eastern border of Bulaq. Recently, the Giza governorate formalized and further accentuated this separation through the erection of a high fence on

Map 2. Map of Bulaq al-Dakrur Central (after CAPMAS, Map of Bulaq al-Dakrur).

the Bulaq side of the tracks (here and there, on the far side of the tracks, a wall-type barrier demarcates the western limits of Doqqi). Thus, crossing by foot to Doqqi from Bulaq requires that one traverse a fairly wide boundary zone (approximately fifty meters) intersected lengthwise by the irrigation/drainage canal, a fence, and two or three sets of railway tracks. During the period of my fieldwork, there were, in fact, three bridge crossings for pedestrian traffic between the central part of Bulaq and Doqqi. One was a wooden footbridge, called *al-Kubri al-Khashab*, which traversed the al-Zumor canal at the southern end of central Bulaq close to where the canal meets Tir'at Zanayn Street. Pedestrians who used this bridge to exit Bulaq (or to enter) were still required to cross the tracks at their own discretion. This meant watching for passing trains or, if the train was stopped at the station, making one's way around it; waiting for it to move on; or, if pressed for time, boarding a train car on one side and exiting on the other.[7]

In addition to the footbridge, two overpass pedestrian bridges spanned the canal and railway tracks and linked Tir'at al-Zumor Street in Bulaq to Sudan Street in Doqqi. One was located at the intersection of Nahya and Tir'at al-Zumor Street, at the northern end of central Bulaq, and one was located to the south of this intersection, near Hamfirst Street. Using any of these crossings, especially the wooden footbridge, was made difficult by the congestion of microbuses positioned at exit/entry points and by the presence of vendors and their stalls along the bridge spans and at access points. Two-way pedestrian traffic on the overpass bridges makes passage rather tight—a virtual squeeze-in at times. Also, the climb up the access stairs can be arduous for elderly people or anyone with a leg or knee ailment. However, for many, the crossing is a necessity. Buses to destinations throughout Cairo can be caught on Sudan Street in Doqqi. A new metro (subway) station is also located there. The difficulties that pedestrians encounter in leaving Bulaq are viewed as approximating conditions of internment. Aggrieved citizens expressed the view that the government might as well close the main entry points and declare the internment of the entire area (*al-Anba' al-Dawliya*, 24 April 2000).[8]

The elements of physical separation render Bulaq semi-closed to the rest of the city.[9] Indeed, taxi drivers are reluctant to accept fares into Bulaq because of its traffic congestion, unpaved roads, and unfamiliar street layout. The fence, the railroad tracks, and the canal are barriers that residents must negotiate on a daily basis in pursuit of

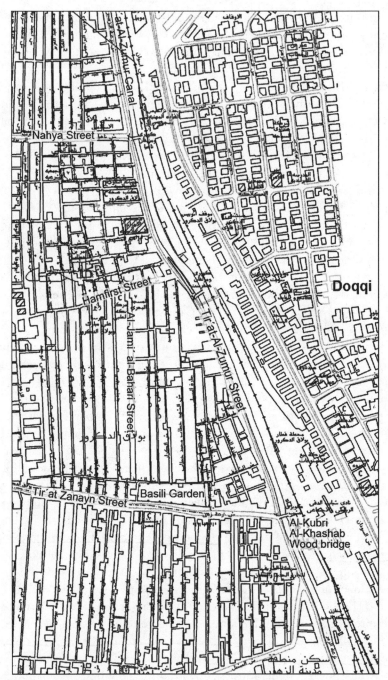

Map 3. Map of boundary zone and crossings (extract based on CAPMAS, Map of Bulaq al-Dakrur).

Figure 1. Bulaq residents returning home on a quiet Sunday afternoon, crossing the tracks that separate their quarter from Doqqi).

their living. These same barriers make it unlikely that residents of the neighboring communities would venture or stumble into Bulaq while walking or taking a leisurely stroll. In fact, from the outside, Bulaq is visible only to the occupants of high rises on Sudan Street in Doqqi. Their view of the quarter may be an unhappy reminder of the reasons for the devaluation of their privately owned condominiums.

Spatial and physical markers serving to contrast Bulaq from its immediate neighboring communities enhance the quarter residents' sense of separation from the city. Street layout and environmental conditions bear clear distinguishing markers. The rising heaps of refuse accumulating in and along the al-Zumor canal imprint the space as unattended to and neglected, particularly if compared with Doqqi and Muhandissin. Indeed, many of my informants pointed to the condition of the canal as a sign of state neglect.[10]

Street layout represents another marker of distinction. Unlike its well-off neighboring quarters, which boast paved streets and wide boulevards, most Bulaq streets are narrow, winding, and unpaved alleyways. The quarter has one paved boulevard, Nahya, and five semi-paved main streets. These main streets represent the commercial centers of the quarter and furnish the residents with much of their daily shopping needs. Along two of the main streets, Tir'at Zanayn and Tir'at al-Zumor, are found informal fruit and vegetable markets, while shops and kiosks line two others: Ten and Hamfirst Streets. Hamfirst Street is very dense with businesses, in particular textile and ready-made clothes outlets and shops selling household wares. The fifth, relatively wide commercial street is that of al-Gam'iyya, which is occupied by a variety of enterprises, including furniture shops, eateries, coffee shops, and auto repair shops. Routes in the interior of the quarter are usually not more than three meters in width. Among the few exceptions is Al-'Ashra or Street Ten, named for its width. Beyond the interior, connecting Bulaq to the contiguous new quarter of Faysal, is the similarly named Street Twenty. The main streets benefit from a small number of electrical light poles. The alleys have no electricity poles, however, and are lit by the light bulbs of front entranceways to private homes.

The Hara *as Lived Space*

The everyday life of Bulaq residents is organized around the micro spaces of the quarter. The most important spatial unit is the *hara*, or alleyway. Rules and regulations relating to a wide range of social relations and practices are inscribed in the spaces of the *hara*. Modes of sociability, conceptions of the public and private, and rules of propriety governing gender interaction are determined in relation to the spatiality of the *hara*. Before proceeding to consider the *hara* as lived space, it is worth recalling something of its historical meaning and evolution over time. In her groundbreaking study of the *hara* in modern Cairo, Nawal Al-Messiri Nadim (1979) notes the multiple denotations of the term as well as its historical inscriptions. She points out that the precise meaning of *hara* can only be grasped in the various sociohistorical contexts of its development and usage. In the medieval period, the *hara* referred to a quarter or division of the city. Until the early modern period, Cairo had a number of clearly defined *hara-s*. They numbered between ten and fifteen in the twelfth century and increased to thirty-six in the fifteenth century and to fifty-three in the nineteenth century (Al-Messiri Nadim 1979, 48). Historically, the *hara* represented an administrative unit inhabited by homogenous groups that shared common occupational and ethnic characteristics (ibid.;

Raymond 1968). In terms of social background, the residents of the *hara* included both rich and poor families. However, by the eighteenth century, aristocratic quarters were distinguishable from poor areas (Abu-Lughod 1969).

During the Ottoman period, the *hara* came to constitute a political unit as well as a social and administrative one. It was organized along residential lines and along professional and religious lines. Thus, professional communities, constituted on the basis of craft membership, were juxtaposed to residential neighborhoods. As it was a political unit, someone would serve as the *hara* head, appointed by and responsible to the city governor. Also, the *hara-s'* political character arose from the fact that they were identified with gangs of youth, known as *futuwwa*, whose potential for political action was actualized at periods of unrest (Raymond 1968). Spatial characteristics—in particular the hierarchical street system, with a main branch (*darb*) from which small alleys (*'atfa*) and dead-end alleys (*zuqaq*) branch off—helped render the *hara* a discreet unit. This hierarchical street system allowed for the maintenance of social autonomy and the enforcement of rules regarding gender relations (Abu-Lughod 1987; Ismail 2000, 370). André Raymond (1994) argues that the forms of organization found in the nineteenth-century *hara* make it possible to consider and represent Cairo as a city administered by the communities inhabiting it. Raymond's observation, it can be argued, holds true today if we consider that many of the needs and concerns of *hara* residents are managed internally and entail eschewing state authorities. Indeed, this is lent further support if we examine how in the 1980s and early 90s, Islamists succeeded in implanting themselves in new popular quarters like Ayn Shams and Imbaba. By investing themselves in quarter spaces and appropriating existing governing institutions and practices, militant Islamists were able to draw on the mobilizational and oppositional potential of everyday forms of social organization. However, as the next chapter demonstrates, inasmuch as everyday forms of social organization can provide the infrastructures of oppositional action, they may also be harnessed to the purposes of the government of the state.

Although today *hara* designates a smaller unit—the alley—it continues to represent a defined social space with rules that regulate the social life of its inhabitants. In common usage, *hara* continues to be associated with old, historical sections of the city, such as Sayyida Zaynab

and Bab al-Shi'riyya. However, it has also come to be associated with
new popular quarters like Bulaq al-Dakrur. In the public discourse inflected with the signs of modernity, _hara_ has acquired pejorative connotations of being a relic of traditional street planning and a site of
unruliness. The image of the _hara_ has been transformed from that of
the repository of authenticity to a place of social deviance. For example, it is common to invoke the idea of "being brought up in a _hara_" to
convey a sense of bad upbringing (Al-Messiri Nadim 1979).

In Bulaq al-Dakrur, _hara_ refers to an alleyway between two and three
meters in width and running, potentially, for some distance of a section
of the quarter. For example, al-Jami' al-Bahari Street (actually an alley)
in Old Bulaq extends from Tir'at Zanayn Street in the south to Hamfirst
Street in the north, intersecting with a number of east-west alleyways
and running through most of the Old Bulaq section of Bulaq al-Dakrur.

The average-sized _hara_ has between fifty and sixty residential buildings on each side. In older sections of Bulaq, buildings are between two
and three stories high, while in newer sections they are between four
and six stories. The alleyway is both residential and commercial. Located within it are grocery stores, various kinds of workshops, clothing
retailers, coffee shops, food kiosks, and repair shops (for automobiles,
appliances, and so on). In addition, peddlers display their goods in the
front entrances of their homes. At the same time, the alleyway is a space
of sociability. Residents, particularly women, children, and young men,
spend a great deal of time in the alleyway, congregating at entranceways
to homes, next to shops, and at various junction points. The proximity
of the homes and the sharing of _hara_ space bring neighboring households into close contact with each other. By virtue of this closeness, the
lives of _hara_ residents become, in a sense, intermeshed. Residents share
a great deal of information about their lives with each other. When I sat
with the women at the front entrance of one of their homes, they chat-
ted about everyday happenings as well as personal matters.

The spatial organization of the _hara_ and the modes of everyday sociability characterizing the lived space give rise to particular understandings and experiences of privacy and the boundaries between the
public and the private. Adjacent homes share common walls and connecting roofs while upper-floor balconies overlook homes on the op-
posite side of the very narrow streets. Such proximity means that a
certain degree of privacy is not possible to maintain. This was captured
in the words of Layla who stated: "Our laundry is out on the line and
there is nothing hidden. We carry our burdens, and the people of the

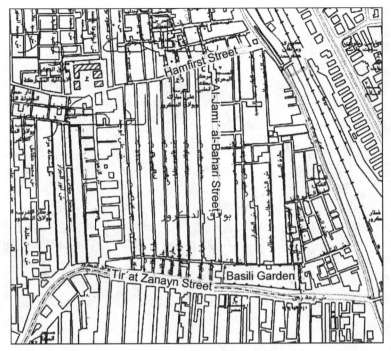

Map 4. Map of Hara (extract based on CAPMAS, Map of Bulaq al-Dakrur).

area know how we live." This conveys the sense that the lives of *hara* residents are lived on the outside. Another resident put it this way: ". . . the homes are inside each other" (*al-biyut guwah ba'daha*). In the newer sections of Bulaq, residents hang curtains on the outer frames of balconies to secure the privacy of the dwelling, in the sense of providing a cover from neighboring eyes. All the same, the spatial proximity and the modes of sociability contribute to the visibility of individual conduct and its coming under public scrutiny. — *MALTA!*

Layla's comment should not be interpreted to mean that the residents of the *hara* cannot enjoy any privacy or that there is a complete lack of private space. Rather, she, like other residents, is articulating a particular sense of private space. The meanings of privacy articulated by my female informants were, to some extent, situational and their concern for public scrutiny had spatial underpinnings. In certain narratives, private space was symbolized by being able to close one's door so that others could not know about one's private life. Private, in one narrative, was thought of in terms of economic conditions: being of

Figure 2. A *hara* in Bulaq. The dynamics of the private and public are played out: peddling merchandise displayed in front of homes, curtains hanging over upper-floor balconies.

limited means but not exposed to the pity of others. This was how Um Mustafa, a migrant from Qalyub, articulated her sense of privacy. She felt that urban living, as opposed to rural, allowed her privacy. Um Mustafa's experience of privacy is associated with covering up need or poverty. For her, attaining this sense of privacy was possible in Bulaq, but not in her village of origin where she would come under the scrutinizing eyes of her extended kin. For example, when she was pregnant and about to deliver, she was visiting her village. She was relieved that she managed to return to Bulaq to deliver her baby. This saved her the embarrassment of not being able to conform to the sociability conventions of serving *mughat* drinks to her guests or having chicken to eat. Shielding her poverty from exposure to the gaze of others was her privacy. Yet this same experience brought exposure and public embarrassment nonetheless. Um Mustafa delivered her baby in the Bulaq al-Dakrur hospital but had to sneak out with the help of a nurse because she could not pay the twenty-pound fee. As she recounted this episode, Um Mustafa's eyes filled with tears. This account brought back the feeling of humiliation that the public exposure of one's poverty can produce.

In Um Mustafa's narrative, privacy is achieved by being able to live
behind closed doors. In contrast, this sense of privacy did not appear
paramount or, at least, its importance was downplayed by Layla when
she said "our laundry is out on the lines." Layla is convinced that she
and her neighbors know about each other's intimate lives. While this
may be a source of embarrassment for Um Mustafa, Layla considers it
a fact of their sociospatial living arrangements. She deals with the exposure by viewing it as a common experience and, hence, as something about which one should not worry. Yet, Layla is anxious to keep
some things private. When she approached me to help her find domestic employment in Zamalek or Muhandissin, she stressed that I
should not mention her request to any of her neighbors. She was
aware that this information could be used to stigmatize her and, more
importantly, her children. In the case of Layla and many other women,
privacy is sought outside the neighborhood, when taking a job in another quarter, for instance. Um Hasan similarly has opted to peddle
her wares in outside markets to avoid the gaze of her neighbors. She
explained that her choice is a means of dealing with the negative image of women peddlers held by the neighbors. The social construction
of women's work—entailing a stigmatization of certain types of employment such as peddling and domestic work—places constraints on
women's work options. While this type of stigmatization is not particular to Bulaq, when outside the quarter, Layla and Um Hasan feel less
constrained by the public gaze. In defying social codes of gendered
subjectivities, Layla and Um Hasan distinguish between different public gazes: the gaze of neighbors and relatives and the gaze of strangers.
They seek to avoid the former but, in doing so, invite the latter.

The normative constraints experienced by working women like
Layla and Um Hasan indicate that the *hara* continues to operate as a
social unit. This is confirmed by the fact that the residents themselves
are engaged in maintaining rules of propriety relating to gender relations and the conduct of women (as will be elaborated further in this
chapter and in my discussion of the governance of morality in chapter
2). Further, the residents' appropriation of quarter spaces is structured
by social relations of power within the *hara* and the quarter. It is also
structured by interaction with state authorities (elaborated in chapter
5). A fuller account of Bulaq as a social unit can only emerge when we
turn to an examination of power relations in subsequent chapters. In
what follows, I examine how the rules of the *hara*, and modes of living

Figure 3. Bustling commercial space: shoppers at the east entrance to Hamfirst Street. Signs advertise meat prices, and the banner promotes a newly opened day-care center.

in it, also enter into how the residents perceive life in the quarter as a whole and how they construct quarter relations with the rest of the city.

The Quarter and the City: Inside-Outside Constructions of Bulaq

Separation and contrast in relation to the rest of the city are recurrent themes in the residents' discourses, articulating a sense of difference and emphasizing divisions within the city. The railway tracks, and the experience of crossing them, are evoked by the residents to signal this separation. As one resident put it, "Here, the train line separates two worlds." This view is also expressed in the phrase *hina 'alam wa hinak 'alam tani:* "Here is one world [referring to Bulaq] and there is another [referring to the outside]." How the residents construct these two worlds, however, is not given to simple dichotomies of good and bad, beautiful and ugly. Rather, the residents articulate an elaborate discourse on norms, social relations, and the good life. What emerges in the narratives about quarter relations with the outside are images depicting modes of life and forms of social organization in various spaces. The residents' sense of the space is shaped by the public gaze and the subjectivities this gaze projects into their lived spaces. As will be discussed here, my informants invoked the terms in which they were viewed by others and they were conscious of their stigmatization in public discourse. At the same time, they cast a critical eye on other quarters and city spaces and on their modes of living.

In articulating their sense of lived space, residents organize their representations around inside–outside distinctions. These distinctions relate to neighborhood relations, to public morality, and to contrasting images of various city spaces. The units of reference most often alluded to when discussing relations with the rest of the city were the *hitta* (neighborhood), the *mantiqa* (area), and *hay* (quarter). The *hitta* is used to refer to the immediate neighborhood, encompassing one's *hara*, neighboring *hara*, and the nearest thoroughfares. *Mantiqa* and *hay* are often used interchangeably to refer to a wider area, to a subdistrict, or to the quarter as a whole, depending on the point of contrast. It is in comparison with other quarters of the city that Bulaq is constructed as a locality that embodies terms of reference and identification for the residents.

In distinguishing between their lived space and other quarters of the city—in particular, the spaces of the well-off—many stressed the relations of solidarity found in their neighborhood in contrast to the lack of concern for others that they perceive to be characteristic of the attitudes of residents in the city's more prosperous areas, such as Muhandissin, Zamalek, and Garden City. Solidarity is thought to be evidenced at times of illness, death, or need. Dunya, a young woman of eighteen studying in industrial school, articulated these themes in her descriptions of the quarter. "Here, if I fall ill," she affirmed, "I will find a lot of people around [for support and comfort]. There, in Garden City, I will not find a neighbor to be kind to me (*hinak mish halaqi gara ti 'tif 'alayya*). Mona would do everything she could [referring to her friend and next-door neighbor]." For Dunya, in areas like Muhandissin and Garden City, the neighbors do not know each other. This view was shared by many of the residents I interviewed. It was also expressed by activists I interviewed in Imbaba, another new popular quarter. According to Hasan, a worker in a local development association there, anonymity and the aloofness of neighbors were problems in the richer areas of the city. "There," he said, "someone would die, and no one would know until the corpse begins to smell."

The distinctions drawn between Bulaq and other city spaces extend to the sphere of individual morality, particularly in reference to sexuality and gender relations. In comparative terms, when evaluating conduct and mechanisms of sexual control, young men in Bulaq thought that their neighborhood conformed better to the moral code. For instance, in Rida's view, women in Muhandissin and Garden City came home late at night and no one in their families objected. Also, the neighbors in those areas tolerated such transgression. In Bulaq, however, such conduct would result in intervention on the part of the neighbors. From the standpoint of young women, this attempt among men to exercise control over women was one of the drawbacks of the area. For Dunya, the tendency to gossip about a girl who came home late was one of the faults of the quarter ('ayb fi al-mantiqa). The norms governing women's conduct are worked into perceptions of the city spaces. For Ahlam, a seventeen-year-old student, the difference in rules regarding gender interaction serves to distinguish Bulaq from Faysal, a developing adjacent district. "There, talking to men is normal ('adi), but here, people think in old ways. They think that when a girl stands with a boy, it is wrong and shameful ('ayb). Here, there is fear. Girls are repressed and do not have sufficient freedom (mafish huriyya kafiyya)."

Schemes of representation of the city and the quarter, as reflected in residents' discourse, are organized around spatially inscribed social practices and lifestyles. These, in turn, are shaped by values and norms, economic means, and individual aspirations. For Raga', a twenty-nine-year-old house cleaner, Bulaq is confining, tight, and limiting:

> Here, [neighbors] are too close. They ask where you are going. All is too tight together (Kuluh laziq fi ba'duh). There is boredom and extreme repression (kabt fadhi'). In other areas, below, people live freely (nas 'aysha bihuriyya). They can afford to go out. Going out requires expenses, clothes. Below, they are able to satisfy this. Financially, they are comfortable. If there is a chance, I will leave Bulaq. I would go somewhere else and get a new start on the right basis—not too much interaction [with neighbors] so there would be no intervention.

Raga's comments and her desire to move out of Bulaq emerge out of the intersection of a multitude of factors: the material difficulties of the lived space and the normative and symbolic constraints that the code of gendered social mores imposes on women. The governance of morality that brings the intervention of others into the lives of neighbors and family members creates the sort of Panoptican discussed by Michael Peletz (2002, 234–36) in reference to Malaysia. The gaze experienced here is not that of Big Brother, but that of "intimate and not so intimate Others" (ibid., 234). It is the kind of gaze under which one's every move or act is assiduously scrutinized and evaluated by others in terms of conformity with or transgression against the moral code.

In the social representation of the city, the distinction of urban space into *sha'bi* and *raqi* constitutes a symbolic referential system for apprehending urban divisions and constructing spatially based identities (Labib and Battain 1991). Within this system, the character of Bulaq as a popular area (*mantiqa sha'biyya*) emerges as the subject of tensions and disagreements among the residents. On the one hand, Bulaq is characterized as *sha'bi* (popular) when compared to "high-living" or "posh" areas (*manatiq raqiyya*) such as Muhandissin, Garden City, and Zamalek. However, in comparison with old popular quarters of the city, such as Sayyida Zaynab, al-Hussayn, and Bulaq Abu al-'Ila, Bulaq al-Dakrur does not appear as *sha'bi*. The old places are viewed as authentic and as having roots (*mi'asala*). Bulaq, meanwhile, is a new quarter whose population originates from a diversity of places, including villages, other cities, and old quarters of Cairo, and therefore lacks common roots. For the local councilman and other residents in the area, particularly figures of authority, the population lacks cohesion because of its dispersed origins. In this sense, Bulaq is seen as *lamma*—that is, having people of heterogeneous origin. This characterization appears to be commonly articulated by residents of other new popular quarters as well. In her work on the quarter al-Zawiyya al-Hamra, Farha Ghannam points out that the notion of *lamma* was put forward by its residents to evoke the lack of authenticity of their quarter in comparison with the city's older quarters. Their comparison made reference, in particular, to Bulaq Abu al-'Ila, the quarter from which they had been forcibly removed by the state some years earlier (Ghannam 2002).

In asserting the character of Bulaq as *sha'bi*, residents made a distinction between *sha'bi qadim* (old popular) and *sha'bi gidid* (new popular). Bulaq's identity in relation to the city develops through a complex referential scheme, in which various quarters of the city are used as points of reference. This is captured in the terms through which Ra'id, a twenty-two-year-old university graduate, characterized Bulaq:

> Bulaq can only be compared with Imbaba. The two areas compete in negatives. I have friends in Imbaba and spend time there. There are conflicts between Imbaba and Bulaq because of drugs and *bango* [a kind of hashish]. Youths from Bulaq go

to Imbaba to have fights and vice versa. The Bulaq youths go there to get drugs and do not pay for them. Then the Imbaba dealers come here to find them and beat them up. The youth gangs also go to Imbaba at times of weddings to start fights. Areas such as Garden City and Zamalek also have drugs, but there, everything is done undercover. No one sees or feels what is going on. So, *bango* is there, but in a civilized manner. People buy it and pay for it and do not beat up someone to get it for free like they do in Imbaba and Bulaq. Zamalek and Muhandissin seem like quiet areas from the outside—but all happens on the inside.

In discussing their quarter in relation to other quarters and their positioning in the urban symbolic configuration, my informants were aware of the public gaze as it was fixed on them and as it fixed them into various positions of "othered" subjectivities. Mona noted that in the public gaze her quarter affiliation was incriminating: "Outside, the people see us as thugs (*baltagiyya*), but we are not like that. If I were to tell someone from Zamalek that I was from Bulaq, she would walk away from me." As we will see in chapter 5, in its effort to effect spatial control, the state deploys a public discourse on *baltaga* (thuggery) in which the new popular quarters are identified as sites of unruly conduct and the natural habitat of *baltagiyya*. The awareness of this state-sponsored stigmatization was also expressed in Ayman's assertion that when having to carry out a transaction outside Bulaq (in this particular instance, he was referring to a visit to a police station in Doqqi), he can gain respect because "I was well dressed and I do not have Bulaq al-Dakrur written on my forehead." In other words, the Bulaq association has to be rendered invisible or masked if the incriminating and stigmatizing public gaze is to be avoided.

In defending their reputation and responding to the incriminating public gaze, Bulaq residents are involved in processes of internal othering. The other—the transgressors who are responsible for the area's negative reputation—is identified as the residents of the huts under the bridge at Hamfirst Street. This claim was a recurrent theme in the discourse of many. According to the local Councilman, the huts and their residents are the sources of all the problems of the area. They are associated with a wide range of moral transgressions. Also, the huts were used as an example of the state turning a blind eye to infractions. In fact, it was hinted that the huts were part of a plot devised by some proprietors in Bulaq to seize land by having squatters occupy it. Hajj Sayyid, a coffee-shop owner, did not think the occupants of the *everyone has their "exampe"*

huts were poor. He believed they were drug dealers, thieves, and other types of "deviants" (implying that there were also prostitutes among them). The hut residents were characterized in similar terms by Muhammad, a lawyer on Tir'at al-Zumor Street.

Representations of the inside and outside are not uniform, nor are they dichotomous in the sense of expressing praise for the inside and condemnation of the outside. Indeed, among other things, "the other side" is admired for its wide boulevards and clean, well-lit streets. What the inside-outside discourse illustrates, rather, is how people articulate their relations to the space as well as their experience and sense of it.

Bulaq's Integration into the City: Spatialized Practices of Exclusion

too much emphasis on state institutions

Our understanding of Bulaq residents' experience of the city should take into account factors shaping their spatial mobility and, in particular, spatialized practices of exclusion deployed by state agencies with the objective of effecting spatial control. My inquiry is intended here to highlight the residents' links with the rest of the city, the kinds of contacts they maintain with other quarters and the constraints they face in their everyday-life movements. In assessing the degree and character of spatial mobility, we are able to understand the dynamic of the residents' integration into the wider urban setting. Spatial mobility is determined by a number of socioeconomic factors, but also by pretexts of sociability and sociopolitical position within the overall urban configuration. Key to this inquiry are the questions raised by David Sibley (1995, x) in his discussion of the geographies of exclusion:

but that's say what you want your ct.

. . . who are places for, whom do they exclude, and how are these prohibitions maintained in practice? Apart from examining the legal systems and the practices of social control agencies, explanations of exclusion require an account of barriers, prohibitions and constraints on activities from the point of view of the excluded.

In other words, we should examine ". . . forms of socio-spatial exclusion as they are experienced and articulated by the subject groups" (ibid.).

In examining the forms of inclusion and exclusion that the residents of Bulaq face, the spatial dimension of the interaction between gender relations, socioeconomic position, and cultural practices comes to the fore. There is a clear intersection between the gendering of space and the gendering of work. Gendered employment is projected into gendered spaces. Bulaq-based employment is significant given that there is a large number of businesses and trades in the area. However, the type of employment offered is geared toward males, as many of the businesses are engaged in activities that are gendered and carried out mainly by men (e.g., auto repair, butchery, electrical appliance repair). This concentration of male employment in the quarter has encouraged the territorialization of economic activities and certain forms of male sociability. Places of work are also sites where fraternal ties are forged and fraternities established. They develop in workshops, in coffee shops where workers take their breaks, and in alleyways and on street corners where young men congregate. These practices of territorialization are reinforced by state practices of spatial exclusion that target young men from popular quarters. Police surveillance and monitoring of crossings to "the other side," as well as the execution of stop-and-question policies, inhibit the mobility of a considerable segment of the population (see chapter 5).

Apart from one youth club, there are no places of entertainment and recreation, such as cinemas, in Bulaq. Thus, residents, and young people in particular, must seek leisure activities outside the quarter. This is constrained, however, by economic means and sociopolitical position. For instance, male youth with intermediate levels of education expressed a preference for Bulaq as a locus of social activity. Tradesmen stayed in Bulaq, frequenting coffee shops and spending leisure time nearby their places of work. Only a few of them indicated that they had been to cinemas outside the quarter. The territorialization of young men's sociability practices in Bulaq has developed in response to spatialized practices of government and control pursued by state agents and agencies. For example, some of the tradesmen considered crossing to the other side risky because it could bring them into contact with government law-and-order agents who would ask to see their identity cards. Social distance from the spaces outside seemed to represent an added inhibiting factor. In my interview with Sabri, a motorcycle repairman, these divisions and considerations were clearly articulated. Sabri is twenty-five years old. He dropped out of primary school. Like many other tradesmen, his outings are confined to Bulaq, consisting mainly of visits to coffee shops. Sabri's preference for Bulaq outings is explained by his desire to avoid coming into contact with the police. According to Sabri, going to "the other side" runs him the risk of being stopped and questioned by the police. Sabri is especially concerned about contact with the police because he did not present himself for military service and, as such, may be charged with draft evasion if ever he is stopped.

The experience of being stopped and questioned when crossing to Doqqi or Muhandissin is common to the young men of Bulaq. A number of them noted that there were police checkpoints set up at bridge entrances during the night. Young men crossing the bridges were stopped, questioned, and asked to present their identity cards. Identity checks of this type could lead to arrest if the law-and-order agent considered the person to be a possible suspect.

The territorialization of men's economic and leisure activities contributes to the structuring of Bulaq public spaces as male-dominated. At the same time, women's practices of sociability, localized in the *hara*, in front of homes, entranceways, and the like, creates an ambiguous space between the public and the private. In addition, women's spatial practices and experience of the city remain constrained. Those who are in formal employment tend to be working in economic sectors that require mobility (government, education, and retailing).[11] The extent of women's participation in the informal labor market is not fully discernible. However, certain economic activities in the informal sector appear to have a high level of female employment. In my interviews, I found peddling and domestic service to be two main areas in which women from low-income households are engaged. These activities draw women into city spaces beyond the quarter, but, again, in constrained terms. Women working in domestic service were often employed by upper-middle-class households in Muhandissin or Zamalek. Women peddlers, meanwhile, either stayed in their neighborhoods to sell their wares or traveled with their merchandise to markets in Giza.

Women are subject to exclusionary practices in the public space that arise out of the gendering of space, spatialized state practices of control, and the sociospatial urban divisions that express socioeconomic positions and demarcate an individual's social location in terms of lifestyle and consumption patterns. The constraints on women's experience of the city become further apparent when we consider practices around leisure and shopping. Young women, on the whole, considered that there were no opportunities for outings in Bulaq, given that coffee shops, the principal spaces of public sociability in the area, were male-dominated. This contrasts with coffee shops in downtown commercial districts and in other well-off quarters where it is

commonplace to find gender mixing and women smoking water-
pipes. Young women from Bulaq are not likely to frequent these places
because of their limited financial means and because of the monitoring to which their movements are subject. They also experience exclusion in terms of municipality and governorate practices that
inscribe socioeconomic divisions in urban space. A good example of
officially sponsored, spatial exclusionary practices is the decision to
close off the green space found on boulevard islands in Muhandissin.
Fences were erected around these spaces to prevent anyone from
making use of them. Bulaq residents understood that they were targeted by this measure. As women often organize their outings with
family and friends and with parks as their destination, they experienced this closure intensely. In lieu of these proximate, but now
fenced-off spaces, women considered trips to the cemetery in Old
Cairo as a social outing.

Women experience their exclusion in terms of the separation of
city spaces into *raqiyya* ("posh") and *sha'bi* (popular), with *raqiyya* areas
being ones they generally would not frequent. For purchases, shops in
other popular areas are preferred (e.g., the fish market in Imbaba,
clothing stores in 'Ataba and Muski). The choice of shopping areas is
determined largely by economic means and the symbolic divisions between *raqiyya* and *sha'bi* areas. These spatial divisions and their association with class-based patterns of consumption function as markers of
identity. My female informants spoke of 'Ataba as a shopping area for
"*sha'bi* people like us" and of Twenty-Six-of-July Street in downtown
Cairo as suitable for "*al-nas al-raqiyya*" (well-off people).

Despite the various constraints on spatial mobility and the exclusionary practices invested in city spaces, the inhabitants of Bulaq expressed a desire for the city. The young men and women yearn for the
spaces of the global city—fast food restaurants in Muhandissin, the
shopping mall, and Dream Park were all noted as places for special
outings and personal treats. Newly married and engaged couples considered going to the cinema in Muhandissin or in Manial and having
a meal at McDonald's or Kentucky Fried Chicken as outings of a special kind. In the social imaginary of young men and women, frequenting eateries in Muhandissin and shopping in city boutiques are
favored, perhaps because these spaces function as sites of sociospatial
integration. In subtle terms, the lifestyle of ease and the public representation of these spaces are the locus of the desire to escape the

stigmatization that the Bulaq modes of living, and associated markers have formed in the public gaze. Recall Ayman's remark: "I do not have Bulaq al-Dakrur written on my forehead," a remark made in relation to being able to gain positive public recognition. In modern city spaces like cafes, boutiques, and malls, it may be possible to perform a kind of "passing" and dissociate temporarily from the Bulaq markers of identity. It is in relation to this kind of performance that we can understand the attraction of malls to young residents of the popular quarters. According to one analyst, the mall offers youths ". . . self-contained, exclusive spaces . . ." allowing them to ". . . enter a world of simulated social promotion. Here, they feel as though they can participate in a better world, even if in most cases that participation goes no further than window shopping" (Abaza 2004).

The proliferation of malls and supermarkets in Cairo is part of a wider process of urban transformation—an overall reconfiguration of the city. In this respect, the terms of Bulaq residents' integration into the city should be considered from the perspective of the quarter's location in a reconfigured Cairo. In the following section, I sketch briefly the elements of the ongoing remapping of the city and the hierarchies of space that have developed as a result.

Reconfiguring Cairo: Between the Local and the Global

Bulaq's emergence as a quarter on the semi-periphery of the city should not be understood in the reified terms of the "urban problem" —that is, as a symptom of the processes of modernization, in particular, rapid urbanization. Manuel Castells (in Susser 2002) has suggested that cities emerge at different conjunctures of capitalist production. This insight applies to Cairo's transformation and reconfiguration. In other words, developments in the city are closely tied with its positioning in the international economy and cannot be understood independently of it.[12]

In the modern period, Cairo's planning and expansion was greatly influenced by the nature of Egypt's integration into the international economy, first as a kind of vassal state of European powers and later as a colonized state. In emulating western models of organization, Egypt's rulers and urban planners sought to create a modern city. Thus, they devised wide boulevards for a new downtown, and "garden city" style suburbs for new residential areas. As noted previously, discipline and order were key objectives of city planners. In the neoliberal phase, during the Sadat period in the first instance, <u>a facelift for the capital was viewed as necessary to signal Egypt's return to the Western fold</u>. The "better-looking" Cairo required the removal of blemishes from its face. This beautification entailed the removal of old buildings and their residents from visible spaces. For example, as Ghannam (2002) demonstrates, sections of Bulaq Abu al-'Ila were removed to make way for the new internationally oriented urban projects.

Cairo's urban history during the colonial period was narrated along the lines of a tale of two cities: the traditional and the modern or the medina versus the European center (Abu-Lughod 1965). Extended into the contemporary period, this tale incorporates the new spaces, the popular quarters within the dichotomized vision of planned versus unplanned, regulated versus unregulated, and formal as opposed to informal. The oppositions are superimposed on the dichotomies. This vision, however, leaves out the multiplicity of spaces and their crisscrossing lines. Rather than approaching the city through oppositions and dichotomies, we should pay closer attention to the multiple strategies of appropriation of space and to the acts through which competing values are spatially invested. An example of this is the ongoing repositioning of Old Cairo, an element of the conventional, traditional–modern city polarity. Old Cairo today is the site of struggle among a multitude of actors ranging from state heritage and culture officials, to international conservationists and heritage institutions, to the inhabitants and users of the space. While the officials prioritize buildings over inhabitants and are moved by the drive for global consumption of the heritage, the conservationists are exercised over questions of authenticity. In the meantime, the stakes for Old Cairo's inhabitants are nothing less than the preservation of a mode of living and the very elements of their livelihood (see Williams 2002).

The expansion of the city under the project of modernity, as embodied in the master plans, was isomorphic with industrialization. As noted by el Kadi (1990), great importance was placed on planning industrial zones around the capital. The industrialization program went hand in hand with the planning and execution of low-income housing projects designed to house workers and lower-ranking state functionaries. Thus, entire residential zones were erected in the areas surrounding such industrial poles as Helwan, Shubra, and Imbaba. By the early 1970s, with the policy of economic opening, real estate speculation became one of the principal means of capital accumulation (el Kadi 1990,

201). The state's laissez-faire orientation encouraged the spiraling up of real estate prices as well as an explosion in urban construction.

Looking at the dynamics of what some urbanists call "the neoliberal age" of the city, we are confronted by questions on the changing nature of urban development (Denis and Moriconi-Ebrard 1995). Using the category of the local/intermediary, Denis (1998) argues that Cairo is undergoing a reconfiguration characterized by a breakdown of regulation and master plans in favor of multiplication of interventions by social elites and private actors. A ghettoization of urban life is occurring, whereby the elite want to live "*entre-soi*," abandoning the city in favor of Dreamland and, in the process, polarizing the capital. Denis argues that with new cities and industrial zones, malls and condominiums, and informal areas, the features of dispersal that mark the global city are imprinted on the face of Cairo. These territories coexist in tension with each other. Yet, the informal sites of residence, work, and production are necessary for the global city spaces of the elite.

In the reconfiguration of Cairo, Bulaq al-Dakrur spaces, not unlike a number of other new popular quarters, are linked to the service needs of the inhabitants of better-off neighboring quarters. The auto repair, welding, and carpentry services and the like produce too much noise to be tolerated by the residents of Zamalek and Muhandissin. Yet, they need the services to be located nearby. The hierarchy of space that characterizes the latest phase of urban development has seen the movement away from the old center of affairs and business in the modern downtown (*wist al-balad*), to a new center more in tune with the globalization of consumption (see el Kadi 1995). This new center is a belt of businesses and residences situated immediately to the west of the Nile, in the neighborhoods of Muhandissin, Doqqi, and Zamalek. Located there are travel agencies, the new technology service companies, and international advertising, architectural, and interior design companies, along with the shopping malls, fast-food restaurants, European style cafes, and cinemas. Bulaq al-Dakrur and Imbaba are situated further to the west of this belt, servicing the tertiary sector by providing the "lower-end" services, such as: auto repair, domestic and cleaning services, and construction work. In its social composition, Bulaq attests to this urban transformation and the new sociospatial hierarchies. Many of its residents come from the old quarters such as Bab al-Shi'riyya and Bulaq Abu al-'Ila. Others come from Dayr al-Nahya, a section of Doqqi that comprised huts and whose residents were served with eviction orders.

Bulaq's integration into the burgeoning commercial and service sectors is also evidenced by its peddlers who are part of the networks of commerce and trade that are imbricated in the global trade networks. The new patron-merchants of 'Ataba and Muski procure cheap goods made in China, Taiwan, and Indonesia. They are then linked to mass distribution networks by the peddlers—often women and refugees—who sell the goods from house to house, street to street, and market to market. The peddlers in this way serve as retailers for wholesalers. They also consolidate the informal credit system that rivals the banks and financial institutions. The informal credit system achieves, through trust and face-to-face contact, that which the banking system in Egypt has not yet achieved. Egypt's financial institutions have not developed the regulatory means to provide personal accounts and lines of credit to all segments of the population, in particular to those in informal employment who have no formal guarantees.

Urban expansion in Bulaq is marked by imperatives, social divisions, and forms of differentiation similar to the rest of Cairo. Since all available space in its old and new sections has been exhausted, the surrounding lands have become the targets for further development. The dynamics of this development highlight the ongoing social transformations and the struggles of the actors involved. We find Bulaq residents seeking to secure housing when they marry, to acquire land and build a family dwelling, or simply to become an owner. For these purposes, the northwestern extension of Nahya and the areas of Kafr Tohormous and Saft continue to provide affordable options. Contractors in these areas are subdividing lots and selling them to families who construct housing for personal use or to rent out for additional income. For young men with limited financial means, renting a home in places like the new extension of Nahya is their only option for moving out of their parents' home and establishing separate households. They are usually required to pay between 1,000 and 3,000 pounds in advance on their rent to be deducted as the equivalent of half of the monthly rental over a certain period of time. Meanwhile, the southwestern extension of Bulaq from Zanayn Street via Street Twenty to the district of Faysal is dominated by large contractors. They are putting up high-rise buildings and selling them as condominiums, with those located on the main street selling for up to 150,000 pounds. Inside the subdistrict, on secondary arteries, condominiums with unfinished interiors are selling for about 70,000 pounds.

The continuing expansion of urban areas onto agricultural land, as well as the differentiated character of this expansion, as found in the case of Bulaq and other popular quarters such as Imbaba, should be set against the background of the policies of urban development as they unfolded during the last two decades of neoliberal government. In the 1982 Master Plan, the needs of the less-advantaged citizens were to be met by the establishment of ten new settlements. According to the institution in charge of the Greater Cairo master scheme, the IAURIF (Institut d'Aménagement et d'Urbanisme de la Région de l'Île de France), this was to put an end to the conversion of agricultural land and to informality (Belliot 1993). However, the new settlements did not attract their targeted population. By the early 1990s, four of the proposed sites were abandoned and the remaining ones became sites for medium-cost and luxury housing. Initially, the state was to provide the infrastructure for the New Settlements and sell serviced plots to citizens. This plan, however, gave way to a reallocation of the sites to housing projects targeting the upper classes (Doorman 2002, 159). The New Settlements so far appear to repeat the experience of the new cities envisioned in the Master Plan of 1971. Under this plan, infrastructure was built to service industrial zones for local enterprises. The zones later came to house joint ventures and foreign companies.

The different patterns of growth that characterize Bulaq are embedded in the ongoing transformation of the Greater Cairo agglomeration as a whole. A hierarchy of space and the growing division between the haves and have-nots guide urban planning whether state sponsored and regulated or privately managed and unregulated. In Cairo's "architectural renaissance" (*nahda 'umraniyya*), to borrow Eric Denis's term, segregation defines expansion projects favoring the well-off sectors of society. It is also the outcome of a configuration of housing and planning policies that leaves out lower-income social groups and hence contributes to their condition of informality. The planned growth of the city, as in the "New Cairo City" with its luxury housing, caters mainly to the upper and upper-middle class. Places like Qattamiyya, Mena Garden City, and Sheikh Zayed City have all been favored by the Egyptian elite as sites for the construction of spacious villas in settings that are provided with the most advanced infrastructure (Doorman 2002, 25). New projects like Dreamland and Beverly Hills promote an urban lifestyle detached from the city and its problems, It also affords separation from the less well-off strata (see Mitchell 2002; Denis 1998).

Conclusion

To a large extent, the location of the new popular quarters has been determined by housing policies, real estate markets, and transformations in the national political economy, all of which are shaped by the exigencies of neoliberal economic policies at the international level. On the whole, the new popular quarters were established on the peripheries of Cairo after housing policies designed to slow down peripheralization came to a halt. The location of the new quarters on the edge of the city has to do with employment possibilities and modes of earning a living at a time of shift in the role of developer assigned to state authorities. This shift has been accompanied by an expansion of the informal economy and emerging patterns of territorialization of economic activities in the service and trade sectors of the economy. Part and parcel of the political economy transformations is a remapping of the city whereby new lines of division and fragmentation of the urban fabric have emerged. Various forms of spatial exclusion have crystallized in the city. For the residents of Bulaq, their experience of the city is mediated through closures of green spaces, fence separation, constraints on mobility, and territorial marking of space into *sha'bi* and *raqi*. Measures aimed at disciplining the inhabitants of new popular quarters and bringing them under control have been adopted by state authorities. The discourse of *'ashwa'iyyat* underwrites these oppressive measures and occludes the efforts undertaken by residents of popular quarters to fashion for themselves a lived space.

The public discourse of *'ashwa'iyyat* deploys the tropes of violence and terrorism to frame the populations of the new popular quarters. In questioning this frame, we should direct our attention to the actual living conditions in the quarters, to the efforts undertaken by the residents to change these conditions and fashion modes of living in the face of grinding political and economic constraints. The examination of the quotidian in the following chapters sketches ordinary citizens' engagement in governance activities, their daily struggles to improve their living conditions, and their encounters with the everyday state.

Chapter 2

Internal Governance: Forms and Practices of Government in Everyday Life

EXAMINING THE EVERYDAY PRACTICES of government and forms of social organization in the new quarters is essential to our understanding of the patterns of interaction between quarter residents and the state. One of the key questions that guided this inquiry was that of whether and how everyday-life practices and structures at the level of the quarter give shape to a certain measure of autonomy in the community's governance of its internal affairs. I use *internal governance* to refer to the exercise of social and moral control and to the management of basic needs and services within the boundaries of a defined social space, such as the quarter. A focus on internal governance is a first step toward exploring the political dimension of citizens' interaction within the quarter. Indeed, the political dimension arises precisely out of citizens' engagement in organizational and governance activities and through interrelations and interactions involving quarter-based figures of authority. I investigate community-based forms of organization that address issues of concern to the citizen (e.g., security, mutual aid, observance of rules of propriety) and that underpin the economic and social activities of the quarters. The analysis demonstrates that these forms embody social hierarchies of power. Thus, rather than presenting community as the bedrock of solidarity and resistance against the state, I give attention to the divisions and conflicts that express hierarchical relations and that attempt to effect a social leveling from within. I have been conscious, at once, of Sherry Ortner's (1995) cautionary remarks about the sanitization of the politics of subalterns and of the need to avoid being wooed by what Lila Abu-Lughod (1990) calls "the romance of resistance."

Internal governance through community-based institutions is effected by both the elders of the community and the rising notability—the latter comprising, in large part, merchants. The examination of internal forms of governance shows that in some cases they intermesh with state practices of government. Further, positions of power within the community are embedded within formal and informal institutions. Equally important for our investigation of power relations and forms of internal governance is how social and economic hierarchies shape citizens' interaction with the everyday state.

This chapter begins with an overview of forms and modes of governance relating to the resolution of quotidian and local conflicts and to the control of public morality. In the subsequent section, I explore how social hierarchies shape the residents' relations to each other and to the everyday state. The final section examines state strategies of co-optation and infiltration into societal spaces and the blurring of boundaries between state and society. It highlights the rise of community figures of authority to the position of notables and their incorporation as intermediaries between state authorities and the people, noting that local politics appears as a form of mediation but not of representation. At the same time, in scrutinizing episodes from the life of local government, we come to see that the sliding from the formal to the informal in practices and sites of government emerges as a feature of local government.

Everyday Forms of Governance

The Management of Quotidian Conflicts

The questions I posed to residents of Bulaq regarding problems they faced at the level of the street allow me to ascertain that they have developed forms of organization that are designed to deal with a range of recurring problems, many of which may be grouped under the general category of disputes among neighbors. These arise on a daily basis and have to do with such quotidian happenings as fights between children, apparent transgressions between neighbors (e.g., water and dirt from an upper floor balcony falling onto a lower balcony), and the misbehavior of youth (e.g., teenage boys being disruptive on street corners). When children or youth are involved, adults are often "dragged into the disputes." Men tend to view women as the instigators of the more serious fights concerning children. However, it is clear from respondents' narratives that men also get involved. When they do, physical fights may ensue, sometimes involving the use of weapons. In general, physical fights do not bring disputes to an end, as aggrieved parties are usually left seeking redress, which may prolong the conflict. At the level of the street and the immediate neighborhood, mechanisms of conflict resolution have developed to bring an end to such disputes once they occur. The individuals who are called upon to mediate conflicts are referred to as the "elders of the area" (*kibar al-mantiqa*). Disputants usually know them personally or by name.

The sequence of incidents, and the range of possible actors making up a dispute, is exemplified in the following story, the details of which were recounted to me by various interlocutors. Ahmad, a boy of thirteen, got into a fight with Ali, a boy from the neighborhood but living in a different alley. Ali's mother intervened in the fight and began to hit Ahmad. Ahmad's sister, Dunya, was notified about the fight and tried to intercede. She got into a physical altercation with Ali's mother and was pushed or pulled to the ground. Then Muhammad, Ahmad's older brother, came by and pushed Ali's mother in order to rescue his sister. In the evening, various male members of Ali's family marched to Ahmad's house seeking revenge against his brother Muhammad. They were carrying clubs and knives. Muhammad's father offered himself in place of his son. Then men from neighboring houses came out and chased away the men who were after Muhammad. The neighbors' loyalty was to Muhammad's father since the rival party came from a different alley. However, the situation could not be left at that. Muhammad's father arranged for a *musalaha* (conciliation) at the home of Mustafa 'Urabi, an elder of the area. He met with the aggrieved party and apologized for his son's behavior. Other residents interceded and convinced the aggrieved party to accept *sulh* (reconciliation).

Conflict resolution meetings usually take place at an elder's home where the disputants are brought together for the purposes of reconciliation. The residents' narratives about this manner of dealing with neighborhood disputes crystallize a particular rationale of reconciliation and a mode of action. In brief, the rationale emphasizes neighborhood-based reconciliation and expresses a particular view of relations to state authority. It consists of the following line of reasoning: (1) the men live in the same area, which creates a sense of fraternity and makes them brothers; (2) they will not gain much from going to the police to resolve disputes among themselves; and (3) they are likely to help each other if faced with a problem outside the neighborhood. The mode of achieving *sulh* follows a simple strategy: (1) the elders avoid going over details of who did what to whom; (2) they do not repeat the previous exchanges between the conflicting parties; and (3) they advise the disputants to start anew.

Mediators as Figures of Authority: Someone 'Biytkabarluh'

Reconciliation meetings are not the only institutions of conflict resolution. Informal tribunals known as majalis 'urfiyya (customary councils) or majalis tahkim (arbitration councils) are convened to deal with conflicts where stakes are higher or where disputants are of some influence in the community.[1] These councils, which are used in other popular quarters of the city, follow a specific logic of interaction. Arbiters in the majalis are chosen on the basis of the respect they are accorded as well as their status and standing in the community. They are referred to as someone biytkabarluh (to whom one defers or, more precisely, to whose authority one must subject oneself). Thus, in determining the membership of a majlis 'urfi, it is important to find individuals to whom the conflicting parties tikabar (defer). This is key to the attribution and acceptance of guilt in the matter. In Imbaba, another new popular quarter, I also found that majalis were set up to deal with conflicts and that workers in various civil associations, such as the local development association, were involved as mediators in disputes between neighbors, spouses, and so on. One local activist in Imbaba, Hamid, saw his authority as being focused in a muraba' (literally, a square), meaning a number of contiguous streets. Any problem in his muraba' is referred back to him for consideration and resolution. He is capable of bringing together the conflicting parties or of tracking down an offender or transgressor. The person will usually come to see him and will be reproached and dealt with.

Hamid's authority comes from his engagement in the local development association and from his efforts to act as an intermediary between residents and state authorities—securing permits for wedding celebrations on the street, for example. This is true also of his colleague Sabir. Hamid and Sabir assert that they do more work than the police in their neighborhood. I asked Sabir how their role as intermediaries and their relations with the people compare with Sheikh Gabir's interventions. Sheikh Gabir was an Islamist activist and the emir of an al-Jama'a

Islamiyya cell in Imbaba. He was arrested in 1992 at the height of security sweeps that targeted Islamist activists. Sabir viewed his and Hamid's role as similar in kind to Gabir's and expressed a positive view of the latter's activities. Both Hamid and Sabir considered that their status was acquired, not inherited. Nor was it wealth-based. Rather, in their assessment, a number of factors contributed to the establishment of personal authority: position in government, connections to government, wealth, and people's respect and appreciation. For their part, Sabir and Hamid indicated that their position in local society was based on *ihtiram wa taqdir al-nas* (people's respect and appreciation). Sabir presented a highly normative account of the terms by which this status is achieved. According to him, trust is invested in a person who has the people's respect, which, in turn, has to do with the person's sense of justice and fairness. In Sabir's own words:

> The person must be just and fair no matter what the circumstances. For example, he will forthrightly indicate the source of error even if the erring person is his own father. He will also state bluntly what he thinks without fear, and he would not likely compromise his own sense of fairness to please a relative or someone in power.

Thus, ethical principles and norms of social interaction figure prominently in accounts of mediation and in explanations of how an individual accedes to the position of someone *biytkabarluh*. However, as I point out later in this chapter wealth and connections to government are also important factors.

Hamid and Sabir may convene a tribunal to deal with a case of conflict, or they may be asked to attend arbitration meetings called by others. If their power or influence does not hold sway over a transgressor, they will seek the help of someone *biytkabarluh*—someone to whom the concerned parties *bitkabar* (look up to or are respectful of), whether in general or in particular. This is a strategy of deploying influence based on affective expectations and on norms and conventions. When a *biytkabarluh* person is brought into a conflict resolution case, the offending person is likely to yield. He will say *"irift tiksarni"* ("you were able to break me"). In other words, this strategy works to weaken and soften a person involved in the dispute because a *biytkabarluh* person is someone who "cannot be made small" (*ma yisagharush fi al-qaʿda*). That is, he cannot be diminished or belittled at a gathering by being contradicted or not listened to.

Majalis 'urfiyya tend, in some sense, to work within the frame of the local power hierarchy. The stakes in the disputes considered by the *majalis* are usually high (e.g., commercial property rights, money, residential proprietary claims, reputation) and, at times, involve persons of influence. The arbiters chosen for these councils are individuals of some standing in their communities by virtue of assuming positions of leadership in local organizations, or because of their material wealth and the contacts they maintain with government officials.

The following account of a conflict illustrates the working of the arbitration councils and the role of the *muraba'* leader in resolving disputes of this kind. The conflict in question involves a woman pharmacist from Muhandissin and a man from Imbaba who was something of a *baltagi* (thug). The focal point is a commercial property in Imbaba, owned by the woman and set up by her as a pharmacy. At some point, she closed the business, but continued to pay the mortgage installments on the property. During the time that the premises were empty, however, the *baltagi* took them over and established a store for electrical goods. The woman attempted to regain the premises with the help of her family, but the man refused to leave. She was wary of taking legal action because a court decision would likely take a long time. She finally looked for someone from the area to intercede and was advised to approach the workers in the local development association. There, she found Hamid, the *muraba'* leader mentioned previously, who agreed to help. Hamid knew that he would not, on his own, have any influence over the *baltagi* since he was not from the same *muraba'*. So he approached hajj Maqsud, a local contractor and the leader of the *muraba'* where the man resided. Hajj Maqsud got hold of the man and faced him with the proprietor's demands. In a meeting attended by Hamid and other local personalities, hajj Maqsud, a self-fashioned *futuwwa*, asked that the *baltagi* vacate the premises. The man agreed, acknowledging that hajj Maqsud was his *kabir* (elder) and that he had to yield to him.

My interviews with individuals who served as members of *majalis 'urfiyya* and with community activists allowed me to gain an understanding of the position of *biytkabarluh* individuals and to construct a kind of profile of their trajectory and mode of accession to that status. Most important in building this profile is what it reveals about the sources of authority on which someone *biytkabarluh* draws. These include having wealth and using some of it for charity, but also having visible contacts with and links to state officials such as police officers.

These contacts are crucial to the recognition of the person as a protector at gatherings and ceremonies such as weddings and as an intermediary in encounters with the authorities. In a sense, the person has the status of notability and is recognized as such by the authorities. Both the state and the people call on him for mediation. People seek and accept his intervention because he is recognized as a "man of good" (ragil khayr) by virtue of his charitable work and as a "man of power" by virtue of his connections with the state. State authorities seek him out through local informants in the community and develop patronage links with him. Hajj Saleh, a community notable whom I interviewed, concluded a story about his mediating role with the police during wedding events by saying that people acknowledge his influential position when they pose the following rhetorical question about him: "Who was able to dismiss the government after it had shown up [at the event]?" (min al-khala al-hukuma timshi ba'd ma gat?). In other words, he is in a position to dismiss the state or at least to coax it to go away. This intermediary role played by someone biytkabarluh has now been incorporated by state authorities, through co-optation and infiltration, into their strategy of control in popular areas. This will be discussed further in a subsequent section.

Hajj Saleh owns a shoe factory and provides employment to some members of the community. In his own account, he attributes his earned position to his role as a benefactor to those in need. He also framed his narrative around the notion of hub al-nas (people's love), saying that "if there was no people's love, there would be no recourse" (law mafish hub al-nas mafish ligu'). He talked of reciprocal respect (ihtiram mutabadal) and underlined the importance of giving people the moral rights and respect they are due (i'ta' al-haq al-adabi). As noted previously, the hajj's status does not rest purely on symbolic and normative criteria, but is materially inscribed. For instance, his status is enhanced by his success in business. He surrounds himself with "people of distinction," namely a group of lawyers and other professionals from the area. More important are his contacts with representatives of state power, in particular, the police. The moral and ethical criteria figure not only in hajj Saleh's own account of his status but may also appear in the discourse of the people who seek his help. As will be elaborated in chapter 5, normative and ethical issues frame many residents' views of the state. The absence of mutual respect between the residents and representatives of the state, as well as these representatives' failure to recognize the residents' dignity, are recurring motifs in descriptions of relations with the state.

Hajj Saleh's interventions as a mediator are aimed at resolving conflicts for which the courts are not likely to provide satisfactory outcomes. One example is the case of Nabil's dispute with his landlord. Nabil rented a flat for which he paid 12,000 pounds key money. He and the landlord agreed that 50 percent of the monthly rent would come out of the key money over a certain period of time. A dispute eventually developed and the proprietor sought Nabil's eviction from the building. The matter went to court. There were no documents to prove that Nabil had paid the key money, and, in court, the proprietor was able to demonstrate that the rent had not been paid in full for some time. The court supported the landlord's demand for eviction. Nabil sought to get back the balance of the key money he had paid, so he contacted hajj Saleh and his group of helpers. The hajj tried a number of strategies to influence the proprietor. Ultimately, after several months, he contacted someone from the proprietor's region of origin, Asyut, to try and prevail on him to refund the money. A number of meetings were held and, with the help of mediators, terms of settlement were negotiated. The mediators used the religious angle. They invoked "religious and ethical constants" (*al-thawabit al–diniyya wa al-adabiyya*), knowing that the proprietor was devout—a "God-fearing man." According to the hajj, the proprietor had intended to reimburse Nabil, but he was planning to do so in installments, over a long period of time. For Nabil, however, this was not a practical solution as he needed the money immediately to rent another flat. Moral pressure was brought to bear on both parties, and a final agreement was written up and signed.

In the ethos surrounding someone *biytkabarluh*, accepting the authority of an elder has an individual and a collective dimension. The offending party, in yielding to the elder, affirms a relation embodying rights and responsibilities and carrying a history. Community members use a common frame invoking the responsibility of the elder. They see the position of elder as confirmed by the individual's adherence to rules and norms governing it. For instance, in a discussion I had with a couple about the position of elders, Samira, an engineer, questioned her husband's view that hajj Salem, a grocer and shopkeeper in the neighborhood, was an elder. She stated that an elder must be willing to open his home to the conflicting parties for a reconciliation meeting. He should be ready to incur the material costs of such an event. The reference here is to the hospitality costs of hosting the conflicting parties in one's house. Samira contended he should be someone that you acknowledge as an elder in his place of residence (*tikabaruh 'anduh*) and not in your own place (*lakin mish 'andak*).

The reconciliation meetings and the *majalis 'urfiyya* represent alternative means of regulation to the police and courts. In cases where matters escalate and reach the police, community efforts are mobilized to withdraw affidavits and other declarations complainants may make. Complainants who pursue cases through the police and the court system risk community sanction. At the same time, community modes of conflict resolution do not cover all conflicts that occur. Indeed, while most interviewees confirmed the existence of internal mechanisms for dealing with conflict, they spoke of people's reluctance to intervene in violent street fights among young men. During the period of my research, in 2000 and 2001, there were numerous incidents of violent altercations. Violence among minivan drivers seemed to have escalated according to my informants. For example, a number of killings were attributed to disputes between drivers over places in the minivan queue. Residents and drivers stated that the drivers' widespread use of *bango* (a kind of hashish) made it difficult for people to intervene to end an altercation. In reference to one street fight between a vendor in the market and a group of youth, Um Mona commented that *bango* had "wiped out the young peoples' brains."

However, even in the advent of violent conflicts, residents do not consider police intervention to be helpful. Interviewees expressed the view that police are inclined to let the people fight or to arrest everyone indiscriminately. On the whole, the police are not seen as providing protection in the area. Eschewing the intervention of the police and relying on internally constituted social institutions, however, does not equate with achieving absolute autonomy. As we will see in the final section of this chapter, inasmuch as these modes of organization can provide the bases of opposition and collective action, they can also be harnessed to the purposes of state governance.

The Governance of Morality

The domain of moral governance covers relations between the sexes, codes of sexual propriety, and public and private morality. This consists especially of the regulation and monitoring of women's comings and goings, their attire, and their interaction with men. The alley is a space from which to monitor women's movements, their associations, and their observance of modest dress. Gender interaction in the *hara* is cast as an extension of family interaction. Enforcement of norms in this domain is undertaken both individually and collectively. For example, a young man may escort a female neighbor home if she is found in the company of a man who is not her relative. The woman's family may be notified of the transgression. In interviews with young men, this mode of intervention was constructed as necessary. However, these same youths also cited a growing tendency among families in their neighborhood to reject such intervention. They view this development as a sign of deteriorating morality. The issues surrounding both the monitoring of young women's mobility and the anxiety the young men feel with regard to what they perceive to be signs of moral laxity are examined further in chapter 4 when we turn to the subject of ongoing changes in gender relations entailing a renegotiation of masculinity and femininity.

Gossip, social ostracism, and threats of eviction from the neighborhood are devices used by *hara* residents to enforce conformity with the morality code. For instance, there was a case in Bulaq of a woman being confronted by her neighbors over her conduct and asked to quit her rented accommodations. This mode of action is found in old popular quarters of the city as well and is documented in historical studies of other Arab cities. In eighteenth-century Damascus, for instance, residents of an alley collectively approached a city judge to order the eviction of residents who transgressed morality strictures (Rafeq 1990). Similarly, in nineteenth-century Cairo, the residents of popular quarters denounced their transgressing neighbors to the police (Fahmy 1999). In the accounts I gathered on these matters in contemporary Bulaq, eviction was undertaken by the neighborhood without recourse to the courts or police. For example, Ra'fat, a tile-layer, residing in an alley of central Bulaq, confronted his female neighbor regarding her late-night male visitors. He threatened to report her to the morality police (*bulis al-adab*). The pressures that Ra'fat and other neighbors placed on this woman caused her to move away. Ra'fat's intervention, it should be said, does not necessarily arise out of strict personal observance of the rules of propriety. Indeed, during the second phase of my fieldwork, I met Ra'fat by chance on Gam'iyya Street and, in our brief exchange, he informed me that he had moved out of his old accommodation, a room on the roof of his sister's home, because of a dispute with his sister over his own female visitors. In this case, his sister feared for her family's reputation, particularly for that of her yet unmarried daughter. Ra'fat's failure to abide by the moral code was seen to have put his niece's prospects of finding a suitable husband in jeopardy, and his sister intervened to correct his potentially damaging conduct. As the owner of the house, she was in a position to put pressure on him to leave.

Preoccupation with morality issues among parents and youths partly explains the appeal of Islamist groups in popular neighborhoods. At the height of their activism, militant Islamists engaged in morality governance. They monitored conduct and intervened to punish transgressors. They counseled repentance to women who were deemed to have been unrighteous and tried to guide them onto "the true Islamic path." In some cases, al-Jama'a members married transgressing women in order to encourage their repentance. As I have argued elsewhere (Ismail 2000), these governance practices are grounded in existing social practices; therefore, in adopting and instituting them, Islamists weave themselves into the social fabric.

Relations of Power and Social Hierarchies: Internal Governance and the Everyday State

The previous discussion shows how the community developed forms of governance that allow it to eschew state authorities when resolving internal disputes and in managing morality issues. However, some modes of conflict resolution work by implicating state agents and calling on state resources and offices. These modes hinge on a number of factors that are indicative of power relations and social hierarchies structuring the community.

Relations of power within the neighborhood determine the ability of community members to invoke state power in dealing with internal conflicts. In many instances, members of the community are unwilling and incapable of calling on the state or invoking its powers. Individuals at the lower end of the socioeconomic ladder feel unable to use state resources to settle conflicts with those positioned higher in status. Various narratives illustrated this point. In one incident, Rawash, a boy of fifteen, accepted to drive a minivan for one of the owners in the neighborhood even though he lacked driving skills. Upon taking charge of the vehicle, he hit a parked truck belonging to a well-off family. As retribution for the damage, one of the truck proprietors hit Rawash in the face and gave him a severe beating. In dealing with this aggression, Rawash's mother, Um Sha'ban, chose not to report the beating to the police.

Rawash did not go to the clinic or the hospital, as he was afraid of having to name his assailant. According to Um Sha'ban, he did not want to drag the minibus proprietor and his assailant into the police station because the latter was a relative of Um Ashraf, a next-door neighbor. Um Sha'ban conceded that Rawash was at fault for driving without a license, but she pointed out that the punishment was severe and could cause permanent eye damage to her son. Um Sha'ban said she did not report the assailant out of respect for Um Ashraf. However, she indicated that she planned to take Rawash to a clinic below the railway crossing (in Doqqi). If the examination revealed permanent eye damage, she would pursue the assailant. Um Ashraf, in whose house the account was given, said she did not take the side of her relative (the assailant) and that both he and Rawash were sons to her (*dah ibnina wa dah ibnina*). Um Sha'ban said the man must have considered himself powerful (*qawi*), but there must be *ili aqwah minuh* (someone who is stronger). This was not a reference to God but rather to someone who would settle things with the aggressor. Justice was to be implemented in the hierarchical order of power. Later on, when Um Sha'ban left the gathering at Um Ashraf's home, the neighbors gave a different explanation of why she did not seek redress through the police. They contended that the aggressor had "back" (*luh dahr*), meaning he had family and connections that Rawash's family could not match. The latter had little to gain from going to the police and risked retaliation from the stronger family. Um Hisham commented that Um Sha'ban was showing a lot of bravado and that, in the end, she was not going to proceed with a complaint.

In another case involving sexual transgression against a young boy by an older boy, the complaint to the police was dropped under pressure from neighbors who upheld the higher status of the alleged aggressor's family. Two of my informants, Karima and Manal, felt indignant about what they considered double standards in dealing with this instance of sexual transgression. They confronted their neighbors for failing to uphold the right of the young boy's family to seek legal redress. In accounts of this type of moral transgression, power and sexuality are intimately linked. In fact, one interviewee,

Ra'd, a university student, associated power with the ability to get away with transgressions against the moral code, in particular, sexual transgressions. For him, the power of a local personality, a wealthy butcher on Nahya Street, was evidenced by the fact that the butcher's neighbors chose not to report his son's assault against a married woman. Rather, it was the woman who was forced to leave the neighborhood. In this case, as in the previous one, a sexual transgression went unpunished, and no legal steps were taken due to the aggressors' position in the community. According to Ra'd, in the assault case, the powerful person's family was active in the ruling party and in Parliament, and "this made it possible for him to do whatever he wants."

Citizens in Bulaq sometimes seek to involve police in disputes as a means of threatening or intimidating an opponent positioned on an equivalent step of the social ladder. For example, Um Sha'ban, who was reluctant to pursue her youngest son's assailant, filed a complaint against one of her own elder sons for beating her up.[2] She also threatened to implicate a neighbor with whom she was on bad terms. False accusations of physical assault may also be made against opponents in order to put pressure on them. This occurs where relations of power among family members and neighbors are unequal. For example, in a dispute between two neighboring families over water dripping and dirt falling from a second-floor apartment on to the first, the women of both families got into a verbal altercation, which was followed by some physical pushing and shoving. Upon learning that the family of the first floor had filed a police complaint, the young women from the second floor went to the public hospital to be examined for injuries that they accused their neighbors of having inflicted on them. However, in private, the young women admitted that the bruises were self-inflicted in order to press assault charges against their neighbor and thereby even the score. What view of state power informs these practices? Implicating the police in false accusations is partly guided by the knowledge that the police are corrupt and that the rules they seek to enforce are improvised. Indeed, in narrating an episode of a marital dispute, one of my female informants reported that in response to her husband's threats to take a second wife and bring her to the marital home, she threatened to plant *bango* on him and report him to the police. Interestingly, this kind of ruse is also an entrapment tactic used by the police to neutralize young men on the street. False accusations underline the tactics of mutual ensnarement that entangle rulers and ruled. This will be discussed further in chapter 5.

In general, making formal accusations against family members is ill viewed. Registration of complaints with the police leads to the parties concerned being called into the station for interrogation. This will result in a *mahdar* (police report) being drawn up, which is considered to be bad for the reputation of the person against whom the charges are made. The person who brings such disrepute onto a neighbor or a family member is likely to suffer reproach from those around him or her. Thus, involving the police in a dispute before seeking a neighborhood-based resolution is frowned upon. Even after a complaint is lodged with the police, individuals are often pressured by neighbors to withdraw it. Refusal to do so could lead to being ostracized.

State Strategies of Incorporation and Infiltration

As shown in the previous discussion, everyday forms of social organization provide the residents with institutions designed to deal with a wide range of concerns, needs, and problems. In a sense, they could be viewed as representing an alternative to formal structures of government since they afford residents a means of avoiding state authorities. However, as noted earlier, the locally developed institutions do articulate with "formal" authorities. To some extent, this could be explained in terms of these authorities' strategies of incorporation and infiltration. At the same time, it should be recalled that the boundaries of state and society are blurred and that the formal has been shown to slide into the informal in actual instances of government.

Contradictory and complementary dynamics are at work in the modes of governance at the local level. On one hand, Bulaq residents avoid calling on the state to resolve many of their quotidian disputes. On the other, links to state institutions through mediators are important for the containment of certain conflicts. Furthermore, it is partly through these links that mediators accede to positions of notability. The picture becomes increasingly complex when we realize how societal practices of government intermesh with state governmental practices, as when *biytkabarluh* figures are sought out by the police or when notables act as auxiliaries to the state in containing potential conflicts. This modality of governance at the local level has given rise to what could be identified as "local power compacts" that are integrated into state government.

The phenomenon of "state in society" discussed by Migdal (2001) blurs the boundaries between government/rule and the governed/ruled. In my examination of these blurred boundaries, I point out that this blurring brings "society in the state"—a reversal of Migdal's formulation that nonetheless confirms the idea that government does not obtain through neat boundaries between state and society, but through an intermeshing of authorities and a morphing in the forms it takes. The picture that emerges is that of government as being a messy business. In some respects, the state is colonized by local notables and functions within the framework developed by notables and their associates. The state is brought down to the level of the people, where it becomes a site of everyday squabbles and disputes. Meanwhile, the public looks on, sometimes interjecting with ridicule, sometimes remaining silent and withholding consent, both in a show of contempt and in a manner of upholding the farce.

In this section, I take a closer look at the dynamics of governance at the local level. In the first instance, I sketch the wider socioeconomic context in which mediators have come to represent a local notability. I then examine how "traditional" forms of authority and local power arrangements could be harnessed to the purposes of state. Following that, I illustrate the blurring of boundaries between state and society by detailing some episodes from the life of local government that show its improvisational character and the process by which serious business may become farcical.

Mediators as a Lesser Notability

As we have seen, the role of *biytkabarluh* figures is integral to the community's forms of organization. The importance of these figures goes beyond their mediation of local disputes to include their functioning as auxiliaries to state authorities in matters relating to political government. By virtue of their work as intermediaries with state authorities, these individuals have come to represent the local notability. The discussion in the first section highlighted a number of factors that enter into the constitution of mediators: having contacts and links with state agencies and agents, possessing material wealth that is partly invested to acquire symbolic capital, and successfully accumulating symbolic capital. We need to inquire further into the material bases of the emergence of local mediators as a notability and situate this emergence in the context of the wider socioeconomic transformations that have been taking place in Egypt over the last three decades.

To begin, my usage of the term *notability* inevitably recalls and evokes an earlier usage, in particular that of Albert Hourani (1981) in his classic study of "the politics of notables" during the Ottoman period. Briefly, in that study, Hourani differentiated the notables of that period into three groupings: a religious stratum made up of high-ranking *ulama*, a military stratum comprising the local garrison leaders, and a secular stratum of wealthy landowners and merchants. For our purposes, the most important dimension of the account is what Hourani identifies as the defining feature of the notables—namely their mediating role with the central government in Istanbul. It was as representatives of the people that the notables could get a hearing at the center. At the same time, their links with the center gave them a privileged position and contributed to their influence among the local populations. They did not necessarily have absolute allegiance to the center and could elect to mobilize their local followers at times of disagreements with central decisions. However, their mediation was necessary for the exercise of political government. Based on my discussion of the mediators as figures of authority, we can draw parallels between them and the early notables, but we need to address some questions in a direct and clear manner. The questions that my usage of the term *notability* throws into the open are the following: How do today's notables compare with the notables of the Ottoman period? How are they constituted? What roles do they play in relation to the state? Are they representative of any particular constituency?

In comparison to the notables of the Ottoman period, today's notables are of a lesser social status in the sense that they do not issue from prominent families with a long, established history. Further, their interventions in their local communities are not of the same scale as the interventions of the earlier notables. Although a few of the contemporary local notability have managed to enter national politics through elections to the National Assembly, they could not be referred to as national figures. In light of these distinctions, they would be better thought of as lesser notables.

Let us now consider the factors that make certain local community figures in contemporary popular quarters of Cairo notables. Undoubtedly, the most important element is their mediating role between local communities and state agents and agencies. As noted, these agencies seek the help of local figures in negotiating issues of potential conflict and confrontation. The acquired status of these figures most often has to do with economic distinction—being well-off merchants and workshop owners. In her historically grounded study of contemporary elites in Egypt, Amira Sonbol (2000) places this stratum of *tujjar* (merchants) below the merchants and entrepreneurs who make up the commercial bourgeoisie and who are close to or are located within the circles of power. This second-echelon *tujjar*, as we may call them, appear in Sonbol's analysis as having no links with the ruling classes (ibid., 199–200). While Sonbol is correct in distinguishing between various echelons of *tujjar*, her contention that the lower-ranking merchants do not have links with the ruling classes and the apparatus of power should be nuanced. In fact, individuals from the second echelon of merchants have acceded to positions of influence that are partly based on contacts with the state apparatus and the ruling elite. Undoubtedly, their contacts are limited relative to those of the new commercial bourgeoisie that has risen to prominence following the *infitah* (open door) policies of the 1970s. Along with some new entrants into the entrepreneurial strata, the first-echelon merchants enjoy close links with the ruling elite and have input into decision making, especially in the areas of investment and privatization. The notability I am identifying here is lower in socioeconomic standing but pursues modes of operation similar to those of the first echelon or new bourgeoisie. At the same time, their status is locally embedded.

If we zero in on the composition of this lesser notability, we find that it is comprised of real estate contractors, workshop owners, and wholesale-retail merchants. In other words, they come from a social stratum whose ranks have expanded with the economic liberalization and privatization policies. The trajectories of those who have fared well within this stratum, share some common socioeconomic features. Some belong to merchant families that have been in business for two or three generations. This is true of Mr. Ashraf who has a clothing store in al-Azhar and an outlet in his own neighborhood. His cousins and uncles are in clothing manufacturing and sales, dealing primarily in children's wear and women's *'abaya*. Mr. Ashraf and his family members have a working partnership that allows them to pool their capital to secure the purchase of merchandise from large private workshops. Resource pooling is a common strategy among these medium-sized merchants, allowing them to avoid having to take out business loans with banks. In this respect, they articulate a different business ethos from that of the upper-echelon entrepreneurs. The large entrepreneurs have routinely used bank loans, and some of them have been involved in highly publicized cases of loan fraud. In distinguishing themselves from the large entrepreneurs, the medium-sized merchants, some of whom in interviews used the term "super merchants" *("al-tujjar al-super")* to refer to the big entrepreneurs, deploy religious idioms to frame their modes of operation. For instance, the preference for pooling capital was explained in terms of a desire to avoid financing that entails interest payments and that would implicate them in usurious, and hence un-Islamic, practices. These merchants continue to rely on personal contacts. They also use simple credit notes (*wasl amana*) to register credit arrangements and payments. This mode of operation accounts for the consolidation of family businesses and the building up of influence in a community. The idea that a merchant's name represents capital is invoked to signify the value of reputation.

Merchants have their own economic and social networks through which they consolidate their positions in their neighborhoods. Links between merchants are forged in collective activities such as raising money for charity. Merchant families like Mr. Ashraf's invest in building their status by donating to charitable activities inside and outside their quarters. One merchant stated that the big merchants of his area collected funds to be donated to particular institutions such as the Orphans Institute or the Cancer Hospital. Through the local mosque they may organize other collections for activities in the neighborhood. For example, groups of merchants organize meals for charity, such as *Mawa'id al-rahman* (the Merciful's tables) set up during the month of Ramadan. On these occasions, the merchants host the poor residents of their area and serve them personally. This is considered a sign of their humility and an expression of their goodness. Finally, they cultivate links with state authorities, for instance, organizing banquets to which the police commissioner (*ma'mur*), the head of the police investigative unit, and members of the local and national assemblies are invited. In the words of Mr. Ashraf, the organization of these activities "allows for direct relations with the leadership" (*'ilaqat mubashira ma 'a al-qiyadat*). Through their contacts with public institutions and their position in the community, merchants are sought out by their clients to resolve problems. Mr. Ashraf's interventions are of the kind we found with hajj

Saleh. Indeed, he maintains the same kind of links that hajj Saleh has with the authorities, in particular with the police. His links are also visible as he has public meetings with the leadership, and his civic work is of a public nature. Through this work and his "good deeds," Mr. Ashraf has acceded to the position of notability. In that position, he may be sought out by the police to mediate their relations with the community.

In addition to merchants, real estate contractors have also sought to join the ranks of the new notability. A number of real estate contractors in the quarter were identified as individuals of influence. One of them, who also happens to be a textile merchant, is referred to as the *umda* (mayor) by friends and neighbors. He had acquired large plots of land, subdivided them, and sold them on credit. Investment in real estate also contributed to the rise of a local entrepreneur, hajj Sultan. He acquired a position of influence with the municipality and the governorate, although he was not identified as a mediator. Sultan began his working career as a textile merchant; according to some accounts, he started out as a peddler. He then seized on the opportunities available during the early days of the quarter's development and purchased property lots for subdivision and resale. It is worth mentioning here that the member of the National Assembly who won a seat in 2000 after running as an independent and then joined the ruling party has a similar trajectory to Sultan's. He was also of modest origin and built up his wealth through real estate investments. His business ventures today include proprietorship of a private language school.

Seeking a seat in the National Assembly appears to be a strategy for consolidating and formalizing positions of authority. In this respect, the lesser notability could be said to be following in the steps of the commercial bourgeoisie. Over the last decade, large entrepreneurs and business persons have run, in increasing number, in elections to the National Assembly. As a consequence, their share of seats has been rising. In 2000, this entrepreneurial class won seventy-seven seats, accounting for 17 percent of the total. This figure increases if we take account of the twelve seats won by bankers as well as those won by professionals, many of whom have their own consulting and investment firms. Merchants and contractors from popular quarters have joined the business class in running for the National Assembly seats. This entry of the lesser notables into national politics should be interpreted as a confirmation of their role as intermediaries with government, not as political representatives. The notability is also active in party politics, as members in the local assembly and as secretaries to the ruling party local branches.

What should be highlighted about the lesser notables is the mediating role they play, the links and contacts they cultivate with the state, and the resources they deploy locally to achieve notability status (e.g., donating to charities and visibly demonstrating their influence on government). A notable is both "a man of good" and "a man of power." His symbolic capital is enhanced by the public exhibition of religious devotion. He contributes to the construction of mosques, to the sponsorship of orphans and to charities that support poor families. Many in the notability carry the title *hajj* in reference to having performed the pilgrimage.

If the mediating role with government is the defining element of the lesser notables, we still need to inquire into the position of those who have many of the other elements that enter into the constitution of notability but who do not have apparent links with government or have broken ties with it. The question arises when we compare the role of notables as intermediaries with the state with the role of Islamist activists as mediators and arbiters within their communities, although occupying an oppositional positioning from the state. As I point out in the discussion that follows, by virtue of their mediating role and influence within their communities, Islamist activists like Sheikh Gabir gained prominence and acquired a popular following. This inevitably led to confrontation and clash with state authorities. One conclusion to draw here is that the state authorities could not tolerate the rise of a contending leadership, but we may also argue that in assiduously co-opting local figures, state authorities seek to inhibit the rise of independent leaders.

In Algeria, a rising notability established ties with the Front Islamique de Salut (FIS). Martinez (2000) speaks of "notable-entrepreneurs" who were anchored in their local neighborhoods. These notables contributed financially to the FIS. The profile that Martinez draws of one of these notable-entrepreneurs (ibid., 26–28) bears many similarities to that of the lesser notables. Although, historically, the notable-entrepreneurs had links with the military, they hedged their bets on the Islamists. Through an alliance with the FIS, they sought to confer the symbols of legitimacy on their wealth, deploying symbolism that validates their trade in Islamic terms—the same terms used by conservative Islamist entrepreneurs in Egypt

(Ismail 1998). Further, the Algerian notables used the networks of informal trade to consolidate their standing in their neighborhoods, employing youths in the trafficking, and importation of goods.

In Bulaq and in other popular quarters of Cairo, some commercial networks are identified as being run by the *Sunniyya* (literally meaning follower of the *Sunna*, or Tradition, of the Prophet). The designation *Sunniyya* is another way of referring to someone who has Islamist associations; *sunni* is the predominant sect of all Egyptian Muslims but in this context denotes the religious character of the individuals and networks. These merchants run wholesaling-retailing firms for clothing and light household goods. They sell at low rates of profit and engage in charitable activities. They have no clear connections to government. From narratives I gathered from a number of the women who worked as peddlers in these chains, there is indication that the *Sunniyya* merchants are engaged in the governance of morality. They require women peddlers who sell for them on credit to don the veil. Their transactions with women peddlers are constructed as giving assistance to poor women who have no male guardian and who are in need of support to safeguard their morality. The *Sunniyya* networks appear as part of the re-Islamization process and there is no indication that they are linked to active Islamists. However, reports of the al-Jama'a al-Islamiyya activities in Imbaba in the late 1980s and early 1990s point out that they were tied to *Sunniyya* commercial networks.[3]

Islamically oriented commercial and financial networks are inevitably drawn into power politics. For example, in the 1980s the Islamic Societies for the Placement of Funds (ISPF) maintained close contacts with high-ranking government officials and prominent sheikhs. For various reasons, the ISPF's economic activities came under scrutiny, and the government intervened to bring an end to its speculative investments. The ISPF did not represent an oppositional force, but there were concerns about its growing economic power.

The informalization of trade and business undergirds the rise of the lesser notability whose politics cannot be easily pigeonholed. For, while a number of these notable works within the ruling party and in conjunction with state authorities, their work ethos and public self-presentation—as devout, God-fearing, honest, and fair dealing—underscores a religious-oriented performance that would be in line with hedging their bets on an Islamist political force. Here, we can see the similarities with the Algerian experience. We should highlight some

features of the changing social configuration tied with informalization, namely the expansion in ranks of tradesmen (*hirafiyyin*) and the
contraction of public sector workers as a result of privatization, in
addition to the rather large share of commerce in the informal economy, with wholesale-retail accounting for more than 40 percent of all
nonagricultural economic activities.[4] These features point to the crys-
tallization of certain new social forces whose political agency is now
forming. We find the evidence for this agency in the changing composition of militant Islamist groups from being comprised predominantly of students to having an increased number of *hirafiyyin* (Ismail
2000). I suggest that merchants and contractors, as a class of lesser notables, are emerging as political actors. The politics of the lesser notables deserve closer analysis. We should follow certain developments, in
particular, their involvement in national politics. The question that
arises here is: Can the existing political arrangements accommodate
their ambitions? If not, to which other channels or modes of political
activism would they turn? My analysis points to the following. First, the
political arrangements cannot accommodate them fully. This is at-
tested to by the fact that many of them could not secure the support
of the ruling NDP to run as its candidates in the National Assembly
elections and had no option but to run as independents. Second, the
symbolic links with conservative Islamism make them potential allies
with an Islamically oriented party.

In his novel, *'Imarat Ya'qubyan*, 'Ala al-Aswani (2003) draws a por-
trait of a religious entrepreneur, hajj Azzam, an owner of a large
wholesale-retail chain in Cairo, selling clothes at cheap prices. The religious entrepreneur cultivates the image of a devout man—fair dealing and caring for his community. In the meantime, he maintains
back-channel links with the ruling elites in order to negotiate consent
for the expansion of his businesses and to secure a foreign-car dealership. Through these back channels, he succeeds in obtaining the
ruling party's nomination for a seat in the National Assembly. Hajj Azzam's political and business rival, Abu Hamiduh, is a wholesale-retail
merchant who is credited with having encouraged thousands of
women to don the veil. This account is thought to have been inspired
by the circumstances of a real-life owner of a wholesale-retail business
with a chain of stores, many of which are located in Cairo's popular
quarters. In the novel, the narrative of the rise of the religious entrepreneur traces a trajectory that ends in a face-off with power. As the
entrepreneur consolidates his businesses and builds an independent

base, he begins to question the terms of the deal he has with the big powers. When he insists on a meeting with "the Big Boss" ("*al-Ragil al-Kabir*"), he ends up in a room where the Boss can be heard, but not seen. Invisible, but omnipresent, the Boss dictates the terms of the deal. The entrepreneur must submit to the terms. This outcome is possible in part because, in this encounter, the entrepreneur is alone, but also it would appear because he has a compromised history, having been implicated in the drug trade. The question we are left pondering is: What happens if he is joined by others in this face-off with the Boss? The salience of this hypothetical question becomes apparent when we turn to the position of the notables in the local power compacts that are integrated into political government.

The Notability in the Local Power Compacts

In my sketch of the profile of hajj Saleh, we see that local notables act as mediators in community disputes and participate in *majalis 'urfiyya* (customary councils). In this role, they may be seen to be furthering the autonomy of their local communities. However, in acting as intermediaries with state authorities, the notables are integrated into a sort of local power compact that serves as an auxiliary to formal government. To illustrate, let us consider the activities of governance in which they are called upon to participate, by state agents as much as by their fellow citizens.

Notables like hajj Saleh perform multiple services that are spatially inscribed. For instance, their presence in public space is sometimes essential for mediation with state agents, as when popular forces hold social festivities or other events. The presence of individuals like hajj Saleh is seen as necessary at such occasions when there is an increased likelihood of conflict between citizens and state agents. The status of a person like the hajj is utilized and validated at public social events such as weddings. The hajj sits at the front of the tents in which street weddings are held. The reason for his personal presence and visibility is that weddings are occasions for various kinds of encounters with the state. Weddings last until late into the night, often past midnight. This is a time when the police undertake the dispersal of public gatherings. The electricity used to light the tent is often tapped from the electrical boxes in the street without authorization. Further, there is always the possibility of a brawl or scuffle breaking out, which may invite police intervention. The hajj's presence signals mediation. His positioning at the entrance of tents and other venues allows state representatives to find negotiators when they engage in spatial tactics of control or when the state "comes down to earth" before being dismissed from the premises.

As sites of the investment of authority, mechanisms of conflict resolution (as exemplified by elders and *biytkabarluh* individuals) have implications for state–society relations. These implications become clear if we consider what happens when everyday forms of organization are invested by oppositional social forces as was the case when Islamists inserted themselves into local settings. In Imbaba and Ayn Shams, for instance, Islamist groups came to occupy spaces of mediation and to appropriate positions of authority. In both quarters, leaders/emirs rose to positions of mediator and inscribed themselves within the communities as agents of *tahakum* (arbitration to God's rules) (Ismail 2000). In Imbaba, sheikh Gabir became involved in the resolution of quotidian disputes similar to those in which Mustafa 'Urabi intervened on Harat al-Sharaqwa in Bulaq. Water thrown from a balcony onto the floor below, children fighting with each other, and tenants not paying their rent are all recurring issues of conflict that invite the intervention of mediators. Sheikh Gabir, however, also mediated bigger disputes with higher stakes, such as conflicts with Christian neighbors or fights with Upper-Egypt clans. Here, his role is closer to someone *biytkabarluh,* someone like hajj Saleh. The difference is that hajj Saleh is co-opted by the state, while Gabir's role and actions are framed by ideological articulations that challenged state legitimacy.

Several points can be drawn out here. The community's modes of conflict resolution are the sites of the investment of power. In Imbaba, and also in Ayn Shams, al-Jama'a leaders occupied positions of arbiters in opposition to formal government. In contrast, in Bulaq, and later in Imbaba following the security campaigns of 1992, local arbiters were co-opted by state authorities. What thus obtains with respect to conflict resolution is a kind of mix of "traditional" authority, represented by the majalis and the notables, with "legal" structures, the latter referring back to the state.

We may better understand the role of the *majalis 'urfiyya* and the notables in the internal governance of the quarter if we compare them with the dispute mediation mechanisms in villages in post-Maoist China. As Ann Anagnost (1997, 144–46) details, these mechanisms involve the incorporation of the village compact—a traditional village mediation institution—into local government as a supplement to the legal system. The role of this institution is to deal with conflicts that are too pervasive and too intricate to be dealt with by the legal apparatus. At the same time, it is intended to re-inscribe "traditional" modes of control in communities undergoing rapid social change. In official rhetoric, the arrangement is represented as a model for self-government. Yet, at the same time that the village compacts give communities a measure of local autonomy, they also serve to reassert the power of local party officials while creating a gap between party policy and the law (ibid., 139–40). According to Anagnost, within this gap lies ambiguity as to the scope and limits of the power of village compacts. This ambiguity, she contends, is necessary for the functioning of power. Similarly, in Egypt, state authorities have called on the *majalis* to deal with intractable disputes such as long-running feuds between clans in Upper Egypt. Recently, attempts have been made to use the *majalis* format to try to resolve disputes between prominent entrepreneurs. The intention is to conceal from public view the rapaciousness of some of the business deals. In Bulaq, the *majalis* function, to some extent, as a supplement in the sense used by Anagnost. They are composed of city councilmen and community notables, and they deal with matters viewed as too pervasive or too normatively complex to be resolved by the legal structure. Do the *majalis* reinforce the power of state officials as is the case with the compacts in the Chinese villages? To the extent that the *majalis* supplement the legal system in a way that facilitates political government, they do. However, we have also seen that when Islamists deployed the same mediation practices found in the *majalis*, they represented a challenge to state authorities rather than a supplement. Thus, the workings of self-government may, in and of themselves, be harnessed to state purposes, or they may be mobilized into oppositional tactics.

Mediation structures and processes address conflicts that are woven into the social fabric of quarters and communities. In Bulaq, for instance, two areas of mediation are tribal or clan relations and confessional relations. Both types of conflict were present in Imbaba as well, and accounts of sheikh Gabir's arbitration activities indicate that he was called upon to mediate such disputes. There are instances in which members of the Jama'a al-Islamiyya in Imbaba were themselves embroiled in confessional and clan-based disputes. In contrast to Gabir, who assumed his mediation role in opposition to state agents and structures, hajj Saleh, in Bulaq, was sought by the police to mediate the clan-based disputes involving al-'Adawiyya and al-Tawyala— both Upper-Egypt clans that have established themselves in the area and that are engaged in fights with each other, with others in the area, and with the police. Hajj Saleh was deputized by the police to deal with the clans, in particular al-'Adawiyya; because its members have businesses, including coffee shops, bakeries, and retail shops, in the area, this clan was more likely to come into conflict with the police. Police raids on coffee shops are occasions when clans assert their local power.

A second area of mediation by the local notability is relations between confessional groups, specifically between Muslims and Copts. In one instance, conflict arose in Bulaq over the use of a vacant lot on Street Ten. According to some accounts, the owner of the lot had originally planned to use it for the construction of a mosque. However, because of a change in his financial situation, he put it up for sale. A church located further down on the same street proposed to buy it with the plan of building a library. At that point, the local Muslim notables intervened to raise funds to purchase the land and build a mosque on it. Hajj Shihab, a local councilman, as well as others, saw this intervention as a means of preventing an eruption of confessional conflict. The fund-raising, processing of the purchase transaction, and construction permits were undertaken by the notability. It was said that a portion of the capital came from Saudi sources and, for some, this confirmed that the notables were well connected. This example and the case of hajj Saleh and the feuding clans demonstrate a number of things about mediation and internal governance: the local notability is active in diffusing conflicts that are potentially destabilizing; the notability can secure state cooperation; and the notability-mediators deal with conflicts in a manner parallel to that of the Islamists.

Local Government: Blurred Boundaries

The co-optation of *biytkabarluh* figures into the state is part of a wider regime of governance and control in which state–society boundaries are blurred. In examining such blurred boundaries, Akhil Gupta (1995) points to the problems inherent in conceiving of state–society relations as taking place across divides or boundaries. The fluidity and nonfixity of sites where state policies and politics are conceived, formulated, and put into effect must be acknowledged if we are to understand the workings of the state. I want to zero in on this fluidity and on the sliding sites of the state by reflecting on the local arrangements and the role of state representatives vis-à-vis societal forces. Three episodes from the life of local government provide insights into the coalition of forces and interests that guide the running of daily community affairs. The first episode concerns the Bulaq central market and highlights how state goals of bringing "discipline and order" to the street are served by reinscribing the social hierarchy underpinning economic arrangements. Second, the episode of the collapsed school features the same personages involved in the market affair. However, in this instance, they are engaged in maneuvers relating to the competing claims of public goods and private property rights. In the final episode, the matter of the defective street-lamp posts, the management of a basic service provided the occasion for the citizen-subjects to dissociate from formal government and express their disdain for its corruption and incompetence.

The issues at stake in the market affair are crystallized in accounts recounted to me by two state agents: hajj Shihab, the local councilman, and hajj Hasan, a municipality official and a New Democratic Party local secretary. The background to the market arrangements should be located in the efforts of state authorities to regain control over the use of public space and public conduct. As part of these efforts, a national policy was developed that sought to remove outdoor markets to the edges of the city or to the periphery of neighborhoods in order to effect control of space. Indeed, the location of markets came to be constructed as a problem of urban government: markets were thought of as less manageable if located within residential quarters, and they were seen to occasion modes of sociability that undermine the logic of "ordered space" if they are in places that are visible and accessible to the wider public. In conjunction with this policy, authorities have resorted to the tactic of using local figures of power and influence, to extend state control over territory or to help mediate relations with local forces.

In the case of the Bulaq market scheme, the Giza governorate, the Bulaq municipality, and the Bulaq police developed cooperative relations with strongmen in the area to relocate the Bulaq market on Tir'at Zanayn Street. For various reasons, the governorate's plan to remove the market to the periphery of the quarter was abandoned. Instead, these authorities charged a local strongman-entrepreneur with the task of establishing a "formal" market on the only plot of undeveloped land in the area. It so happened that the land was adjacent to the existing Tir'at Zanayn market. The previous governor had approved the plan of locating a market on the plot, although title to it had been contested in court. The entrepreneur built a wall around the plot and offered to rent spots, not stalls, to vendors in the existing market at a fee of two pounds per day. While some vendors moved into the new market, others remained on the street. All vendors were, however, obliged to pay rent to the market proprietor through his local representative, whether or not they moved into the designated area.

This arrangement embodies local power relations sustained by state authorities. The owner of the new market uses a local strongman to collect the rental fees from vendors. This tactic is known to everyone in the market area—shop owners, local assembly people, and so on. The market owner is said to be close to the vice-head of the municipality and to be paying salaries in the municipality. Undoubtedly corruption is a feature of the market arrangement agreed to by the governorate and implemented by the municipality. However, the arrangement expresses a mode of local government management that delegates the running of affairs in a manner consistent with the existing power relations.

In their narratives of the market arrangements, both hajj Shihab and hajj Hasan noted the informal nature of the agreement that allowed hajj Sultan to use his land for a market (the new market was not registered with the Market Directorate and no official, written permit had been issued). As they pointed out, the arrangements were decided following a verbal agreement with the former governor of Giza and were implemented with municipality backing. At this point in their accounts, the corruption of the government is invoked: "Hajj Sultan pays salaries of people in the municipality" and the vice-head of the municipality is implicated. Thus, inasmuch as hajj Sultan is "the employer" of public servants, he in a sense has replaced the government. There is a reversal of the roles of citizen and state. This modality of government recalls Mbembe's (2001) discussion of "indirect private government."

Fluidity in the sites and the workings of government also marked the maneuvers that followed the "collapse" of a primary school in the quarter. Conflict arose when the lot housing the school was sold to hajj Sultan, a local entrepreneur, market proprietor, real estate contractor, and by all accounts, "a powerful man." The sale agreement was accompanied by an order for the school to evacuate the premises. The sellers of the property secured the order based on a municipality report that the school building was on the verge of collapse. The technical accuracy of the municipality's report of the condition of the building may not be certain; however, securing a report to the effect ensures that the Department of Education's existing school lease would be terminated and the new owner can put up a more lucrative edifice in place of the old.

This type of maneuver is common throughout Egypt's large cities and is typically pursued by proprietors who seek to improve their real estate investments. It also requires the collusion of municipality technicians. As a result of the evacuation order, the students were to be relocated to another school, causing the swelling of class sizes to as many as eighty to ninety students. Hajj Shihab contested the sale in the local assembly and requested that the land continue to be reserved for use as a school. This would have required the intervention of the executive council of the municipality as well as the office of the Department of Education in the governorate. Hajj Sultan's supporters in the local assembly informed him of Shihab's intervention, and he mobilized to stop Shihab from proceeding with his plan to block the school closing. Shihab wanted the state to buy the land and to locate a public school on it. In response, Sultan claimed that he would build a private school on the lot and hence would be providing the needed service (albeit at a much higher cost to the residents). Shihab negotiated with the Department of Education to reopen the school for the students already enrolled so that they could complete their primary education. As part of the deal, no new students would be accepted. The temporary resolution was designed to buy time to find another plot of land on which to locate the school. In this episode, competing claims to public good and private property were fought out, in the open, in the local assembly and in the municipality, and, behind the scenes, through informal channels within these very same public institutions.

What do these episodes tell us? At one level, we may see them as instances of official corruption, as the vain efforts of some seemingly honest individuals to fight corrupt practices, or as the apparent lack of citizen action in confronting a situation of deteriorating public services. At another level, however, we see in the struggles and maneuvers of the local notability a sliding and blurring of formal and informal sites of governance. The state is not a coherent entity—its public institutions do not operate only in public. Much lobbying and negotiations take place behind the scenes. Regulatory powers are not all formal, and informal arrangements are put into effect using formal powers. It may be countered, as noted by Gupta (1995), that the sliding of the formal into the informal and vice versa occurs at the level of local but not national institutions. However, against notions of public accountability through open National Assembly debates, and through public policies, rules, and procedures, myriad backroom discussions and competing claims are negotiated informally. In these less visible spaces, state–society boundaries are blurred.

I want to end my exploration into the sliding sites and blurring boundaries of government by considering the conundrum of the Bulaq streetlamps. I will sketch out some of the details on why the lamps were faulty and why the citizen-subjects refused to collaborate with the state in resolving the problem. The episode began with the installation, by the municipality, of streetlamp posts to illuminate alleyways in some sections of Bulaq. As it turned out, due to a technical error, the lamps did not work—the supply of electrical power was insufficient to light them. As such, it was decided that the electricity would be generated from the public boxes that supplied private residences. To do this, the lamps would have to be connected to the boxes and then to switches outside of people's homes. Homeowners and tenants would be responsible to switch the lights on at night and off in the morning. A municipality technician asserted to me that this plan worked out fine in some alleyways, but not in others. Indeed, some residents objected to certain aspects of the plan. For instance, there was the matter of who was to supply and install the switches and the question of why the residents of private homes should take responsibility for the running of a public service. Withholding cooperation in resolving the problem was, for some residents, a way of dissociating themselves from government inefficiency. Perhaps their reluctance to be implicated in the matter reflected their desire to stand back to watch the farcical production of governmental power. In a sense, the lamp posts became monuments to corrupt, but farcical, power. We may also see in this reaction a kind of *dédoublement* (doubling) to which Mbembe (2001) alludes: subjects of power de-authorize it at the same time and in the same sites that they ratify it.

If rituals of state grandeur and spectacular public projects are designed to bring the people up to the heights of the state's majesty,[5] dismal failures and ineptness in the management of basic services may be said to elicit ridicule and contempt. In returning the gaze back upon farcical power, the citizen-subjects cannot hide that they are not impressed and may, at times, seize the opportunity to express their derision.[6] The lamp posts stood there as a sign of corrupt practices. The contractors, in collusion with the municipality personnel, supplied inadequate electrical connections. Outspoken figures like hajj Sayyid pointed to the posts as evidence of corruption. Indeed, on the occasion of a visit to the market by the head of the municipality, hajj Sayyid publicly confronted him over the posts. Their exchanges deteriorated into insults. Further, in an informal meeting with a municipality technician at his coffee shop, hajj Sayyid accused the technician and his colleagues of being thieves and asked rhetorically: "How much money did you make from the electrical connection?" Publicly, hajj Sayyid took the state to task for its corruption.

The lamp posts episode reveals dimensions of the workings of the state that are resonant with Gupta's (2001) findings that the state may be housed in private locations. When I inquired from a municipality official and from the local assembly representative how the issue of the electrical connection was decided, the response I received pointed to the sliding between formality and informality in decision-making processes and in interventions normally associated with the state. The official explained that a budget allocation for the connection plan was approved at the city level. This was followed by a meeting of "representatives," comprising National Democratic Party members and members of the City Council. The meeting was held either at the City Council building or in the local NDP office. No other individuals— community residents, for instance—were invited to attend and express their views. Needless to say, the NDP office is not a government office and the "representatives" are not all representatives.

Conclusion

In dealing with everyday-life problems and in their effort to manage needs and issues of concern such as security and preservation of the moral code, residents of Bulaq neighborhoods have developed forms of governance, such as *majalis tahkim*, which, to some extent, recall and reinscribe institutions of old. As the chapter has shown, everyday-life forms of organization are intimately tied to social hierarchies, in some instances reinforcing relations of power and domination within the quarter. It is important to underline that while turning to elders for dispute resolution is motivated by the residents' desire to eschew police and state, their separation from or contestation of state power is not one of absolute opposition. Rather, poor families sometimes use tricks and ruse to deliberately engage the police in their disputes, their objective being to gain leverage over one another. In other words, the differently situated subjects of power mobilize their knowledge of the system of rule in their interaction with each other and in their dealings with state authorities. I discuss ordinary citizens' understandings and views of government in greater detail in chapter 5.

Normative rules govern the workings of the institutions devised by the community. For example, the ethos of someone *biytkabarluh* involves rights and obligations on the part of the person occupying the position. Moral deference exercised toward the *biytkabarluh* figure derives from relations of kinship, regional origin, and the moral standing of the person. The profile of hajj Saleh indicates that acceding to the position of someone *biytkabarluh* is materially inscribed. It is the hajj's visible links to formal institutions that are ultimately acknowledged and validated at times of intervention. The hajj's involvement in charitable work earns him the image of "a man of good," while his links with the police establish him as a "man of power." As someone *biytkabarluh*, the hajj is incorporated by the state apparatus of coercion to mediate in disputes with the local population. In a sense, by virtue of their social status and their political role, individuals like hajj Saleh represent a notability of sorts. The political agency of the lesser notables is in the process of forming, and we need to pay attention to their modes of action, alliances, and allegiances. My analysis points to the contextual nature of the politics of the lesser notables and the possible directions that their implication in local and national politics may take.

Through state authorities' incorporation of the lesser notables and through the farming out of positions of authority, an urban regime of government is actualized. Politics in the sense of action taken to affect the conduct of government is a form of mediation but not representation. The image of the state that emerges in the account of the market arrangements, the view of hajj Sultan's influence, and hajj Saleh's induction into the system of government underscores a mode of operation that is characterized by improvisation. It would be difficult to prescribe a unitary logic to how local government is managed on a daily basis. By the same token, the proposition that there is a society that stands outside the state obscures the coalitions that bring "society in the state" to reverse Migdal's (2001) proposition on "the state in society."

So far, we have looked at the ordinary citizens' development of forms of governance designed to meet their needs. This should be understood in relation to the withdrawal of welfare provisions and disengagement of the state from its longstanding commitments in the social sphere. This disengagement is associated with a move toward the privatization of welfare and a reconfiguration of the terms of social responsibility. In the next chapter, I turn to another dimension of state–society relations: the exchanges between rulers and ruled and, more specifically, the changes in the social or moral contract governing those exchanges.

neoliberalism

Chapter 3

Neoliberalism and the Relocation of Welfare

THE IDEA THAT THE PEOPLE should be recipients of the state's largesse and of either free or heavily subsidized services was at the core of "the social contract" characterization of state–society relations in Egypt. Since the 1952 revolution, the Egyptian state has defined itself as a welfare state concerned with its citizens' social reproduction. Welfare provisions were fundamental to the ideological justifications of the ruling regimes in postrevolutionary Egypt. Further, they have entered into the terms organizing state–society relations as embodied in the notion of the social contract. The policies and laws that marked the outlines of this contract conveyed a populist bent reinforced by rhetoric on popular alliances and the elimination of class antagonism. Sociopolitical arrangements that set out the terms of state–society interaction were viewed by scholars as constituting a corporatist structure of sorts (see Ayubi 1995). Indeed, the predominance of singular type associations involved acquiescence, if not loyalty, in exchange for social benefits and for their monopoly over their members and over interest representation (Ayubi 1995; Posusney 1997). However, in the era of restructuring, the reigning orthodoxy of neoliberal economics has counseled a leaner state, one that is withdrawn from the economy. A component of this orthodoxy is to delegate service provision to the market. One question that emerges, then, is what kind of exchanges obtain between "the state" and "the people." In chapters 4 and 5, I attempt to address this question in terms of ordinary citizens' encounters with the everyday state. My purpose in this chapter is to examine the assumptions and understandings about population and society that structure neoliberal rationality in Egypt as well as the techniques of power through which this rationality is inscribed in everyday life.

The chapter traces the contours of the emergence of neoliberalism as a rationality of government in the social and economic spheres. It shows that the emergence of neoliberalism has been achieved through a number of policy moves that include the relocation of public welfare to the private sector, to NGOs, and to other civil associations, and the assignment of "development work" to NGOs.

The first section of the chapter provides a background overview of welfarist governmental rationality in Egypt and its links to the system of rule. That is, it looks at how welfarist arrangements were hitched to a corporatist style of political government. The second section focuses on my findings regarding welfare arrangements in Bulaq al-Dakrur. These findings reveal the existence and operation of an expansive network of charity, run primarily by religious organizations such as al-Gam'iyya al-Shar'iyya and al-Gam'iyya al-Khayriyya. I survey the workings of these associations in the area of poverty relief and social welfare and point to the techniques of discipline they inscribe. The third section discusses the move to private welfare in terms of its grounding in a discourse of philanthropy that mixes two registers: religious conservatism and western philanthropic traditions.

In the final section, I examine the relocation of welfare to the "private sector," especially its articulation with a range of technologies of discipline such as those involved in the engendering of the entrepreneurial subject as the ideal citizen. This, and other new subjectivities, are supported by the marketization of the social (social capital and informality are co-opted into this). Institutions such the United States Agency for International Development (USAID), the United Nations Development Program (UNDP), and Egypt's Social Fund for Development (SFD) are actively developing programs in support of entrepreneurial subjectivities. NGOs are incorporated into the process as intermediaries, while "culture" becomes a resource and an asset (Elyachar 2001). To illustrate my argument, I take as a case study the programs of microcredit promoted by these institutions.

From Welfarism to Neoliberalism

Students of modern Egyptian social history date the rise of the welfare state in Egypt to the 1950s and '60s. This turn toward welfarism came to be understood as the state being committed to the social reproduction

of its citizens (Bibars 2001, 77). However, the origins of a welfarist governmental rationality can be traced back to the constitution of the
Egyptian nation in the latter part of the nineteenth century (Ener
2003). Under the Western gaze, and with the desire to join the community of nations, Egyptian rulers and elites adopted various modes of
intervening in the social, thereby constituting the social body. By the
1950s, these modes of intervention were incorporated into the government of the state. At the same time, property and knowledge were na-
tionalized. Institutions with responsibilities for regulating the social
were integrated into the consolidated state bureaucracy. For instance,
juvenile reformatories became part of a juvenile division in the Ministry
of Social Affairs, a ministry whose purview covered the welfare of the
population, including pensions, social assistance, and surveying and
monitoring civil associations and the like.

The emerging welfare state introduced a wide gamut of provisions,
from guaranteed employment to all university and college graduates
to free education throughout all stages of schooling (with primary education becoming compulsory), literacy programs, and free medical
services to all. Welfare provisions extended also to the subsidization of
foodstuffs, primarily bread and other staples. Regulations in the area
of labor relations stipulated maximum working hours, mandatory benefit payments, and job security. These various welfare arrangements
were seen to constitute the postrevolution Egyptian "social contract"
or "moral economy" (Posusney 1997). However, their logic goes beyond exchanges between rulers and ruled. As studies of government in
the areas of population management and poverty have shown (Dean
1992; Donzelot 1979), the logic of welfare programs involves the de-
lineation of a sphere of government intervention separate from the political but networked with it (Rose and Miller 1992) and having as its
broader purpose the governing of population.

Welfare programs are inscriptions of techniques of rule on the
population. In their workings, they both sustain and modify power relations. Of particular interest here are the workings of social assistance
programs. Public benefits or social security are divided into provisions
that are subject to contributions and other insurance-type conditions
and those that are paid as a citizen entitlement and are part of a welfare or safety net not subject to regular insurance arrangements.
These latter fall under the general rubric of social assistance or welfare payments. In this section, I will focus on the social assistance programs that, in principle, constitute the safety net of the poor.[1]

Social assistance or welfare payments to those who have no insurance are organized under Law 30 of 1977.[2] The law contains thirty-four articles divided into seven main chapters. The chapters stipulate the sectors of the population to which the law applies, and they lay out the special rules concerning monthly benefits and one-time benefits to former workers. The law also identifies categories of beneficiaries of welfare payments. These are listed as follows: (1) orphans whose fathers died and whose mothers remarried or who were born out of wedlock; (2) widowed women under the age of sixty-five and all women who remain unmarried after their husband's death; (3) divorced women under the age of sixty-five; (4) the children of divorced women, if their mother has died, has remarried, or has been imprisoned; (5) elderly people over sixty-five years of age; (6) women (girls)[3] at age fifty who never married; and (7) the family of a prisoner serving a sentence of at least ten years (in this case the prisoner's wife receives a monthly pension) (Markaz Qadaya al-Mar'a 2000). In addition to the law, various schemes and programs were introduced to expand the reach of social assistance. These include the Sadat and the Mubarak pension plans, which primarily target citizens who are over sixty-five years of age or are physically disabled. They exclude the unemployed and daily and temporary workers from eligibility to social assistance.

The welfare law and policies are clearly gendered and conform to the social construction of gender in Egypt. For instance, the head of the household is assumed to be male and is considered to be responsible for his wife's and children's financial maintenance. As such, women who are in need must prove that they have no financial guardian. In other words, married women are presented as falling within the scope of their husbands' responsibility, while unmarried women are the wards of their fathers. Thus, married women whose husbands receive social security are excluded from eligibility for benefits (Bibars 2001, 96). They become eligible only when they can prove the absence or loss of their guardian. For formerly married women, proof of eligibility consists of a divorce certificate or a husband's death certificate and an attestation to being single. The provisions for never-married women over the age of fifty include the condition that the beneficiary be a *bint* (girl), a condition that reinforces gender hierarchies and controls.

In her study of the administration of welfare policies in Egypt, Bibars (2001) documents how administrators interpret the rules in a manner that reflects their personal prejudices and societal biases concerning women, especially divorced women. For instance, they treat divorced women as if they were failures or temptresses (ibid., 97), in the process reinforcing the patriarchal construction of assistance and sustaining moralizing principles of the family. The biases and prejudices are not merely residuals of traditional attitudes but are elements of the regulatory norms of governing through the family. The conditions women face while trying to get social security often cause them to abandon their quest. A number of my informants narrated episodes of encounter with the Department of Social Security in which during interviews they felt humiliated by the clerks and as a result decided to drop their application for social assistance.

In dealing with the hurdle of the social security bureaucracy, the social networks of family and neighborhood have proved to be important to women. They rely on the guidance of others who have some familiarity with the social security department and its workings and procedures. In Bulaq, local activists like Manal, my main informant, were known to be well versed in the system. Manal knew which forms had to be filled out and where to present them, and she had some knowledge of how they were processed. She volunteered this knowledge to help her neighbors and friends. For example, she helped Raga, a divorced woman, get winter aid—a one-time payment given by the welfare department in support of winter expenses such as buying warm clothing or paying school fees for children. For a number of women I interviewed, the social security payment they received was essential to their subsistence. It also allowed them a degree of independence in the family. For example, they gained greater mobility and were less subject to the monitoring of their male siblings. Securing assistance made it possible for some to return to school to further their education and improve their work options.

Overall, the funds allocated by government to social security payments remain negligible. Looking at the data for 1996, we find that the total amount spent on aid and social pensions through the Ministry of Social Affairs was 36.1 million pounds.[4] This represents an increase of 36.2 percent over the previous year's total of 26.5 million pounds. The total number of families benefiting from income support was 250,013, and the average annual benefit amount paid per family was 144 pounds. Additional aid comes from the Ministry of Awqaf (Religious Endowments), which in 1996 totaled 4,347,000 pounds, with an average payment of 40.6 pounds per case. In the governorate of Giza, of which Bulaq is a district, the number of families benefiting from state-run social pensions was 12,116 in 1996. The breakdown by category of beneficiary is as follows: 503 families of widowed women, 6,546 families of divorced women, 3,358 families of physically disabled persons, 1,056 elderly persons, and 229 listed as "Other."

At a glance, the numbers confirm citizens' limited access to benefits. Families in which the husband is unemployed and is neither over sixty-five years of age nor suffering a severe disability are not eligible for welfare. Thus, families in which the male breadwinners are seasonal or daily workers have no recourse to public funding. Further, the criteria outlined for proving physical disability leaves out many whose health condition is poor enough to impede their ability to keep steady work but not considered severe enough to qualify. Thus, the rules and conditions that define the status of beneficiary keep many families outside the official social safety net. Individuals with poor health, but no permanent disability, do not fall into the categories designated for welfare payment and as such do not qualify for assistance.

Early rumblings of a neoliberal shift in Egyptian social and economic policy may be said to have been felt with the removal of bread subsidies in 1977. They were reestablished after widespread public demonstrations. Since then, other food subsidies have had to be reinstituted after their removal—April 2004 being a recent instance—indicating that the shift away from welfarism has not been straightforward. However, a number of measures have been taken as part of the retreat from welfarism. These include the freezing of health spending, the masked privatization of schooling, a cap on public sector hiring, and an accompanying informalization of labor leading to the disappearance of social security for greater numbers of the working poor. The shift to neoliberalism has also been marked by the relocation of welfare provision to the private sector and the assignment of development work to NGOs. The remainder of this chapter looks closely at these moves and the subjectivities that are engendered under the sign of neoliberalism.

Case Notes I   Abu Dunya's Household: Negotiating the Privatization of Health and Education

Abu Dunya works as a driver for a doctor and his family residing in Garden City. He earns 300 pounds per month—equivalent to the average income of the Bulaq households in my sample. Abu Dunya's household comprises himself, his wife, three children, and his mother. Two of the children, his daughter (eighteen years) and younger son (thirteen years), are still in school. Muhammad, the eldest child (twenty-one years), works in a hotel but will be commencing his military service shortly. Abu Dunya's monthly budget allocations are as follows: Um Dunya, his wife, is given 200 pounds to cover bill payments (approximately thirty pounds) and other household expenses, including food, clothing, medical fees, and incidentals; his daughter, Dunya, and his younger son are given allowances of forty-five pounds each, 70 percent of which is used to cover travel, by minibus, to and from school. There is no housing rent to pay as the family occupies the second floor of a building Abu Dunya co-owns with his brother. According to Abu Dunya, his salary is spent within the first five days of the month.

Muhammad contributes to the household income when he gets work. At the time of the interview, he was working in the tourism sector, making sweets in a hotel. His father found him the job through personal contacts. The medical tests required as part of the application procedure for the job cost LE 200. Muhammad entered the labor market before completing high school. He has worked irregularly since then.

Abu Dunya has steady earnings, but they allow him to just make ends meet. He is, in fact, dependent on aid from others, mainly from the couple that employs him. For example, the doctor's wife raises donations to help cover the costs of treatment for Abu Dunya's kidney condition. He requires dialysis treatment three times per week. While fees for this treatment at al-Qasr al-'Ayni hospital are covered by his medical insurance plan, the costs of medication are not. This is so, because the Egyptian government revoked its subsidy program on prescription drugs for insured workers. It was eliminated on the pretext that patients, with the cooperation of some pharmacists, were exchanging the subsidy vouchers for products such as creams and shampoo, instead of drugs. In this context, assistance from neighbors and family has become a necessary supplement to Abu Dunya's employment earnings. One form of assistance that has become important to Abu Dunya is the donations that the doctor's wife raises for him from time to time from within her own circle of friends and acquaintances. This assistance takes the form of clothes for the children, money, or items for the house. This kind of personalized charity is an important supplement to earnings for many whose work involves service to or regular personal contact with the well-to-do. However, being the recipient of benefits of this type depends on a number of contingencies, such as the potential donor's personal attitude toward the poor, his/her willingness and capacity to raise donations from within his/her circle, recognition that the employee or service provider is in need, the demeanor of the potential recipient, and his/her self-presentation as someone in need of some support. Thus, there is considerable discretion built into the practice of personalized charity. In Abu Dunya's case, this means that there are times when, for lack of funds, he forsakes medication in order to cover other necessary costs.

In dealing with expenditures and rising deficits, Abu Dunya's family prioritizes expenses and must make hard choices. Apart from choices having to do with Abu Dunya's illness, this has also meant that Dunya had to choose to pursue her education at vocational college rather than university. In doing so, she has reasoned that "university is open" (al-gam'a maftuha), meaning that there are no limits on expenses and hence it is unaffordable for her family.

For most families in Bulaq, transportation is an additional cost to securing children's education beyond preparatory school since most schools are located outside the quarter. Even young girls who attend vocational school in Nahya are required to take the minibus. The minibus fees range from sixty to seventy piasters per day and may total about fifteen pounds per month. For a family with three or four children, transportation costs could represent a considerable expense—in some cases, one-third of household income. Masked fees in public schools add to the costs of education. As there is a shortage of places in public schools, school administrators have resorted to strategies designed to increase school income. These include instituting a donor's fund to which the parents of prospective students must contribute if they want to secure a place for their child. When Dunya wanted to transfer from commercial secondary school in Aguza to an industrial craft school in Munib, her parents had to donate 200 pounds to process her application papers. Similarly, the parents of Abir, who is a student in Aguza secondary commercial school, had to pay to get her enrolled. In fact, a donation was not sufficient, and her father, an auto mechanic, had to call on a personal connection high up in the Ministry of Education. He also asked his neighbor, who is a teacher in a school in Haram and who knows someone in the Aguza school, to intercede on his behalf.

The masked fees that Dunya, Abir, and many others have to pay to gain entry into a public school are compounded by the fees required to pay for private lessons. The latter have become a necessity given the poor learning environment that results from overcrowded schools and poorly paid teachers. These fees increase household expenses, and because they have become a necessity, parents are faced with the choice of either paying the fees and keeping their child in school or not paying them and taking the child out. It is estimated that the annual cost of putting a child through primary school is 348 pounds and, at the preparatory level, 452 pounds (Assaad and Rouchdy 1999, 26). The average annual income for families in Bulaq is 3,600 Egyptian pounds. The relatively high cost of education, along with its devalorisation, has contributed to an increase in the dropout rate. Faced with the rising costs of living and the deficit in household budgets, many families take the route chosen by the mothers in Madinat Amer (Case Notes 3)—that of not sending their children to school. Such a decision is further rationalized in terms of the need for children's contributions to household incomes and the fact that an intermediate education does not improve work chances (see Hoodfar 1997, 201–2; Assaad and Rouchdy 1999, 26–27).

The Privatization of Welfare: Networks of Charity and "the Deserving Poor"

The literature on everyday-life politics in popular neighborhoods of large cities of the Global South richly documents the flourishing of social networks of solidarity (see Singerman 1995; Tripp 1997; Korayem 2001). It shows that through network exchanges between family members and neighbors, a degree of mutually assured security is achieved. These exchanges are particularly important in the management of the needs of low-income households. However, one dimension of network formation and operation appears to be based on something other than mutual aid. Rather, networks have arisen that can be more appropriately seen as charity-oriented—the product of a hybrid ethic of religious charity and modern philanthropy. Indeed, there has been a reactivation of philanthropy in Egypt as well as a deployment of the religious register of charity. Both of these developments redirect interventions in the social sphere for the purpose of managing the poor in a context of state retreat from the arena of welfare and a reorganization of the economy on neoliberal lines. The propagation of philanthropy, as argued by Jacques Donzelot (1979, 55), rests on the construction of an "assistance pole" that directs citizen demands away from the liberal state to the private sphere. A second pole is "hygien-ist" in nature. Its aim is to enroll the state in the management of social ills that accompany the expansion of the segment of the population engaged in industrial work (ibid., 56–7). In the case of Egypt, we are not dealing with a liberal state as such. Rather, what we find is an ar-ticulation between, on one hand, the exigencies of neoliberalism and its modalities of government in the sphere of welfare and, on the other, the workings of the police state. The latter will be discussed in subsequent chapters.

My discussion of the charity networks in this section of the chap-ter will be focused on the role and workings of a key charitable orga-nization in Egypt, the Gam'iyya al-Shar'iyya.[5] First, however, it is important to make note of the growth of charitable organizations na-tionally, especially those organizations that deploy a religious refer-ence. According to Imad Siyam (2001), in 1990–91, Islamic charitable associations represented 21.3 percent of all NGOs in Cairo, 23 percent in Giza, and 31.3 percent in Alexandria. In some Upper Egypt gover-norates, meanwhile, they accounted for a higher proportion, as in the case of Minya with 51 percent. Overall, Islamic charitable associations accounted for 34 percent of all charity-oriented associations in 1990 and for 27 percent in 1991. Siyam points out that the majority of these associations were established in the 1970s and '80s. This trend in-cluded a growth in the number of *zakat* committees in mosques. Ac-cording to Siyam, the Islamic charity associations operate both to provide charity and aid to instrumentalize charity work on the basis of a religious idea. In some cases there is a direct link between political activism and charitable work. For example, there has long been com-petition and struggle between the ruling National Democratic Party and the Muslim Brotherhood over control of branches of al-Gam'iyya al-Shar'iyya. In addition, Gam'iyya branches have served as bases for local elections and, in some cases, for national elections as well (Ben-Nefissa 2002).

Al-Gam'iyya al-Shar'iyya was established in 1912 by Mahmud Khatab al-Subki, in the Cairo district of al-Darb al-Ahmar.[6] In organiza-tional terms, it has branches in neighborhoods throughout the country, usually located in mosques. In Bulaq, for instance, Gam'iyya branches are based in mosques in areas such as Ard al-Liwa, Zanayn, and Nahya.[7] Much of the discussion concerning the Gam'iyya al-Shar'iyya will draw on an interview I conducted with a woman who is a key figure in net-works of charity in Bulaq and a founding member of an al-Gam'iyya branch in the quarter (henceforth, she will be referred to as the *hajja*). According to the hajja, the al-Gam'iyya branches receive funds from people referred to as the *hujjaj*, meaning literally those who have performed the pilgrimage (*hajj*), but also evoking wider meanings referring to the individual's devoutness and performance of good deeds. The *hujjaj* are residents of well-off areas of Cairo, such as Misr al-Gadida (Heliopolis), Maadi, and Muhandissin, and are known to attend Quranic lessons at mosques in Aguza and at the mosque of Mustafa Mahmud in Muhandissin. What is worth noting is the fact that people eligible for financial support are not necessarily known to individual donors of the Gam'iyya. The desire to perform an act of charity is what lies behind the extension of help. In this respect, the hajja distinguished between regular *zakat*, which is determined and specified according to a percentage of one's income, and the type of *zakat* on which the Gam'iyya's charitable work draws. In technical terms, she called it *zakat gariya* (a kind of current account *zakat*)—a continuing *zakat* that has dividends during one's lifetime and in the hereafter. This *zakat* is paid also in memory of a dead person, usually a relative. The hajja's connection with the *hujjaj* derives from what she calls *majalis al-'ilm* (knowledge assemblies), which include Quranic recital meetings, activities at the Mustafa Mahmud mosque complex, and gatherings at the Rushdi mosque in Aguza. According to the hajja, "the *hujjaj* want to do good. They sponsor orphans and pay people's medical fees. The *majalis al-'ilm* bring people together to better their religious knowledge."

The Gam'iyya's rules, procedures, and mode of operation with respect to applicants and assistance are similar to those of the Ministry of Social Affairs. The organization works in conjunction with social workers and activists at the local level who serve as intermediaries in the identification of people in need of support.[8] A Gam'iyya case worker receives the applications and presents them to the committee members of the local branch. A doctor then visits applicants on behalf of the Gam'iyya and prepares a report on the person's condition of need. The local intermediaries' recommendations are crucial for approval, since they carry out inspections into need and report on the social condition of the households they visit. The hajja told me that to ascertain whether a person is in need or not, the intermediary uses various indices. These include ownership of certain household items deemed unessential, such as TVs and video players. Possessing these items would disqualify an applicant from assistance.

The Gam'iyya operates on the basis of a particular conception of the poor, one reflected in the discourse of the al-Gam'iyya activists I interviewed. This conception frames the administration of assistance and is present, in particular, in the monitoring and investigation of recipients and applicants. The rationale of control at work here recalls liberal practices of government in the area of welfare provision as noted by scholars in reference to both Western philanthropy, beginning in the nineteenth century, and welfare programs of Western liberal states in the twentieth century. Donzelot's observation in reference to the first phase of social intervention by Western charities carries resonance for our case. With respect to the conduct of inspections into need, he states that "[t]he objective of . . . examination, its characteristic novelty was to make the granting of assistance conditional on a painstaking investigation of needs by delving into the life of the poor recipient" (Donzelot 1979, 68). Donzelot notes, further, that the inspection into need was concerned with material conditions but also with moral conditions. In this sense, the inspection was also an inquiry into the moral fault that was determinant of misery (ibid., 69). The inspection into need is framed by the construction of "the deserving poor" as the subjects of charity. In this construction, material indices are used as pieces of evidence of need. In addition, the deserving poor must also appear as "moral subjects" conforming to the subjectivities projected in both secular and conservative religious discourses. To qualify for assistance, the subject must produce herself not only as a supplicant but as a deserving one in both material and moral senses. The deserving poor subjects are more likely to be fixed as children and female, who must present themselves as lacking a male guardian but striving to abide by the moral code.

The moral dimension of control and monitoring operations is illustrated in the following case of orphan support described to me by the hajja. One of the main social programs of the Gam'iyya is the sponsorship of orphans, involving a monthly support payment of ten pounds per child.[9] To illustrate how the orphan support program works, the hajja told me about Wafa, a widow with three children. After registering with the orphan sponsorship program, she was given an entitlement of forty pounds per month in orphan support. As part of the application process, she had to submit copies of her identity card, her residential rental lease, and an electricity or water bill. According to the hajja, Wafa does not want to work outside the home and leave the children alone. Also, she is unlikely to find employment in something other than domestic work in a home in Muhandissin—a type of paid work located at the bottom of the social ladder and subject to much stigmatization. In my discussions with charity activists, many noted that assistance should be conditional on the willingness of the recipient to work. Yet, they also stressed the need to support women with young children for the purpose of guarding morality (understood in sexual terms). Young women's work as domestics or as peddlers in open markets is seen as exposing them to deviance (*yu'aridhum lil inhifraf*). The focus on women and children arises out of the rationality of government through the family (Donzelot 1979, 69) and articulates with the governance of morality, particularly sexual morality.

Other services provided by the Gam'iyya may be considered to fall within the "hygienist pole." These include covering water connection fees, which range between 500 and 1,500 pounds, and paying fees for circumcisions and medical treatment. In a small section of Old Bulaq, eighteen homes received help with water connection fees in a single year. According to the hajja, four years ago an entire street in the Zanayn neighborhood of Bulaq was connected to the municipal water system thanks to the support of the Gam'iyya and the wider charity network to which she belongs. This particular network includes a man in the water company who encourages individuals and charity organizations to apply for connections. He helps process applications and with other bureaucratic procedures. This tie to the water authority is seen as advantageous for securing services at a reasonable cost.

Case Notes 2 Entrepreneur and Supplicant: Um Ahmad in Madinat Amir

The family of Um Ahmad, residing in Madinat Amir, supplements its income with donations from various sources of charity. Um Ahmad's household is composed of eight members (including herself): her husband, who is blind and unable to work, her five unmarried children, and her mother. She is the household's main breadwinner. In addition, she provides help to her married daughter, who lives with her husband in another home but is in need of financial support. Um Ahmad earns about 300 pounds per month from varied sources. She earns 100 pounds from the cleaning jobs she does for a number of companies in the area. Additional earnings come from selling vegetables in the street. She buys radishes from wholesalers for three piasters a bunch and sells them for fifteen. Her mother helps with the selling. Her profit amounts to about two pounds per day (thus, about sixty pounds per month). Um Ahmad's mother contributes the 104 pounds she receives in monthly pension as the widow of a railway company worker.

Um Ahmad's income is insufficient to meet the household expenses, which include twenty pounds per month for the rental of three rooms in a shared dwelling (with no kitchen) and thirty pounds per month in water and electricity fees. Um Ahmad told me that the balance of family earnings are spent on school expenses for the children and daily food consumption. As mentioned previously, she also provides financial help to her eldest daughter, Sara, whose husband is a daily worker and is not earning enough to support the family (himself, his wife, and a new baby). He refuses to let his wife work. "He is Sa'idi," Sara says, "and it is his way of thinking." Um Ahmad's household expenses increased as a result of her daughter's marriage. She had to buy her some furniture, including a stove, and now she must pay off the installments. Um Ahmad has two other unmarried daughters who will eventually require contributions to their marriage expenses. However, Um Ahmad hopes to be able to support her two young sons through school and into university. Her greatest wish is to send one son to the engineering faculty.

In seeking to provide for the education of all of her children and in dealing with the added costs of her daughter's marriage, Um Ahmad has tapped into diverse sources of charity and forms of assistance. For example, she has managed to secure school-fee exemptions for the two younger boys. She is also the recipient of donations in kind from several sources: a shoe factory owner in the area donates shoes for the children once a year; a local cloth merchant, whom Um Ahmad identified as a *Sunni* man (the term is used to denote being religious and devout), donates fabric periodically. During the month of Ramadan, the family received food from a *fa'il khayr* ("someone who does good"). In addition to these donations, Um Ahmad secured a monthly stipend of fifty pounds from the mosque. To access support of this kind, Um Ahmad had to present herself and her family as "the deserving poor" to all "those who want to do good." Indeed, it is precisely in those terms that I was introduced to Um Ahmad by her neighbor Um Ashraf. Although my research purposes in visiting homes in Madinat Amir was explained to Um Ahmad, she preferred to interpret my position as that of a social worker and hence someone who can provide assistance.

> Um Ahmad provided details of all her sources of income and presented
> this information in petitioning me for help with some pressing needs.

The Ethic of Philanthropy:
Neoliberalism Meets Conservative Religious Morality

Links of charity between Bulaq al-Dakrur and other parts of the city
are developing. I was told of money coming to intermediaries in Bulaq from charitable persons in Zamalek and Muhandissin.[10] Similarly,
in Imbaba, a local development association is also the recipient of
funds from people in rich quarters of the city. The idea that charity is
an effective means of meeting social needs is propagated by the media
and by charitable organizations during fund-raising appeals. This has
had the effect of encouraging those in need to look for nonstate
sources of support, whether in the areas of housing or health. For example, I met with members of three families who were seeking housing assistance from Tariq Alam, a television personality who hosts a
program featuring cases of social need and suffering. The three families share a single dwelling, each living in a single room, and are seeking alternative accommodation (see Case Notes 3). In another case,
the family of a young woman who suffered severe burns on her leg
planned to write to Mrs. Mubarak (President Mubarak's wife) to ask
her to sponsor the needed cosmetic surgery. National newspapers promote the recourse to charity to respond to basic needs, particularly in
times of emergency. For instance, *al-Akhbar* newspaper in the 1970s began a campaign for raising charitable donations under the direction
of a prominent liberal writer, Mustafa Amin. *Akhbar al-Yum* has also established a fund, through private donations, for meeting emergency
needs or needs arising from catastrophes. A regular column informs
readers of the cases that are being supported by the fund.

The ethic of philanthropy is encouraged by prominent figures of
the regime. Suzanne Mubarak and Gamal Mubarak, the President's
wife and son respectively, are both involved in philanthropy organizations, in particular ones concerned with housing needs. The Association of Iskan al-Mustaqbal, headed by Gamal Mubarak and actively
supported by a group of businessmen, has undertaken a project to establish low-income housing for dislocated families, such as the victims
of the 1992 earthquake. The housing plan of Iskan al-Mustaqbal is presented publicly as a national plan for meeting the needs of low-income

families (Hammouda 1998). It is implemented in collaboration with businesspeople and the Ministry of Housing. According to official reports, the businesspeople subsidize more than 50 percent of the cost of the units (*al-Ahrar*, 9 July 2003). The financial contributions and the engagement of private businesses in the provision of low-income housing enter into a system of exchange with the state that includes tax breaks in addition to facilitating the acquisition of serviced land destined for private luxury construction and the like. It is interesting to note that some of the charitable projects sponsored by businesses involve the participation not only of the Ministry of Social Affairs but also of police agencies. For example, one association named Gawam' al-Khayr is reported to be setting up *Bayt al-Sadaqa* (House of Charity) to reduce the number of beggars and to get them off the street.

The propagation of an ethic of philanthropy articulates with a redeployment of religious traditions of charity. This articulation should be situated within the broader ideological context in which conservative Islamism is a structuring element of the political and social spheres (Ismail 1998). Also we need to take into account both the religious and secular heritage upon which the new discourse of philanthropy draws. The idea of charity as a religious duty is inscribed in the practice of *zakat* and alms giving. The obligation to give away a percentage of one's wealth is prescribed by *shari'a* regulations. For example, *zakat* is specified on annual capital savings, harvests, and so on. *Sadaqa* is another form of giving encouraged by religious exhortation to support the needy in one's surroundings.[11] The social dimension of these acts of charity allows for the development of bonds and ties between givers and recipients, in some cases taking the form of relations of patronage and clientelism. Historically, merchants accumulated symbolic capital through good deeds. Elite and ordinary people alike established *waqf-s* and other charitable institutions. Such institutions were tied to positions of notability and power hierarchies (see Sabra 2001; see also Bonner, Ener, and Singer 2003). Until the beginning of the nineteenth century, this type of charitable engagement was conceived in religious terms and divorced from political interests (Haenni 1997, 277).

In the nineteenth century, a reformist ethic was added to the religio-moral ethos of charity. This ethic was inspired by western philanthropic traditions. Thus, interventions of merchants in charitable work were framed by ideas of social order and progress (ibid., 277) and motivated by a sense of social responsibility (see Ener 2003). From the late nineteenth century on, philanthropic organizations became increasingly active in the establishment of orphanages and educational and medical facilities for children. Mine Ener (2003, 101) notes that benevolent societies "grounded their activities in religious imperatives of caring for the poor" but also posited action within the framework of national duty. It would appear, then, that moral reform through religion was articulated with social reform through charity and philanthropic work (see Baron 2003).

Patrick Haenni (1997) notes that in the neoliberal period, beginning with the *infitah* in the 1970s, this articulation of modern philanthropy with religious traditions of charity resurfaced. He points out that the new entrepreneurs of this period invoke ideas of charity elaborated in two different registers: Islamic traditions and the Western discourse of modernity. In this regard, the Western codes invoked by the entrepreneurs articulate with the imperatives of neoliberal ideology—namely, the retreat of the state and the rise of a business class. Entrepreneurs like Husam Badrawi deploy ideas of humanitarian activism and emphasize the need for social stability in a context where investment takes place in a global system (based on citation in Haenni 1997, 284).[12] Badrawi also invokes *zakat* as a religious duty that grounds his brand of humanitarian social work. In his view, the funds from *zakat al-mal* (annual payment on capital stipulated in *shari'a* regulations) may be used to finance public goods such as medical care. As noted by Haenni, this vision coheres well with neoliberal precepts regarding the financing and management of public services. Badrawi founded al-Takaful Foundation, an organization aiming at "promoting the social role of the private sector." A conference organized by al-Takaful in 2000 brought the message to the public under the slogan "The Heart of the Private Sector Beats for the Community" (see el-Dali 2000). The theme of the conference—the private sector's role in charitable work—ties in with a concern among entrepreneurs like Badrawi to improve the public's perception of businessmen. The need for social stability is an objective that clearly marks the discourse of activists in secular charitable associations. One such activist warned that unless a program of social aid was maintained by charities "there would be massacres" (*"hayhsal magazir"*). In other words, reducing social tensions and ensuring a degree of social stability that is conducive to investment are key objectives of philanthropic works and activities.

In the contemporary period, the construction of charitable activities in strictly religious terms appears in the discourse of activists associated with religious charitable associations such as al-Gam'iyya al-Shar'iyya. In this discourse, engagement in charity work is constructed as an expression of personal piety and dissociated from any particular social or political project. I asked one al-Gam'iyya al-Shar'iyya activist, Mrs. H., what motivates her engagement. She responded that the religious dimension drove her to be involved in charity work. She added that her concern was to please God. Mrs. H. is a resident of an upper-middle-class suburb of Cairo and holds a key position in al-Gam'iyya al-Shar'iyya branch in her district. Much of the charity work in which she is engaged is directed at residents of poorer neighborhoods. The large scale of the work of the al-Gam'iyya becomes apparent when we consider that the orphan sponsorship program of this particular branch alone covers 8,000 children and has a budget of 97,000 Egyptian pounds per month. Sponsors in this program are part of the social and religious networks of the al-Gam'iyya activists themselves. For example, Mrs. H. managed to recruit sponsors from her bank branch, where employees agreed to sponsor 200 children.

Mrs. H. emphasized that she was aiming her acts at pleasing God (*liwajih allah*, literally "for God's face"). She was also concerned about her balance sheet on the day of judgment. According to Mrs. H., the intention behind the act is important, and the aim of religious charity is to seek God's pleasure. This intention, she averred, is not of the same order as a sense of social responsibility. In seeking clarification of her position, I put to her Sarah BenNefissa's (2002) idea that engagement in the work of charitable associations could be considered as "an alternative citizenship." Mrs. H. rejected this interpretation and denied that there was any political dimension to the kind of work she does. Mrs. H.'s cultivation of religious devotion is evident. In supporting the idea that she was motivated by an ethic of the self developed on strict religious grounds, Mrs. H. invoked her participation in the performance of voluntary religious rituals such as the washing of the body of a deceased person. She pointed out that her learning how to perform such a ritual and then volunteering to perform it was evidence of the strictly religious nature of her charitable activities. It should be noted that the performance of this ritual is one of the activities supported by al-Gam'iyya al-Shar'iyya and by other Islamic charity associations. Performing the ritual itself may indeed have no political meaning; however, the question remains as to how an ethic of the self, formed in religious terms, contributes to political projects

that deploy religious idioms.[13] Further, we should recall that despite
its original desire to stay out of politics, al-Gam'iyya al-Shar'iyya has
been drawn into political conflicts and competition.

The charity work of religious organizations is part of a wider socio-
religious engagement. For example, al-Gam'iyya al-Shar'iyya's activities
include preachers' training. Through her network contacts, Mrs. H. was
able to find premises in her district to house the Center for Preachers,
an organization that trains preachers. Another activity relates to
Quranic memorization lessons. Activists such as Mrs. H. are also involved
in other types of charity work outside the al-Gam'iyya al-Shar'iyya. These
include collecting clothes for poor students and raising funds to provide
small-business start-up loans to women. Conditions are set on the provision of aid. For example, Mrs. H. indicated that married women with
children are expected to work or to send an older child to work.

In its approach to the issues of poverty and social responsibility,
the conservative discourse of charity promoted by religious charitable
organizations shares common ground with the hybrid ethic of philanthropy espoused by the new entrepreneurs. Activists from well-off
backgrounds conceived the problem of poverty in terms of unchecked
population growth, with poor people viewed as having too many children. This, in fact, was the view of both secular and religiously inclined
activists. Mrs. H. tied poverty to moral transgression, in particular, to
fornication and criminal conduct such as theft. Such an analysis, embodying a conservative moral authority, could not be said to emerge
from religious strictures, but must be understood in relation to a
broader public discourse. Indeed, the responsibility of the poor for
their own condition of poverty is also put forward by secular charity activists. The poor are faulted for such things as women having too many
children and men taking more than one wife. Further, a link is drawn
between poverty and criminality, as in a public speech by Egypt's President (see Ali 2002, 36). Mrs. H.'s articulation of her engagement in
charitable work should be situated in the wider context of the propagation of charity as a means of responding to societal needs and development imperatives. In this context, one of the main structuring
themes of public discourse enunciated by the President, intellectuals,
and social work activists is that the government is overburdened by
population growth. In the words of an activist from a secular charity
organization, "the government cannot spend on all this." From this
perspective, both community-based care promoted by religious chari-

table associations and philanthropic work, redirect away from the state the provision of assistance to the poor.

The scope of charitable activities and the nature of charity have widened, covering an ever-increasing range of needs. In addition to the community-based care that charitable associations provide to poor families, large-scale welfare services are now undertaken by the entrepreneurial elite. For example, charitable donations are collected for large public projects such as building the Cancer Hospital for Children or establishing the Institute for Orphans and the oncology branch of al-Qasr al-'Ayni hospital. Some of these charities are associated with known businessmen. For example, the Cancer Hospital for Children was started by the Qabnury Group, a well-known name in the manufacture of aluminum products and kitchen furnishings. Validation for the projects of philanthropy is proffered by religious authorities. For example, prospective donors to public projects such as the Cancer Hospital for Children are assured through a *fatwa* (religious ruling) by Al-Azhar that their donations would count as *zakat*.

With this popularization of charity and philanthropy, private companies have found it beneficial for their public image to participate in charitable work. Thus, we find a private mobile telephone company advertising that some of the charges on mobile calls will go to a designated charity. Along the same lines, the mobile phone company, Vodafone, publicizes its "program of social responsibility" and its valorization of "sympathy with the world around us." Vodafone's program is undertaken in conjunction with the charitable association al-Nur wa al-Amal, which has a long history of affiliation with causes sponsored by the Egyptian elite and, in particular, by Egypt's former first lady, Mrs. Gihan al-Sadat. Private firms such as the Korean auto manufacturing company Daewoo have now integrated charitable activities into their publicity work. In one of Daewoo's charity drives, the public relations department searched for and identified a local orphanage in Old Cairo as the recipient of the company's charitable donations. The drives are not necessarily long term and do not imply a sustained program of activities. Instead, the fund-raising drives and the donations are set up to accompany promotional campaigns. One Internet company with paid subscriptions has set up a line called Internet *al-Khayr* (Internet of Good Deeds), which contributes to charity a portion of the service charges it earns.

Case Notes 3 Supplicants in Quest:
Three Families in Madinat Amir

Forsaking education altogether was the decision made by three families living in a single dwelling in Madinat Amir, one of the poorest neighborhoods of Bulaq. The families had migrated to Bulaq from Upper Egypt. "We moved to where we would find our living" (*'ashan akl il 'aysh*: literally, to eat bread), the mothers in the three families (Um Rida, Um Hala, and Um Shayma') told me when I met them. They explained that they migrated because they could find no paid work in Upper Egypt and their husbands did not own land. In Cairo, the men were all working as *arzuqi* (daily workers) and as *fawa'liyya* (manual workers). However, work was not steady or regular. They earn between ten and fifteen pounds per day, or about 300 pounds per month, during the seasons when demand for construction workers is high. To get jobs, they go to a coffee shop in Doqqi where they wait for building contractors who are in need of a few men to work for a day or so on a construction site—carrying cement, bricks, or sand and doing other kinds of physical labor.

The three families share the first floor of a two-story dwelling, each living in one small room with shared bathroom facilities, no kitchen, and no common living area. There are five to six members in each family. A single mother, whom the women said they do not know, occupies a fourth room on their floor. The women prepare meals in their rooms using small cookers; there is no stove. The tightness of the living space is at the root of occasional tensions between the women. For instance, when their children get into fights, they may be drawn in. But they said they could never be upset with each other for very long. "We fight over the kids because we have nothing else to fight over. After we fight, we reconcile and we become close again (*lama niza'aq, ba'dayn nibqa habayb*). At the end of the day, we close a single door."

The monthly rent for each room is thirty-five pounds, and electricity and water rates amount to fifteen pounds per month. The food budget for each family is set at five pounds per day, spent mostly on bread and legumes. The families do not receive any form of aid. The women stated that assistance from the mosque and from charitable organizations targets widows and orphans; because they are married, they do not qualify. They are unable to take up employment because they have to look after the children. In addition, they maintain the view that the provision of household needs is the responsibility of the men and women should not work outside the home. At the same time, the women indicated that they tried to seek assistance. They said: "We see help on TV. We see programs about helping the poor and we hope for help to come." During the month of Ramadan, they wrote to Tariq Alam's TV show hoping to be entered into a drawing to win accommodation that would allow them some privacy. However, it took them some time to find the program's address, and they had some difficulties getting their letters in order. In the end, they were too late to be entered into the drawing.

The families must make choices to make sure they meet basic needs. One key choice was to forsake schooling for the children. Um Hala put it this way: "*Nidfa' al-igar, wala nakul, wala nishrab?*" (Should we pay the rent, or should we eat, or should we drink?) In other words, the choices come down to basic survival, precluding, in their assessment, the possibility of education for the children. In addition to the constraints on the families' incomes and living conditions, they faced limitations on their patterns of sociability and relations with others. For example, the families cannot have anyone over to share a meal. Um Hala said: "We cannot provide shelter to visitors from Upper Egypt. In fact, when visitors come to our dwelling and see our conditions, they pity us and leave for the coffee shop and try to find somewhere else to stay."

Neoliberal Government of Poverty: Microcredit and the Engendering of the Entrepreneurial Subject

The relocation of welfare to the private sphere and its assignment to charitable religious organizations or to secular philanthropic groups are part of the wider process of the privatization of the social. With the move to a market economy, the question of poverty has been reformulated along new lines that place responsibility for getting out of poverty on the poor themselves. In this context, microcredit has been championed as both the new tool of poverty relief and as the means of empowerment for the most disadvantaged members of society. Within the context of shifts in the discourse of development articulated by development and international aid institutions such as the UNDP and USAID, microcredit is presented as a device for alleviating poverty and as an instrument that would contribute to economic growth.[14] The promotion of microcredit by these institutions is based on the assumption that the informal sector and micro-enterprises are engines of growth in need of "quick and small injections of capital" or "liquidity and flexibility," to use the words of one UNDP document (UNDP Micro Start Assessment Report 2003, 4). It is argued that "increased liquidity enables households to respond to opportunities . . . to take advantage of greater investment options—access to finance can enable households to increase their income" (ibid.). In addition to increased income, microcredit, according to its promoters, contributes to "empowerment, capital efficiency and consumption." The idea of empowerment is explained in the following terms: by giving the poor, and women in particular, access to credit, they are enabled to start a business and eventually achieve financial independence. These propositions follow from the discursive shifts of the development discourse whereby "the social capital" of the poor has become a force to be mobilized through the work of programs of microcredit.[15]

As with the wider discourse of development, the tenets of the microcredit discourse are the subject of much debate and conflicting assessments. Views critical of microcredit draw on empirical findings that do not support the claims of empowerment and autonomy advanced by researchers and institutions promoting the policy. At a deeper level, some critics have questioned the power relations that underlie the promotion of microcredit in the disadvantaged countries of the global South and have raised questions about domination and the engendering of particular subjectivities. In this section, I want to explore the critique of microcredit, drawing on existing studies and on my own interviews with a group of women recipients of microcredit from ADEW (Association for the Development of Egyptian Women) in Manshiyyat Nasser, a new popular quarter.

Before questioning the assumptions built into the microcredit discourse, let us look at the questions that empirical research raises regarding the claims made about empowerment and economic growth. Using the indices flagged by development institutions to demonstrate that women are empowered through gaining access to credit, Mariz Tadros (1999a) examined the impact of microcredit on women clients of two funding NGOs in Egypt. Her research shows that women's position in the family is not necessarily improved. Women were still dependent on their husbands' consent to work outside the home, their overall workload increased, and they had no additional support taking care of family responsibilities. Tadros also notes that women reproduced the patriarchal discourse on women's subordinate status in the family. Among the women peddlers I interviewed, I found that financial independence gave them a greater role in decision making within the family. However, many other considerations that relate to the working of microcredit should be explored. In examining the income generated through the use of loans in setting up or expanding a small business, we find indications supporting the view that microcredit contributes to survival needs rather than improving economic conditions. In some cases, the indebtedness could also be an added burden on the woman (Tadros 1999a). There are stories circulating to the effect that women acquire the credit at the beginning of financial cycles of their households such as at the time of school entry or on the occasion of a son's marriage. In such cases, the credit is used as a loan to meet an immediate need.

In my discussion with a group of women peddlers who use microcredit to finance their peddling activities, I found it difficult to establish the rate of return from the use of the loans. The women peddle clothes, linens, and light household goods such as plastic ware. They procure the goods from wholesale merchants in 'Ataba and Ghuriyya and resell them mainly on credit. In contrast to independent peddlers who raise capital through rotating savings associations that do not charge interest, the microcredit recipients depend on credit managed through a number of NGOs, themselves recipients of foreign funding. The amount of credit obtained from the lending NGO ranges between 500 and 1,500 pounds. The cycle of repayment is six months and includes a 20 percent fee. On a 500-pound loan, a borrower must repay forty-six pounds fortnightly.

The women I met were part of a program that appears to be modeled after the Grameen program. That is, the borrower is part of a group of five women who have a collective agreement with the organization on the responsibility of repayment. If a woman falls behind on her payments, the group pays the installment for her. The experience of women with microcredit is mixed, and it has proven difficult for them to calculate the profit in a clear and certain manner. However, it is possible to establish the parameters defining the financial returns on microcredit.

According to the women, the business cycle extends over six or seven months from the time they get the loan to the time they recover the capital from the market. In a typical cycle, a peddler starts with 500 or 1,000 pounds and uses some of the money to buy goods for immediate sale. Clients then give a down payment and agree to spread the balance over a period of weeks or months. The price mark-up depends on the length of the repayment period. Usually the mark-up is one-third or one-half of the wholesale price. Thus, an item bought for 100 pounds wholesale will retail for between 130 to 150 pounds. At this rate, it would appear that after repaying the loan, the rate of profit is somewhere between 10 and 20 percent. In other words, if a peddler manages to sell goods for 250 pounds per month, she will make somewhere between fifty and seventy pounds profit. Women are expected to use some of the earnings to reinvest in new goods and extend the cycle of sales and repayment. In principle, then, they should be able to accumulate enough savings to allow them to accumulate their own capital. However, the capital remaining after repaying the principal and interest on the loan must be used in contributions to basic household needs. This rate of return confirms the view of the head of one lending organization that microcredit is, at best, a survival mechanism and does not contribute to economic growth or to the improvement of recipients' living standards.[16] By all accounts, the financial returns are limited and should be evaluated in terms of other costs involved, such as the lengthening of women's workdays to more than twelve hours and their anxiety over repayments. These costs are related to the deeper questions that arise around the kind of subjectivities microcredit seeks to create.

In a probing study, Morgan Brigg (2001) points to the subject constructions that the new development discourse promotes. Brigg notes that in this discourse, "there are striking parallels with the production of the liberal subjects" that have been deconstructed in the governmentality literature on liberalism (ibid., 244). The subject positions produced in the development discourse of microcredit institute women and the poor in similar terms of subjectification (the process through which individuals are constituted as subjects) to those found in the liberal discourse of government. The subjects/clients of microcredit are constructed as autonomous subjects who are empowered to take responsibility for their poverty and to carry the burden of the efforts to get out of it. Brigg suggests that we look at how the practices and processes of the new development discourse displace or banish other subject modalities. In this discourse, the subjects of microcredit are those with initiative and determination and thus with resources to improve their situation.[17] This new form of subjectification places the responsibility for ending poverty on the poor themselves. As one NGO worker put it, "the microcredit model has sparked a movement to dismantle development initiatives and to decentralize antipoverty programs with the ultimate privatization of welfare—shoeless women lifting themselves up by the bootstraps" (quoted in Rady 1999). Making the poor responsible for their condition of poverty works concomitantly with cuts in state welfare spending in the process of subjectification.

At the heart of the new subject modalities—in particular, entrepreneurial subjectivity—is the business ethic (Brigg 2001). This is captured in the words of Muhammad Yunus, the founder of the Grameen Bank, the original model of microcredit. For Yunus, what is needed is ". . . to instill in people's minds that everyone creates his or her own job. We can build institutions so that each person is supported and empowered to do this. The more self-employment becomes attractive, wide-ranging, and self-fulfilling, the more difficult it will be to attract people to wage jobs" (quoted in ibid). In the same vein, USAID in Cairo preaches that the family is an enterprise and that a home worker is an entrepreneur (Elyachar 2001). It is important to scrutinize the terms in which autonomy and empowerment are produced in the construction of this entrepreneurial subjectivity now being valorized. Entrepreneurship is seen to allow for autonomy and empowerment and, as such, it is the individualization of the responsibility for poverty that makes it possible to get out of it. As critics of microcredit discourse note, poverty is depoliticized when it is reduced to an issue of lack of credit (Rady 1999). In such a manner, issues of disparities of wealth, the market's inherent imbalances, and the growing exploitation of labor in a globalized consumption society are displaced. The move to the micro level of individual initiative and resources displaces the macro level of inequalities within the world economy.

The operation of microcredit has been associated with disciplinary mechanisms. These include holding groups of borrowers collectively responsible for repayment and thus deploying community pressure on borrowers to be responsible clients.[18] This, in turn, integrates the poor into the financial and economic networks of the development enterprise. It is telling that the microcredit business has been found to be lucrative and that more financial institutions have joined the early pioneers of microcredit while these pioneers themselves have seen their funds expand. It was expected that by the year 2005, microcredit would expand to 100 million of the world's poor. This generated much enthusiasm on the part of microcredit proponents who observed that "the world's most sophisticated capital markets have actually been linked with the promise to pay of a woman microentrepreneur [sic] selling her wares on a street corner in La Paz" (quoted in Brigg 2001, 251).

In studies commissioned by the lending organizations to assess the success of their programs—named, in one case, "impact-tracking studies"—we find a positive picture of the liberating and empowering effects of microcredit. This contrasts with more critical studies that highlight the limitations of the microcredit initiatives in dealing with problems of poverty and in contributing to empowerment. At the heart of the differing assessments and evaluations are varying interpretations of valorized subjectivities. In impact-tracking studies, success is signaled by the borrower's ability to repay the loan and in his/her engagement in getting a larger loan. In other words, greater indebtedness and an inability to break out of the debt cycle is interpreted as a measure of success by the lenders. Yet, different readings come out of the borrowers' explanations of their need to continue borrowing. Many borrowers report that the amount of the loan is too small to bring a profitable return on their investment once mandatory interest payments are included. In their calculation, a bigger loan would help generate more income. This view, however, contradicts with their assessments that the market for a given activity may not absorb a greater investment. Yet, the desire for getting bigger loans is motivated by the need to increase the income gained in order to meet basic household needs.

We may ask, then, how long it takes to cross the poverty threshold and gain a secure income. In optimistic accounts, based on the Grameen experience, it takes eight to ten years to escape poverty. Most microcredit initiatives in Egypt began less than a decade ago, and tracking studies cover a shorter period. Therefore, no conclusive report on the impact of microcredit on poverty alleviation is yet available. The impact-tracking studies highlight improvement in living standards, noting some families' ability to have more than one meal per day, or parents being able to pay for the children's private lessons (National Cooperative Business Association 2003). Once again, we find that structural issues of poverty have been displaced to the individual level. As such, the reports do not question why it is necessary for parents to pay for private lessons, nor why the social cost of education has risen. Nor do they tackle the problem of the association between poverty and blocked access to education.[19]

Conclusion: Neoliberalism, Old and New Subjectivities

The deficiency in the provision of basic services, such as health and education, and the limitations of the social security policies underline the widening gaps in the Egyptian social safety net. Accompanying state withdrawal from its welfare role, an ideological discourse on the role of charity and personal effort is now propagated. *Al-takaful al-ijtima'i* (social sponsorship), a term used by both the ruling regime and charitable associations working in conjunction with government agencies, seems to capture the move away from notions of social responsibility and solidarity (*masu'liyya ijtima'iyya/ tadamun ijtima'i*). The change in public discourse that has accompanied the privatization of welfare signals the rise of neoliberal notions of philanthropy and, in some instances, the articulation of these notions with a religious discourse on charity as a religious duty.

The examination of the scope of charitable activities reveals that they have come to play a significant role in providing for needs previously covered by public sector provisions. However, a closer look at household needs also shows that the contribution of charity is more of a stopgap measure designed to assist "the destitute" but not deal with poverty. For example, charitable donations are not sufficient to provide for a child's schooling or to meet the costs of medical care. Indeed, despite their increased dependence on charity, households have to devise other strategies to deal with basic needs such as health and education. Such strategies entail sacrificing the pursuit of higher education or not sending children to school at all.

In discussions with charity activists, certain areas were identified as being outside their scope of action. They pointed out that the provision of sewage or adequate schools was a public responsibility that should be undertaken by the government. In addition to practical limitations on the ability of the charitable associations to meet people's needs, we have to consider normative issues that relate to citizenship rights and obligations. The relegation of some items of basic needs to the status of a gift, to be received by the disadvantaged from the better-off sectors of society, denies the equality of rights and opportunities fundamental to citizenship. Further, the privatization of welfare undermines the objective of a universal system of rights by setting conditions on the provision of needs that emerge out of particularistic and subjective views of the sponsoring group or individual. This also entails personalization of welfare provision that may take the form of clientelist relations.

Equally important in our examination of the propagation of charity and philanthropy as a mechanism for dealing with poverty and for providing for basic social needs are the constructions of the poor that are deployed in public discourse. In this discourse, the management of poverty is shifted from the macro level of public policies dealing with labor, investment, and subsidies, for instance, to the micro level of the individual who is made responsible for her poverty through personal faults: having too many children, not working hard enough, and being prone to deviance. In these constructions, "the deserving poor" emerge as a subjectivity that must be performed if the citizen is to qualify for private assistance. Under the scrutinizing eyes of charity activists, the poor must engage in public self-presentation that confirms their being worthy of assistance. Thus, they must exhibit their need and prove their moral worth. As the deserving poor, the successful supplicant may also qualify for integration into neoliberal plans of poverty relief. For now, she may qualify for a small loan to produce herself as an entrepreneur.

The relocation of welfare to the private sector articulates with the adoption of a neoliberal rationality in managing poverty. The promotion of microcredit as the instrument of both "poverty alleviation" and economic growth is a case in point. Microcredit programs aim at the engendering of the entrepreneurial subject as the ideal citizen—one who is a trustworthy borrower, who is reliable in her credit dealings, and who ultimately is a citizen responsible for self-provisioning. Programs such as microcredit are consistent with the new emphasis in the developmental approach on ideas of empowerment and strategies of enabling civil society. In some respects, this appears as a rupture with older approaches that regarded the people of "the less developed societies" to be in need of improvement. Yet the pedagogical approach for teaching "the less developed" remains, and has, if anything, expanded in scope and reach. We need only look at the educational and "consciousness-raising" activities of international aid programs throughout the Global South—ranging from education about contraceptives to workshops on the marketing of artisanal goods to apprenticeship in democracy—passing by empowering women using teaching manuals on how to listen to their husbands and engage in civil discussions. These programs and activities signal the transnational character of governmentality at the heart of the neoliberal enterprise.

In the remaining two chapters, I trace the contours of the articulation of security politics with neoliberalism. While we should be careful not to reduce the expansion of the security state to neoliberal politics, we should also be attuned to the complementary relations developing between the two. As argued previously, the withdrawal of public services signals the interruption of some form of social or moral contract between rulers and ruled. Now that the acquiescence of the ruled is not bought off with social support programs, this acquiescence is being produced through techniques of discipline and population control.

Chapter 4

Youth, Gender, and the State in Cairo: Marginalized Masculinities and Contested Spaces

THIS CHAPTER EXAMINES the interplay between young men's interaction with the Egyptian state, their constructions of masculinities, and gender relations. More specifically, it interrogates how gender relations, state practices of control, and constructions of masculinities, as sites of power and domination, traverse one another and contribute to a state of flux that may open up possibilities for challenge and defiance on the part of differently situated subordinate subjects. Gender, as a social category, mediates interaction with the state. In turn, state practices—themselves gendered—shape gender constructions in terms of negotiating masculinity and femininity. Drawing on fieldwork I conducted among youths in Bulaq, I inquire into how their daily encounters with the state interact with the social construction of gender and the enactment of masculinity.[1] I argue that by virtue of their class position and their experience of subordination, young men locate themselves in the power hierarchy through constructions of masculinity that not only express their marginalized position but seek to reproduce hegemonic masculinity. I draw attention to the fact that this construction is contextually shaped and takes the expression of an "injured masculinity" that youths negotiate through acts designed to reproduce their dominance at home and in their circumscribed public space. They also negotiate it through narratives of leveling that aim to achieve vindication of their injured manhood. Meanwhile, the spectacle of injured masculinities combines with ongoing changes in gender relations in the family and in public to open up a space for women to question hegemonic masculinities. The disruption in gender relations and the experience of injured masculinities also inevitably shape young men's meditations on relations with the state. The terms in which they incorporate this experience may be read as ranging from submission to rebellion.

Gender relations and class position are central to understanding the trajectories of youths, their terms of political engagement, and their social activism. Gender constructions mediate the production of social hierarchies. At the same time, they shape and are shaped by interaction with the state.[2] For young men, the construction and assertion of their masculinity is articulated in terms of the preservation of the patriarchal relations of domination over women. These relations are also imbricated in their households' interaction with state agencies and their own relations with the state. My central argument is that young Egyptian men's construction of their masculinity is shaped by a set of interrelated factors: the changing position of women in the household and in public, antagonistic relations with state institutions involving violence, and the rising role of women as mediators with state institutions. As a counterpoint to young men's narratives, women's views on norms governing gender relations, their position in the family, and their role as mediators with the state enhance our understanding of the politics of everyday life, power relations in the family, and social hierarchies.

The analysis is situated in the context of the shift in state–society relations in Egypt, from the politics of welfare to the politics of security. With the state's withdrawal from its role of development agent and welfare provider, its apparatuses of violence expanded their reach and intensified their activities. Indeed, violence was a hallmark of the state's response to Islamist activism and challenge in the 1980s and '90s. By the middle of the 1990s, with the Islamist challenge contained, more diffuse strategies of state control were put into effect. These included the normalization of the country's emergency laws by writing them into the legal system, as was the case with the law on combating terrorism. They also included passing laws targeting young men from popular neighborhoods, namely *Qanun al- Baltaga* (the law on thuggery) of 1998, as well as the expansion of surveillance and monitoring by the police in the form of security campaigns (*hamalat amniyya*) carried out in these neighborhoods.

Youths in the Middle East, especially young men, have been important actors in oppositional movements in the region, particularly in Islamist movements. However, the literature on social forces and the state in the Middle East tends to leave youths out or to incorporate a discussion of youth into wider analyses focused on class or family.[3] Yet, we know that youths have engaged in developing their own forms of organization and modes of activism. These are inscribed in their everyday-life structures and are deserving of closer scholarly attention. Studies of Islamist movements have focused largely on the socioeconomic conditions and ideological beliefs motivating activism. My interest here is not to investigate the factors that have contributed to the rise of such movements. Rather, I argue that an understanding of male activism must inquire into everyday forms of male social organization and sociability, such as fraternities, as well as changing dynamics of gender relations and how these factors come to bear on young men's positioning vis-à-vis the state.

The chapter draws on my ethnographic work with young men and women, aged between fifteen and thirty years, in Bulaq al-Dakrur. The first section explores the role of fraternities in shaping masculine identity and young men's social engagement and political activism. Young men's membership in a variety of Islamic organizations, such as al-Tabligh wa al-Da'wa and Ansar al-Sunna al-Muhammadiyya, and in religious musical bands, as well as the fraternal relations they develop in workshops and in the neighborhood, contribute to a sense of solidarity and to the building of social networks beyond the family. It will be argued that work relations, spaces of sociability, and patterns of spatial mobility reinforce a spatial identity that is quarter-based and linked to a lifestyle and a particular set of social norms. Against this background we can comprehend the constructions of masculinity, gender relations, and interaction with the state.

In the second section, the discussion is structured around young men's discursive constructions of gender relations and the ongoing negotiation of these relations. Two factors are of particular importance to understanding these relations: women's role as mediators with the state and their contributions to the finances of the household. The final section examines young men's everyday-life encounters with the state. My objective here is to show how these encounters disrupt the dominant masculine construct while instituting men in oppositional positions to the state. This disruption helps explain the ongoing process of renegotiating gender relations in the family and in public. Further, these encounters are important to any investigation of the potential for organization and activism among young men.

Youth Fraternities, Sociability, and Family Obligations

Young men develop fraternal relations and establish fraternities around a number of social activities and institutions, depending on their life trajectories and on their position in these trajectories (e.g., employed/unemployed; married/single) at a given point in time in their life cycle. For example, fraternities may take shape in school or, more commonly, develop around workshops among young men who have dropped out of school. In Bulaq, neighborhood fraternities are linked to work, religious activities, and quotidian practices of sociability. These tend to overlap as bases of association. Young men working in various crafts or skilled occupations belong to the same networks because of the spatial proximity of their work. Thus, on Gam'iyyat Street, one of the main commercial arteries of the area, a group of mechanics, grocers, and house painters belong to a common fraternity.

What do fraternities and fraternal relations involve? First, there is a great deal of sociability among the men. They share their meals and spend leisure and break time together. They buy their meals from shops in the area and eat together in their workshops. Sharing a meal entails mutual obligations of loyalty and generates relations of trust as it establishes the bond of *'aysh wa malh* (bread and salt). Spending leisure time together in coffee shops or in their workshops reinforces fraternal bonds. For example, Sameh, Fathi, and Nagi spend their Sundays on Gam'iyyat Street in front of Sameh's shop. They congregate there, even though shops are closed on Sundays, because of familiarity, a feeling of safety, and the sense of having a place that is theirs. Thus, the shop and the street serve as spaces of sociability. This particular fraternity comprises Sameh, Fathi, Nagi, Muhammad, Ra'fat, Sabri, and Hamdi.

By appropriating the street corners or the workshop areas and investing them as safe and familiar spaces, young men produce a territorialized identity as *awlad al-hara* or *awlad al-hitta* (sons of the area). This practice is grounded historically in the organization of the *hara* as a basic social and political unit. The issue of the territorial identity of youth deserves closer attention when examining questions of activism and youth relations with the state. Territorial markings are lines drawn in contest. Thus, to produce a territorial identity is to establish spatial title in relation to others, including the state. In Algiers, *oulad al-houma* (sons of the quarter) constituted the rank and file of Islamist gangs in the period of confrontation with the state (Martinez 2000).

A great deal of the daily lives of the young men in fraternities is spent on the street. For example, Sabri's workplace is in the street, at the corner of a little alley and Gam'iyya Street. He parks the motorcycles that are brought to him for repair under the window of his grandmother's first-floor apartment, located in a building along the alley. He does the actual repairs at the corner where the street and the alley meet; in effect, the street corner is his workshop. He worked in this spot for a number of years. Repairing motorcycles is noisy work, but because of Sabri's social relations with the neighbors and his close contacts with other workers in the area, the noise is tolerated. He had at one time relocated to rented premises outside the neighborhood. However, he did not get a permit for the business and was forced to close the shop. He subsequently returned to the alley. Although his home is in the alley where he works, he spends his break times at the nearby coffee shop, buying drinks for himself and his friends. He only goes home to sleep. Indeed, a significant portion of Sabri's earnings is spent in the coffee shop. In contrast, he makes a contribution of only ten pounds per week to his grandmother's household.

Sabri's own trajectory illustrates the importance of workshop-based ties. He began as an apprentice with a motorcycle mechanic who had a shop in another alley, not far from the street corner where he now conducts most of his business affairs. Sabri says that this mechanic was like a father to him—he taught him the trade and looked after him. Sabri recalls that whenever he would run away from home, his *usta* (master craftsman) would go looking for him and bring him back.

Like Sabri, most of the young men I interviewed spend some part of their income on sociability within the *hara*. Generosity and open-handedness with other fraternity members are qualities that are given importance in these young men's conception of the masculine self. Also important are the traits of *shahm* (dependable), *gada'* (tough and brave), and *kasib* (earner), which all recall the classical *ibn al-balad* masculine construct of the popular-class male who embodies the spirit of the country (see El-Messiri 1978). This aspect of the masculine construct may exist in tension with the household responsibilities identified with being a man, particularly with the role of provider. As noted by Kandiyoti (1994), the demands of sociability and fraternity compete with family obligations. Many of the young men stated that they had family responsibilities and that they had to contribute to their household income. However, as will be shown below, in many instances, sociability demands took precedence over family expectations.

The young men in the workshops were the ones in their families who took a trade in support of parents or siblings. For example, Sameh, at twenty-one, is his family's main breadwinner. He has a high school level diploma in commerce and completed two years of a college level degree before dropping out. He is in charge of the family-owned bicycle repair shop, being the only child who learned the trade from his father. His older brother is a cab driver and is married, so he takes care of his own family. Sameh also has two younger brothers for whom he feels responsible. This includes helping them with their schooling expenses and, eventually, with their marriage expenses. Similarly, Fathi, who earns between twenty and twenty-two pounds per day from his job as a furniture painter, believes that he must assume the expenses for his sister's marriage because he became the household head following his father's death.

Other dimensions of fraternity relations have to do with what Kandiyoti (1994) refers to as expectations of male nurturance. Through fraternal relations, young men secure needs both material and emotional. Their exchanges include help with getting a job, finding a bride, securing purchases, and subverting state regulations. Many of the young men I interviewed found jobs through the help of male friends from the neighborhood. They usually start working at a young age, while still in school or after dropping out. The bonds, ties, and exchanges between the men are constructed around norms of trust, loyalty, and obligation. These relations take precedence over other considerations such as issues of legality. For example, Ali hired Ahmad as a driver of a minivan that he owns even though Ahmad does not have a driver's license (he needs a literacy certificate to obtain one). In Ali's view, trust in a male friend is more important than the legal regulation. Also, Ali introduced Ahmad to his fiancée and influenced him to quit drugs. In turn, Ahmad agreed to guarantee the installment payments on furniture purchased by Ra'fat. He also helped to find and convince a marriage registrar to contract Ra'fat's marriage, despite the fact that the latter does not have an identity card. In this instance, Ahmad put himself forward as a guarantor once again. These exchanges confirm moral obligations and norms of reciprocity. Ra'fat, for example, had visited Ahmad when he was in jail on drug charges and brought him food and cigarettes. In recalling this, Ahmad said Ra'fat and the other men in the group were his family. The young men exercise influence over each other—through advice and moral pressure they may succeed in getting one to quit drugs or another to attend lessons in the mosque.

Drug consumption organizes an alternative form of sociability. There is a widespread view that the majority of young men in the area have, at some point, experimented with or been addicted to drugs. Among the men I interviewed, some were addicted to drugs while others had successfully fought off their addiction. This, to some extent, parallels what Luis Martinez (2000) highlighted about young men in popular neighborhoods in Algiers. There, Martinez points out, youths were confronted with two choices: to join either *hizb al-zalta* or *hizb al-jami* (the party of drugs or the party of the mosque). In Bulaq, the widespread use of drugs has become the subject of concern and action. As noted previously, friends will often try to dissuade each other from taking drugs. They may also take action collectively against drug dealers in their neighborhood. Mahmud, a member of al-Tabligh wa al-Da'wa group, said that by means of nightly street patrols the group had, at one time, been able to chase dealers out of the area. However, their group lost its position and some of its influence in the area as a result of the police presence. The drug dealers, coincidentally, have returned. It is important to note that members of religious fraternities, in particular, have been actively engaged in neighborhood efforts to counter drug dealing.

Drug dealing and abuse have become sources of conflict in the area. For example, failure to pay dealers, competition between dealers and drug addiction itself are all causes of fights in which knives and other weapons are used. In fact, several drug-related criminal cases have involved murder and grave injuries. This situation is viewed as threatening. Area residents think the government is doing little to control the problem and, in some instances, identify the police as part of the problem. This view arises, in part, because police officers are co-owners of minivans used to provide local transport services. Many of the drivers are known drug addicts. In addition, the police use drug dealers as informants. Fathi, one of the young men of the Gam'iyya Street fraternity, tells the story of his attempt to deal with the problem. At one point, drug dealers were congregating across the street from his workshop, using bad language and threatening passersby. Fathi approached a lawyer whose office was located on the same street for help. He wanted to lodge a formal complaint and demand police intervention. He prepared a complaint form, but others in the area refused to sign it. He filed the complaint, but the police did not act on it. In his reflections on this experience, Fathi suggests that people's apathy is part of the problem. He and Nagi figured they would have to beat up the dealers in order to clear them from the area. This type of thinking and activity links with the general concern with moral regulation. As will be shown in the following section, activities of moral regulation are central to both pietist and militant religious groups. Furthermore, the management of public morality, as such, constitutes common ground for much youth activism.[4]

Religious Networks and Fraternities

Fraternal relations also develop around religious practices and associations. The narratives of the young men participating in religious activities indicate that much of the recruitment is neighborhood-based and tied in with relations of sociability. My findings also point out that there is a multiplicity of religious groupings and discourses invoking different understandings of religion. At the same time, the articulations of a personal view of what it means to be a Muslim, a believer, and a *multazim* (person who is religiously observant) are linked to general ethical concerns while also entering into the constitution of moral selves. Through their daily practices, social relations, and interaction, the youths are engaged in the construction of moral selves. In what follows, I situate this construction in relation to the various life trajectories of young men participating in a variety of religious groupings such as Ansar al-Sunna al-Muhammadiyya, al-Tabligh wa al-Daʻwa, and religious musical bands.

Ayman and Mamduh are members of Ansar al-Sunna al-Muhammadiyya, a religious association known for its *wahabi* ideological orientation. Ayman is twenty-six years old. He dropped out of preparatory school and is now a manufacturer of leather jackets. After his apprenticeship in leather-goods manufacturing, he moved into sales, procuring goods on credit from leather manufacturers in Saft, ʻAtaba, and Muski. He used the profits from sales to start his own manufacturing business, which he set up on the first floor of his mother's house. His younger brother Muhammad works with him. At the time that I met him, Ayman had been a *multazim* for three or four years. He had been recruited into a religious fraternity by his friend, Mamduh, who took him to hear a preacher at an Ansar-run mosque. Following that, Ayman, Mamduh, and other friends went from one mosque to another to attend religious lessons given by Ansar preachers. They consider themselves to be followers of Sheikh Muhammad Hasan, a preacher whose taped sermons and religious lessons are in wide circulation. Ayman and Mamduh share their readings and adopt a similar posture in their social relations in the *hara*—abstaining, for instance, from "speaking idly to women." The subjects of their readings underline their concern with issues of ethics and morality and the growing influence of conservative Islamist discourses. Among the titles of the readings they and other friends share are *Reminder on the Conditions of the Dead and the Issues of the After Life, Forbidden Practices Ignored by People,* and *Scenes of Happiness on the Day of Resurrection.* The readings also include commentaries on hygiene and rulings on women's menstruation. Such readings reflect Ansar al-Sunna's emphasis on rituals and on the adoption of the strategy of *tarhib* and *targhib* (instilling fear and invoking desire).[5]

Ayman, along with the other members of his reading group, preach on morality issues. The group was in control of the Gam'iyya al-Khayriyya mosque on Tir'at al-Zumur Street in Bulaq, but was forced out by the police. Ayman's membership in the group integrated him into the family of a preacher whose daughter became his fiancée. He is now a disciple who aspires to become a preacher. He calls his friends to do the prayer and leads all-night prayers called *tahajjud,* which commence at one o'clock in the morning and continue until the dawn prayer. The *tahajjud* consists of prolonged prayers in which the worshiper is expected to show profound humility before God. As noted by Hirschkind (2001), these practices of self-discipline and piety enter into the constitution of moral personhood. Indeed, Ayman indicated that through the religious lessons he learned to distinguish between Islam and *iman.* He explained that *Islam* is to perform the basic duties, or the five obligations, while *iman* "is to believe in the fundamentals of religion, which entails loving God as if one sees Him as one sees oneself." Ayman's understanding of correct practices and beliefs is articulated in his critique of other Muslim groups active in the area, in particular, the *sufis* and al-Tabligh wa al-Da'wa. He sees the difference with them to be fundamental—a difference in *iman* and not just in *fiqh* (jurisprudence).

Ayman advises his family on religious matters. He has also recruited his brother Muhammad into the group. Their preaching activities involve sharing readings with others and distributing tapes of their favorite preachers. However, Ayman stressed that they do not put pressure on others nor use force. Through these activities, they succeeded in recruiting Radi, their seventeen-year-old next-door neighbor, into their group. Ayman and Mamduh introduced Radi to their mosque circle and counseled him on the readings he should do.

Radi's integration into the piety circle was furthered by his listening to the religious tapes. He buys them on a regular basis and has built up a collection. Radi has cultivated the discipline of audiocassette listening and the embodied piety it instructs—for instance, bringing oneself to tears in appreciation of the moral lesson drawn out by the preacher in his explication of a Quranic verse or his narration of religious parables (see Hirschkind 2001).

Other religious activists like Mahmud, an auto mechanic on Gama'iyyat Street, are engaged in preaching and organizing activities. He joined the group al-Tabligh wa al-Da'wa following the 1992 Cairo earthquake. This conversion was helped along by a close friend's intervention. Mahmud's friend invited him to reflect on his lifestyle as a nonpracticing Muslim in light of the earthquake and the possibility that he could have died. Following discussions with this friend, he began attending lessons and adopted the white *gallabiyya* and grew a beard. Also, he stopped talking to women, except to admonish them for their immodest attire, and began preaching to his neighbors and advising them to perform the prayer and attend the mosque meetings. Mahmud was first met by resistance but was able to win support and persuade many of his neighbors to join him for prayers. Mahmud's devoutness has earned him his neighbors' trust. For example, Hind, who is a shop attendant next door, trusts Mahmud with the key to her store. She seeks and accepts his advice on the upbringing of her child and on her family problems. Hind is not veiled, though she concurs with Mahmud's view that the veil is a religious obligation. Mahmud's zeal was moderated when he joined the army and then got married. Now he wears jeans and his beard is trimmed. He continues to counsel veiling for women, however, and speaks critically of declining morality. In addition to performing the prayer at the mosque, he spends one hour there between sunset and evening prayer.

M. Sayyid, a twenty-five-year-old accountant, is a member of a religious musical band that plays percussion instruments only, such as *tabla, duf,* and *simbala* (tambourine), in the belief that electronic instruments are un-Islamic.[6] He joined the band upon the encouragement of a university friend. The friend is a *multazim* (religiously observant individual) whom M. accompanies to the mosque to attend religious lessons. They are not involved in preaching activities, but in *'ibada* (worship) which M. sees as a form of action, namely "doing good." The band performs at weddings, beginning with Quranic recitations and followed by religious songs. The idea is to promote *halal* (licit) practices. He says he is indebted to his friend for encouraging him to pursue a life of good deeds. Such expressions of gratitude, as well as the confirmations of fraternal bonds among male friends, were enunciated by the majority of my male informants. According to M. Sayyid, income from the performances is used to "do good." For example, the band uses part of the money to pay the *hajj* (pilgrimage) expenses of one of their members, selected by means of a lottery draw. In 2002, the *hajj* funds were used to send three members of the group to perform the *'umra* and to pray for all the other group members. M. Sayyid also plays in a secular band, but is unhappy about it and plans to quit. He is aware that his friends in the religious band would not approve.

The pietist groups to which the youths belong are often seen as passive and sometimes as opponents of militant action and jihadist-type Islamism. However, this view of the groups does not address the central question of how the cultivation of piety shapes self-positioning in social and political terms. I do not wish to argue that religiosity and devoutness create a predisposition to militancy. Rather, I want to draw attention to the possible passage from *multazim/mutaddayin* (observant/devout) to active Islamist. The records of membership of the various militant groups, from al-Jama'a al-Islamiyya and al-Jihad through al-Najun min al-Nar and al-Samawiyya to the reconstituted Vanguard of Conquest, all attest to movement among members from belonging to groups such as al-Tabligh wa Da'wa and Ansar al-Sunna al-Muhammadiyya to joining militant Islamist groups (see Ismail 2000).

Some features of this movement could be traced here. Typically, it starts with members of the pietist groups meeting *jama'at* members in mosques and then accepting invitations to attend prayer at other mosques. Studies have shown, and my interviews confirm, that young men move from mosque to mosque in search of teachers/preachers. Equally important is the fraternal base of action. The recruits in Islamist groups come from fraternities that developed around neighborhood spaces in the *hara*, such as the workshop, and then expanded to new areas and districts of the city. A certain commonality in training through the reading of the same texts creates affinity among the various groups. For instance, Ansar al-Sunna's basic stock of readings is the same as that of Jihad and Jama'a. However, some of the readings of youths in Ansar are less learned and more accessible. Modes of recruitment employed by both Ansar and Tabligh follow the same pattern as the *jama'at*, namely recruiting friends and neighbors to attend lessons in the mosque and preaching to women on the question of the veil. Convergence on issues of morality and gender relations has helped to consolidate ties among the group members. Issues of morality occupy a central place in all Islamist discourses and, as the following section shows, the management of public morality, understood as the control of sexuality—women's in particular—constitutes a major preoccupation of young men.

If we look at the practices of the youths in religious fraternities and musical bands, we find signs of the ongoing processes of re-Islamization whereby signs and symbols from Islamic traditions are reinvested in various domains of social life. For example, the grid of *halal* and *haram* (licit and illicit) is applied to musical instruments and wedding celebration rituals. Also, the Islamic position on the permissibility or impermissibility of various practices is developed. This ongoing re-Islamization attests to the sociality of Islamism and to the fact that its significance cannot be assessed only in terms of the fortunes of militant Islamist groups. As noted, the religious fraternities and organizations to which the youths belong do not adopt a militant posture on issues of state. Moreover, their activities are focused on transforming social practices in a manner that conforms to their understanding of "true" Islam or what constitutes correct practice.

Members of religious groups follow particular preachers, listen to their sermons, and read their pamphlets. They may invoke their authority in choosing a course of action or determining the appropriateness of an act. Undoubtedly, the re-Islamization of cultural practices and the interpretative frameworks articulated in reference to Islamic traditions are variables that help make Islamist movements appealing. Moreover, militant Islamism's capacity to mobilize and ability to ground itself socially were strengthened as a result of the convergence of certain of its ideological practices and local cultural practices (Ismail 2000; 2004). A good example of this is the control of women's conduct. Islamists' involvement in the monitoring of gender interaction and the management of relations between the sexes is inscribed in realms of governance that continue to be important (Ismail 2004).

Religious networks that may not have an explicit political agenda can be mobilized for a host of reasons and can therefore be a source of recruits. Thus, pietist groups such as Ansar al-Sunna and al-Tabligh wa Daʻwa present opportunities for fraternal solidarity and doctrinal training. The question we may ask is whether this could serve as a foundation for Islamist activism. No members of these groups whom I interviewed belonged to an activist Islamist group or militant cell. Yet their discourses shared some common themes with those of the Islamists. They also found organizational and social engagement using a religious idiom to be attractive. Most importantly, they articulated some oppositional views to the state. Indeed, some of them had come into confrontation with the state as exemplified by the case of Mahmud, the auto mechanic who belonged to Ansar al-Sunna and who was arrested in 1992. Mahmud was not an advocate of violent action and may not have endorsed the necessity of overthrowing the regime, but he contributed to the movement by spreading elements of the Islamist message and contributed to the diffusion of its practices (this discussion draws on Ismail 2004, 392–93).

The socio-political position of Mahmud, and of many other young men, confirms that the micro-context of mobilization is favorable to protest activities and movements. An important factor here is that oppositional positioning vis-à-vis the state (examined further later in this chapter) is shared by many youths. At the same time, there are constraints on mobilization. First, state policing of protest presents serious constraints on the broadening of collective action beyond the neighborhood. Second, militant groups' confrontational and violent strategies foreclosed other courses of action that were necessary to widen their base of mobilization (e.g., the *jama'at* was not open to entering into an alliance with the Muslim Brotherhood on university campuses; rather, its members clashed with MB members). These kinds of constraints help explain the current impasse of militant Islamism. We should also take into account the strategies adopted by official Islam to discredit the militants.

Youths and Gender Relations: Marginalized Masculinities and the Community of Women

In my discussions with young men, issues surrounding gender relations appeared to be of utmost concern. In discussing the problems of the quarter, young men spoke repeatedly of declining morality. Occasionally, this assessment was qualified in comparative terms, by reference to well-off districts of the city where, they observed, there is less morality. The sign of immorality evoked most often was the dress and public conduct of women. The narratives of women's transgression tended to follow a common line of girls and young women dressed immodestly and going out with boys. Fathi noted that women wear a "body" (a tight-fitting top, '*biyilbisuh al-body*'), stretch pants, and tights, in addition to makeup. He commented that "a girl speaks to one boy and ten more." Nagi stated that girls were too forward in their interactions with boys—they approached or would "go after" boys (*huma il-biy'aksu*). Similarly, Mahmud's main criticism with respect to morality is focused on women's attire and loose behavior. He gives examples of women in coffee shops in Muhandissin "smoking *shisha*" and women in Bulaq "using bad language."

A number of young men did not think the veil was a guarantee of women's morality and good behavior. In fact, they related abundant stories of women using the veil as a cover for compromising conduct. Sameh tells of seeing *munaqabat* (women wearing a face cover) removing their face and head covers in coffee shops in Muhandissin. M. Zayid said women took off their '*abaya* (loose fitting overdress) once they crossed to "the other side." The motif of women removing their veils in particular settings is not present only in the narratives of Bulaq male youth, however. It is incorporated into other men's commentaries about women and sexual morality. For instance, I have been told similar stories by taxi drivers referring to the conduct of women clients in their taxis. The accuracy of these stories is not the main issue, but the sociosexual imaginary that generates them is. The predominant motif of this imaginary is of women as potential transgressors and as strong candidates for breaking the moral code. This somehow becomes a sign for something else, namely everything that is going wrong in the country.[7] In other words, the narratives invoke existing constructions of women, found in repertoires of patriarchal discourse on womanhood, to undermine women's claims to modesty through the adoption of the veil.

Another recurrent theme in the men's narratives is that of intervention to correct transgressive conduct by young women. Young men recounted instances of approaching young women and admonishing them for what they consider improper behavior. This performance constitutes a public enactment of their manhood, by which masculine identity is territorially inscribed: the young men perceive their assertion of their masculinity in taking steps to reinstitute the moral order in their neighborhoods.[8] For this enactment to take place, other performances are undertaken, including the monitoring of the comings and goings of women in the neighborhood. From the vantage point of their workshops and the coffee shop, Fathi and Mahmud appear to be

performing this monitoring of young women. If they see them immodestly dressed or speaking to a stranger, they talk to them. Here
they find another sign of moral decline. This emerges in the responses
of the young women's families to their interventions. A number of
young men said parents objected to their intervention or accused
them of trying to sully their daughter's reputation. Again, this twist in
the tale is narrated by young men from different parts of Bulaq. It attests to persistent motifs and themes. One young man said he did not
walk out with his sister for fear that others may mistake him for a
boyfriend. The negative response of parents has caused some to re-
frain from intervening and keep to themselves. In this respect, the ritual of masculine enactment is denied.

Let us recall that the Islamists' appeal to young men had to do with
this kind of masculine enactment (Ismail 2000). A common practice of
Islamist activists was to patrol the streets together as a group with the
aim of managing public morality by enforcing the veil, ensuring the
separation of the sexes, and punishing transgressions. In the absence of
this kind of organized monitoring, the men expressed concern in terms
of the effects that parents' objections to this practice of intervention
would have on women's morality. The main worry, as stated by Nagi,
Fathi, and Sameh, is how to find a good wife. They represented the
search for a moral partner as a bigger problem than getting a flat. Given
how difficult it is to obtain an affordable flat in Cairo, it would seem that
these young men consider it almost impossible to find a good wife. In
this respect, their monitoring of neighborhood women is also designed
to locate a potential partner, someone who has not been out with another man and who, in principle, would not go out with them either.

The majority of the married young men in the area chose their
wife after a period of monitoring or upon the recommendation of a
trusted friend. Most of the chosen marriage partners come from the
area and are part of the family network. For instance, Hamdy's wife
came from the neighborhood and was the sister of a man who married
one of his cousins. Muhammad's wife, meanwhile, was a customer in
his grocery shop. She was veiled, and Muhammad noted that she was
polite and religious (confirmed by the fact that she prayed). When
compared to other girls in the area, she appeared to him to be more
virtuous. Both he and Hamdy, like many of the other young men, did
not want their wives to work outside the home. Yet Muhammad's
mother attends to the work in the store for part of the day.

These views on gender relations are shared by both educated and uneducated young men. The desire to restrict women's mobility is also expressed in these young men's rejection of having working partners. Sayyid, a school teacher, will allow his wife to work until they have children, while Wahid, a welder, says that "the free craftsman's wife does not work" (*al-sanay'i al-hur miratuh ma tishtaghalsh*). The men framed their rejection of women's work in terms of familial roles; that is, women are seen as child raisers and men as breadwinners. They also did not wish to have wives out in public, seen by or interacting with other men. Ra'fat expressed his desire to limit women's public presence and relations with other men by saying "I do not want to marry a *gam'iyya* (cooperative)." It is also within the familial role of women as child raisers that they explained their preference for having educated wives. They all thought that the education of women was important and wanted to have educated wives who can help the children with their schoolwork and be good mothers. Many of the men were uneducated, yet they married women with intermediate levels of education. They will also educate their daughters, but would leave it up to their future sons-in-law to decide on the work question.

Young women's views on the need for the social control of women were diametrically opposed to those expressed by young men. They considered talk about young women's conduct, especially among young men, as gossip and as a social practice designed to control them. They did not see any harm in speaking to boys from the area, although they had reservations about interacting with outsiders. In many respects, young women engaged in activities that challenged notions of male authority in the household and confronted male practices of control. Dunya, an eighteen-year old who studies crafts in high school and sees a boy from the *hara*, took judo lessons and believed herself to be a man's equal. Huwayda, a divorced single mother, sought financial independence through employment and securing social security from the Ministry of Social Affairs to support her children. She viewed financial independence as important to her freedom of movement, especially her ability to go out without being asked by her brothers about her comings and goings. She went back to night school in order to improve her employment opportunities. Raga', a young divorced woman who lives with her brothers, accused neighboring men of gossip and objected to their interventions regarding the fact that her brothers received male friends in their house. For these young women, work and education helped them achieve their independence in the family. Many worked as peddlers to supplement the household income, in defiance of negative attitudes about this kind of economic activity. In doing this, they sought to contribute to the marriage expenses of a son or to secure the capital needed by a spouse to start a business. Young men's views that women were idle and contributed little to the household were in contradiction with the fact that women acted as intermediaries with the authorities, processing and procuring papers and permits for such things as water and electricity, and that many were working as employees or peddlers and contributing to their families' livelihood.

How should we interpret young men's denial of women's contributions and their elevation of the problem of finding a suitable marriage partner to an overarching level, high above the challenge of finding housing or secure employment? In puzzling out the youths' emphasis on the need to control women's morality and sexuality, the concept of marginalized masculinities sheds light on the apparent tensions in male youth narratives. "Marginalized masculinities," as R. W. Connell (1995, 80–81) defines it, refers to a configuration of practices through which men in subordinate positions negotiate their position in the power hierarchies of class, gender, and race.[9] Through a reassertion of practices of patriarchy, they seek to reproduce the dominant position of men, that of hegemonic masculinity. Yet, this connection with hegemonic masculinity is scarred, bearing the wounds inflicted through its articulation with class and state power. In response to my inquiries as to why they identified this or that person as a figure of power in the community, my informants narrated tales of sexual transgression on the part of the named person or a member of his family. One tale told of a powerful person's son having harassed a woman in the neighborhood and then going so far as to commit an act of aggression against her in her home. The community failed to support the woman's demand for retribution and she was constrained to move out of the neighborhood. This theme in men's narrative of power, as symbolized and enacted in sexual transgression, bears the marks of marginalized masculinities. Figures of power, then, are identified as those who can get away with transgressing the sexual code. The violence of sexual dominance is linked with a higher power and, in this instance, is a confirmation of the inability of dominated men to stand up to a violation of their masculinity. In this tale there is recognition that money and connections support a patriarchal hierarchy.

Marginalized masculinities are inflected with the humiliation experienced at the hands of agents of the state and with the absence of any shield from state repression such as higher class status. The role of women in mediating this experience of state domination is pushed out of men's narratives. Rather, male youths insist that women are idle gossipers, doing little but displaying their feminine wiles. In contrast to the denial of women's work, male youths affirmed through their narratives the male's responsibilities in the family. Lower-class men's masculinity is constructed in relation to their position as providers for the families and as guardians of their women. Women's work could be seen, thus, as a challenge to this construction, especially when women become the main breadwinners of the household. Indeed, women have articulated this challenge by deploying a critique of husbands who fail to contribute and thus do not live up to the image of the masculine self. In one poignant account, Iman Bibars (2001) quotes one of her female informants saying *"la mu'akhtha huwa malush lazmah"* (pardon me, but he is useless) in reference to her husband who failed to contribute to household expenses. Failing to provide for household needs disrupts the masculine construct. This failure has its costs, such as the questioning of male prerogatives of control. Married women whose husbands fail to provide financial support have felt that their spouses' sexual expectations are inappropriate. A husband who fails to provide should not expect compliance with sexual "obligations" within the marital bond (el-Kholy 2002). Women's questioning of their sexual obligations by invoking husbands' inadequacy as providers may be interpreted as women finding an opening, in a context of changing social conditions, to interrogate patriarchal terms of domination.

The position of youths in the urban setting and their construction of masculinity under conditions of subordination should be contrasted with earlier constructions of masculinity by subordinate urban youths. Historically, young men from popular quarters fashioned themselves in valorizing terms as *awlad al-balad* (sons of the country) (el-Messiri 1978). *Ibn al-balad* (son of the country) was the ideal male figure. This masculine self came to be associated with the figure of the *futuwwa* (el-Messiri 1977). The *futuwwa* was a strong-bodied male who displayed physical strength and exhibited his manliness through acts of honor and courage—watching out for his female neighbors, intervening in neighborhood disputes, and so on. *Futuwwa*, in its etymology, signals an exultation of youth; its root, *fata*, means a male youth.

The organization of *futuwwa* groups into brotherhoods claims a historical lineage that extends back to the first century of Islam and to the figure of Ali, the fourth caliph. *Futuwwa* gangs played an important historical role in the *hara* of Arab cities and, at crucial historical junctures, were a force of political contestation with which rulers had to contend. I have argued elsewhere that, in contemporary times, the Islamist activists' interventions in their neighborhoods have sought to reinscribe *futuwwa* practices, such as mediating disputes, monitoring women's conduct, and maintaining local order (Ismail 2000). These interventions should be seen as practices of masculinity under conditions of subordination.

Young men's narratives about their interventions in cases of women's transgressions highlight the actions taken by men to reinforce the moral order of hegemonic masculinities. What is at stake is the exercise of male authority not only in the home but also in the community. If the fraternities have no formal political power, they have disciplinary power in which checking the potentially transgressive conduct of women is an important dimension. In other words, the monitoring of women emerges as a technique of internal governance that is continuous with the patriarchal dominance of hegemonic masculinities.

Women as Mediators

I became aware of the role of women as mediators when I asked Um Hasan why it was she who did all the running around to process her application with the water authorities to get a water connection. Um Hasan responded: "The *harim* are tough. They can take the abuse at government offices, put up with being told off, and spoken to badly for the sake of getting the service." Also, women have acquired the cultural capital needed for negotiating the bribe, learning who gets it and how much to pay. In describing her performance as mediator with state agents, Um Hasan constructed womanhood in terms of strength, resilience, and appreciation of household responsibility. This construction should, however, be put in the wider frame of Um Hasan's family arrangements and the broader gender narratives of the family. Through her earnings as a peddler, she managed to acquire the home in which her family lives. Her husband, meanwhile, is an *arzuqi* (daily laborer) with an irregular income. He used to drink heavily, which meant that this income was mostly unavailable to the family. Similarly, the sons' position in the household does not conform to the public narrative. In Um Hasan's words, one son is a bum (*sayi'*). He does not have a steady job and does not make any contribution to the household. The second son is enlisted in the army and is engaged to be married. To help him with marriage expenses, Um Hasan has set up a small business in her home. The youngest son peddles with her. Um Hasan's view of the *harim* (a word used to refer to women in a patronizing way) as "tough" inverses the conventional gender assignations of strength and weakness. Women's striving to get basic public services in the face of hostile and abusive authority places higher value on family needs than on an individualized articulation of honor and self-respect. Self-respect, in Um Hasan's narrative, is about meeting the needs of the household.

The mediating role of women takes many forms. For example, in Layla's account of family/household matters, especially as they concern household expenses and contributions, we find an instance of women's role in mediating police-youth relations. During my midday visit to see her daughter Samia, who had just come out of the hospital, Layla informed me that neither of her two working sons contributed to household expenses (one of them was quietly watching television and smoking while this discussion was going on but did not offer any views on the topics of Samia's hospital expenses or marriage plans). She went on to explain that she did not demand a contribution: "I do not want to take from their income. They use the money on cigarettes and drinks at the coffee shop. If I take from this income, then they may not have enough to cover their expenses. Then they would get into trouble and the police would say it was their mother's fault." Not only were the boys exempted from a contribution, the police was given as their alibi. Layla is conscious of the dominant narratives that place responsibility for male youth's conduct on the mother. She anticipates the blame and rehearses the accusations that will be made against her. She has decided to protect herself from societal and state charges of her being an accessory to any potential transgression on the part of her sons. At the same time, Layla's withdrawal of any financial claims on her sons was her way of mediating between them and the police.

In opposition to the practice of masculine concealment, women question the terms of their subordination and point to the contradiction built into the claims of marginalized masculinities. I think that Shirin's understanding of her position in the family with respect to the male members—her father and brother—points to this questioning. Shirin is a fifteen-year-old peddler selling sunglasses on a main boulevard in Giza. She was set up in this trade by her father who was selling out of a street stand until the police forced him to shut down for lack of a permit. Shirin now sells the goods for him, displaying them in the street. Her father sits close by for part of the day. On her way to her place of work, she passes by her mother, who sells paper tissues by the railway crossing in Nahya. This daily encounter with her mother's own harsh reality and struggle captures her imagination as well as her love and sympathy for her mother and other struggling women. In Shirin's account of the different roles assumed by the members of her family, her father appears as an irresponsible parent. He plays dominos and gambles in a coffee shop, spending, and sometimes losing, the money earned from sales. He has been trying to get a permit for a vendor's kiosk but has not yet succeeded. Shirin is not confident that he is actually working to get the permit, and she has grown tired of his promises that he would get one. She thinks that her father uses the kiosk permit as an excuse for not working. As trust is absent in their dealings, she keeps some of the profit from sales to give to her mother to help with household expenses. Her withholding of some of the earnings from the proceeds is sometimes discovered, resulting in beatings from her father.

Shirin thinks she was taken out of school to educate her brothers. She has come to question this preference for her male siblings after starting to attend night school, where she has learned from her teacher that women are just as important as men and that they will change society one day. She is now determined to continue her schooling and is helping her younger sister, who has dropped out, to enroll in school again. She teaches her what she learns. Out on the street, Shirin is exposed to different situations, including being harassed by men. The experience has taught her to stand up to her father and tell him what she thinks of him. She says this shows that she is courageous and better than her older brother, who beats her up if she is out late but does not stand up to his father. She critically notes: "he acts as a man dominating me" (*'amil 'alayya ragil*), pointing out the contradiction in his behavior. Shirin's contribution to the household and her work on the street have repositioned her in relation to the men in her family. She feels morally justified to question patriarchal claims. Her exclamation about her brother's conduct aims at the heart of masculine enactments of domination.

By assuming a greater role in public and contributing to their household expenses, women have also opened up spaces for questioning constructs of femininity anchored in frames of domesticity and banishment from public space. In response, social practices aimed at managing this change attempt to hold on to older constructs of femininity. I read the terms in which my key informant was cast by her family and neighbors as representing such practices. Manal is a local activist and a quintessential mediator who has taken on a public role that involves supporting women in their pursuit of social services, mediating local disputes, and presenting herself as a resource person. Her role, and her family's and neighborhood's acceptance of it, is framed in terms of gender crossing. "She is a man" (*hiyya ragil*), they say, to justify her public engagements, her interventions to resolve disputes, and her social activism. But her undertakings are precisely those from which men have withdrawn. She accompanies women on their visits to various government departments, because, as she puts it, their men folk have no stomach for government. But acceptance of her role comes at a cost—the negation of her femininity and the conferral on her of a symbolic and honorary masculinity.

The conferral of a masculine identity on Manal is an attempt to negate a self that challenges conventional gendered constructions of men and women. All the same, this induction into the fraternity of men is not an absolute one. There are embodied limits to Manal's honorary masculinity.[10] For instance, she is not allowed to dance at weddings and if she transgresses the prohibition on dancing, she is beaten by her brother or slapped by her mother. However, her security and independence are guaranteed within the patriarchal order. Manal's freedom of movement is ensured by the acquiescence of her father, which cannot be challenged by her brothers. Her mother's support is also central. Indeed, her mother is cognizant of the rules of governance at play. She prays for Manal that "God will spare you (Manal) the evil of oppressive rulers" (*Allah yikfiki shar al-hukam al-zulam*). The expression *al-hukam al-zulam* (oppressive rulers) mentioned in this proverb could potentially apply to Manal's brothers.

In tracing transformations in the city globally, Manuel Castells remarked that what has emerged is "the city of women," where women are workers in the informal sector and heads of households (in Susser 2002, 378–79). As I reflect on the narratives of men and women and on my observations of the daily practices, I am led to think that I have encountered the community of women—a collectivity that transcends sisterhood and sororities and that is by no means in opposition to the male fraternities. Rather, the community of women is about resistance against the grinding conditions of everyday life; it is about overcoming. The women's return to school, as in the case of Sawsan, Manal, Nihmaduh, Samia, Raga', and Karima, is illustrative. Each of these women viewed education as empowering as a means to improve their employment prospects, to learn and broaden their intellect, and to allow them to speak to men and to answer them. Further, by rejecting gossip as a strategy of social control and by taking up work as domestics or peddlers in defiance of social sanctions, these women challenge practices of control aimed at their subordination.

In male discourse about gender relations, the contention about the idleness of women and the affirmation of male familial responsibilities as breadwinners covers silences on women's contributions. We see this, for example, in Ayman's account of how he set up his leather jacket business. In this account, he makes no mention of the financial contribution his mother made toward the business. However, there was a twist in the tale—a twist that is becoming common but is often left out of narratives of household and family life. Some of the capital for the business came from the dowry Ayman's sister received when she married a man from the Arab Gulf.[11] In fact, raising capital through marriages to Gulf Arabs has become a more common practice among women of poor neighborhoods like Bulaq. Layla, for instance, also neglected to mention that Samia had contracted a previous marriage to a man from the Gulf, one from which she had to be rescued.[12] The practice of women marrying wealthy men from oil-producing Arab countries has become a strategy of raising family income, a transaction that benefits other members of the family. As a new family member, the husband is asked to invest in a business venture or an existing enterprise such as a mechanic shop or a bookstore. On the whole, young men were silent on the idea of women being used as asset raisers if not as asset substitutes.

The changes in marriage arrangements have contributed to further questioning of gendered roles. Marriage remains an important social institution that engages the efforts of many families especially for raising the necessary capital. This has traditionally put most of the responsibility on prospective male partners who were to pay a dowry, make an engagement offering, and buy the substantial items of household furnishings. In addition, procuring housing had been the man's responsibility. These arrangements are now changing as women are making major contributions to the financing of the marriage, buying household furnishings, and selling their engagement offerings to pay the housing down payments. The contribution of women changes the power relations in the households. In fact, el-Kholy (2002) found out that women seek to increase such contributions to enhance their position in the household vis-à-vis their husbands and in-laws. One indication of the ongoing changes is the decision among young men to contract marriages with older women. Such marriages reduce the engagement offerings and other contributions that men must make toward the union, since the women usually have residences and furnishings of their own.[13]

Youths' Everyday-Life Encounters with the State

In this section, I want to sketch out the quotidian encounters between young men and the state. These encounters take place in markets, coffee shops, and alleyways. As residents and workers in a popular neighborhood that developed as a result of people's initiative, the youths, along with other residents, are the object of state regulatory practices aimed at bringing them under control. Such practices include raids on markets by the utilities police as well as patrols by other police departments, including the security police. Here I focus on the practices aimed at young men.

As part of Cairo's informal economy, young men work in unlicensed shops and use public space in contravention of utilities regulations. For example, Nagi set up an unlicensed kiosk on Gama'iyya Street to sell audiotapes. He called the kiosk 'mashrou' shabab', in reference to a state-sponsored program designed to support young people who want to establish their own businesses. In fact, Nagi does not have a vendor's license, and his tapes are most likely pirated copies. He reasoned that he would not get the license if he applied, so he saved himself the trouble. Sabri and Ra'fat use the street for their repair business, again with the threat of being arrested by the utilities police. Fathi's furniture-painting jobs are on a commission basis and remain within the informal sector, while Ayman's leather goods manufacture is unlicensed. In many instances, the spatial dimension of these informal economic arrangements brings the "irregular" nature of their work into public view, open to inspections and monitoring practices of the state. Indeed, the management of young men's public presence is a particular preoccupation of state authorities, especially, the police (this will be elaborated in chapter 5). Undoubtedly this has to do with the fact that Islamist activists are drawn primarily from the ranks of young men in popular neighborhoods. Thus, the monitoring of young men's activities and conduct has been integrated into the general security objectives of state. Practices of territorialization are a related concern. They are seen as potentially oppositional tactics, as when youths form gangs or groups that encourage challenging authority. Much spatial maneuvering occurs on all sides.

Young men's encounters with the state follow the general patterns found in their communities' relations with state institutions, but also have their specificities. Youths in the markets and on commercial axes share the experiences of older vendors and traders in dealing with supply police raids and utilities police campaigns. However, they face additional and particular forms of police repression, discipline, and monitoring that have to do with their age and certain state policies targeting youths. For example, police raids on coffee shops and "campaigns to arrest suspects" have young men as a primary target. Also, the practices of requesting identity cards and "suspicion and investigation" (*ishtibah wa tahari*) procedures are concentrated in popular neighborhoods and aim at the control of young men's presence in public.

A number of my male informants were of conscription age but did not present themselves for military service as required. As a result, they try to avoid contacts with the police. Sabri, the motorcycle repairman, avoids going to "the other side," below the railway tracks that separate his neighborhood from contiguous areas and the rest of the city. There, he is likely to be stopped by police and questioned. On a number of occasions, Sabri has been asked by police about his military service status. In response, he claims that he suffers a medical condition that qualifies him for exemption and that his papers are being processed. However, he knows that this ruse may be discovered so he maintains a low profile in his movements.

Sabri's brother Ra'fat, an auto mechanic, does not have an identity card nor a driver's license. Like many others in the neighborhood, he needs a literacy certificate before he can apply for a license. Ra'fat has been arrested several times for driving without a license. He is treated badly by the police and believes it to be because of his job. He says *al-sanay'i mithan* (the craftsman is humiliated). Similarly, Hamdy drives without a license and has been stopped and arrested.

In commenting on these encounters and experiences and the continuous police patrols of the area, Hamdy says that this is the time of government (*da zaman al-hukuma*). Many minivan drivers in the area are not licensed and, as such, are subject to police surveillance and raids, culminating, sometimes, in chases and clashes. One driver, Sobhi, complained of being humiliated by the police. He said he was free and could not accept humiliation. Sobhi describes the situation for young men as being marked by a persistent fear that the police will exercise its powers of suspicion and investigation (*ishtibah wa tahari*) against them. These powers allow the police to stop and question any person they deem to be a suspect. He related an experience of humiliation by an Amin Shurta (a policeman below officer rank) who subjected him to insults. Sobhi viewed this as infringing on his dignity and sense of self. He described himself as "*ibn balad wa dami hur*" (son of the country and my blood is free).

The experience of arrest is not limited to those whose status and licensing papers are not in order. For example, Mahmud, an auto mechanic, has an identity card and a driving license but has been arrested several times. In one instance, he was arrested while transporting a friend's motorcycle in a pick-up truck. He was only released from police custody when the friend showed up at the police station and confirmed Mahmud's story. He was also arrested during security raids when he was bearded and wore a white *gallabiyya*. Mahmud's experiences with the police lead him to conclude that during raids they arrest everyone in sight: "They take the good and the bad, check and verify later." Others have been arrested on suspicion of drug possession or drug dealing. Adel was arrested and only let go because of the intervention of a high-ranking officer known to his father. Most of the arrests are carried out within the remit of police powers of *mahdar ishtibah wa tahari* (suspicion and investigation). Accounts found in police reports of the *ishtibah wa tahari* process highlight its use by the police as a means of disciplining young men.

The arrest procedures and the new regulations relating to public order appear to target young men. In 1998, the law of *baltaga* (thuggery) was passed in Parliament. One intent of the law is to deal with young men's presence and conduct in public. Under its provisions, displays of physical strength for the purpose of intimidation are identified as acts of thuggery punishable by up to five years in prison. This should be situated in relation to the history of confrontation between the state and the Islamists. From the standpoint of state authorities, young men in popular quarters embody opposition. Drawing on its own experience, and a particular reading of it, the state deals with young men as a potential oppositional force that must be tamed. We can say that the state has developed the analytical skills of social scientists and has reasoned that young men have a window of opportunity to resist: the period in their life when they have entered into adulthood but have not yet assumed family responsibilities associated with marriage. Young men's lifestyles during this period are seen as potentially threatening. Recall that this state, under emergency rules, considers a gathering of three or more people as potentially seditious, having outlawed all public gatherings and required a permit for any public meeting. By congregating on street corners and forming fraternities of sorts, young men are engaging in acts that could be unruly from the state's point of view.

To manage this public presence, the state deploys a wide range of practices of control. The state's management of young men draws on its experience with Islamist activism reworking strategies and practices deployed against the Islamist activists. The Islamist activist as a lawless, violent enemy of the state was, in the ideal type constructions, a young man from popular quarters (sociological profiles initially cast him as educated but the profile changed later on). The Islamist activists were viewed, in blanket terms, as terrorists. With the 1998 law on thuggery, the Islamist terrorist was replaced by the young *baltagi* (thug)—a social terrorist—as the rising threat to national security. This representation underwrites the official violence inflicted on young men in public. The objective of the police raids on coffee shops, stop and investigate operations, arrests, and beatings are to render the potentially resistant bodies into obedient bodies restrained by fear of physical sanction, public abuse, and humiliation. The framing of young men's infractions of public order in terms of thuggery represents a discursive strategy on the part of the state. This framing is intended to deny young men the more positive image of the *futuwwa*. The effect of such policies marks both the discourse of young men and their practices. The young men of Bulaq, for instance, avoid crossing to "the other side"—to Muhandissin or Doqqi, for example—retreating instead to their neighborhood alleyways and staying close to their homes. They also avoid presenting themselves in public offices. As noted previously, the spatialization of sociability practices takes the form of a territorialization of activities in the quarter and the creation of safe zones in alleyways and around workshops. For young men, urban space is mapped out in terms of zones of relative safety or danger. The map guides them through their everyday-life movements. Yet the evasion and concealment designed to shield their injured masculinity and, indeed, humanity deepens the injury. The wounded masculine self seeks recovery/restitution in the home and alleyway through enactment of control over women's mobility and over their presence in public.

Young men's experience of arrest and humiliation by the police lead them to avoid dealing with government. In narrating his encounter with police, Ayman, a tile layer, stated that he was badly treated when trying to get an identity card. He compared this with the better treatment he received when he went to Doqqi police station on some official business. There, he points out, the officers showed respect and restraint and treated him properly, perhaps, he suggests, "because I was well dressed [and also because] I do not have Bulaq al-Dakrur written on my forehead." For Ayman, being well-dressed was a device of hiding an identity that is spatially inscribed.

Young Bulaqi men's antagonism toward the police has parallels in youth-police relations in Algeria. Martinez (2000) notes that youths who spend a lot of time on the street (popularly known as *hittistes* in reference to the fact that they lean on the *hit* or wall) joined the FIS (the Islamic Salvation Front) and, later, armed groups as an expression of their opposition to the police. Within the framework of the Islamist groups' activities, they were able to pursue their grievances against the police and carry out acts of leveling that were motivated by the sense of humiliation or *hugra* they felt in their encounters with police officers. Similarly, in Egypt, support for Islamist groups in the 1980s and early 1990s was associated with their confrontational stands with the police. Islamist groups active in popular neighborhoods drew support from youths in the markets and streets (Ismail 2000). Joining an Islamist group offered the youths an opportunity to band together and challenge police incursions into their spaces. *Ihana* (insult and humiliation) and *mahana* (humiliation) were the terms most frequently used by my informants to describe the sense of infringement they felt in encounters with the police. This humiliation is embodied especially in such police tactics as roughing up, beating, and slapping. The construction of the body is gendered, and the physical attack or affront is experienced as an attack on a masculine self. This is well illustrated in the statement "It is the craftsman who is humiliated" (not the poor citizen, for example). In Sobhi's account of dealing with a police officer, we find that the *ibn al-balad* identity informs the injured masculinity and contributes to a state of affairs in which redress is required and for which narratives of acts of leveling provide some relief.

As noted previously, avoiding enlistment in the army puts young men in a precarious situation, because of the possibility of being charged with draft evasion. At the same time, the draft experience of many young men has proven to be a source of resentment toward the state and its agents. This subject requires detailed and in-depth study. My discussion here is limited to sketching out some of the themes that arise in relation to the draft experience. Referring to his draft experience, Ra'id said he lost any respect for the state and no longer felt bound to the country. For him, the humiliation and exploitation endured during that period discredited the entire system of government. Sobhi's account of his travails in the service highlights the theme of exploitation. He was assigned as a foot soldier to a high-ranking general. In this assignment, he was asked to perform cleaning tasks in the general's home. When he refused to comply, charges were laid against him, and he faced court martial. His case is still being considered.

The use of conscripts in private service as personal drivers, cleaners, and errand boys for high-ranking officers is a common experience and has come to constitute an important frame of reference organizing relations with the state and figures of authority. On one hand, the experience of military service socializes young men of poor backgrounds into marginalized masculinity. On the other, the narrative of this experience allows for imagined acts of leveling. These narratives indicate that the households of the high-ranking officers occupy an important symbolic place in the young conscripts' imaginaries. Motifs and themes that organize their narratives of this experience could be interpreted as vindicated masculinity. In these narratives, the young conscript is desired and pursued by the officer's wife. A reordering of masculine hierarchy orients the emplotment of this narrative whereby the sexual relation established with the superior's wife moves the conscript up the ladder to a position of dominant masculinity.[14]

Young Men: Between Submission and Rebellion

How are the daily encounters with the state incorporated into the construction of the self, in particular, the masculine self? How are these encounters negotiated in relation to criteria of manhood? Unlike the beatings experienced by Palestinian youths when confronting Israeli soldiers, the humiliating and violent encounters between Egyptian youths and police have not been turned into "rites of passage." Unlike the Palestinian male youths studied by Julie Peteet (2000), the Egyptian males do not seek confrontation. Rather, their agency takes the form of evasion—staying away from public thoroughfares and only frequenting coffee shops in their neighborhood alleys. They narrate the experience in terms of humiliation and injury and not as an experience of sacrifice that must be endured. Does this mean that the violence inflicted on them is internalized in terms of inferiority and submission? Is it incorporated, to use Peteet's words, as "subjectivity without interpretation and challenge" and hence submission to "the dominant performers' meaning"(121)? The tactics of evasion do not exhaust the responses of the youth, and there are instances of defiance. For example, a number of young men refused to act as informants for the police. In turning down police offers of remuneration in the form of farmed out positions of dominance within their neighborhoods, they rejected co-optation as an option. In their view, police informants are thugs who betray the ethic of fraternity and the values of manliness associated with the traditional manhood of the *futuwwa*.

Two particular episodes of encounter highlight the complexity of determining positions of submission and rebellion. The first episode involves a young man, M. Abu Zayd, a third-year law student and manager of a family business on a commercial thoroughfare in Bulaq. From the vantage point of his shop, Abu Zayd witnesses the daily police campaigns in the market. In his account of the police presence in the area, he told of one intervention in which the police arrived and sought to confiscate the weight scales used by an eighteen-year-old woman vendor. When the young woman resisted and tried to prevent the seizure of the scales, she was beaten up by a police soldier. As he watched the assault, Abu Zayd felt angry and was indignant at the aggression. However, he stopped himself from intervening. He reasoned that his intervention would bring him into conflict with a police officer in uniform, an action that would jeopardize his career prospects. We may read this response as one of submission or at least of feigning submission and of engaging in a public performance scripted in the culture of fear.

In another encounter, Ayman was standing outside his home early one evening when a police patrol passed along the street. Ayman and one of the officers exchanged looks. The next day, the police patrol came by again and, once more, Ayman and the officer exchanged looks. Then, the officer approached Ayman and asked to see his identity card. Following that, he ordered Ayman into the police car. Ayman was arrested, charged with drug possession, and brought before the prosecutor. He interpreted his arrest as a result of daring to look back and failing to keep his head down. Here, it would appear that Ayman, when challenged to be submissive, responded with defiance.

Abu Zayd's and Ayman's responses are mediated by the logic of the situation and do not necessarily reveal the positions of submissive or rebellious subjects in the abstract. What the episodes show is that the young men occupy antagonistic positions vis-à-vis the state. I want to end this section with Ayman's reflections on the state and collective action. During our discussions, Ayman expressed the view that the idea of changing government through elections was unrealistic and that people of his background would never get elected. When he watches broadcasts of the People's Assembly, Ayman said, he sees there the ineptness of government and the lack of representation. This lack is also reflected in the images of public institutions and in hosts and guests who appear on TV talk shows and news programs. Ayman pointed out that no one like him is interviewed on these shows, except on rare occasions and, then, only briefly. This extends to sports, especially football, where coaches are chosen by manipulation and with disregard for the fans. Ayman attributes economic problems to corruption and adds that "if government was conducted according to God's edicts, there would be no problem." Although he is not religious, he still thinks that the *shari'a* should be applied. He does not pray, but would do so if government was conducted according to the *shari'a*. Ayman has never elected an MP or a local councilman. He does not have an electoral card and suggests that most people in his *hara* do not have electoral cards. In reflecting on how change would come about, Ayman said, "One day we will all rebel like 'Urabi, but we need a leader, a Salah al-Din to guide us." The construction of the relation to the state in Ayman's reflections clearly expresses antagonism. His narrative anticipates confrontation of a revolutionary nature. It may be that in invoking the eventual arrival of a leader, the narrative displaces the confrontation indefinitely. However, it highlights the oppositional positioning that he, along with other young men, occupies vis-à-vis the state.

Conclusion

In looking at the lifestyles of young men in popular quarters of Cairo, we gain insights into their position from the state and the potential for action. The youths inhabit a space of dissidence that can become a space of confrontation. Their presence contradicts official rules of law and order such as congregating on street corners and working in the middle of the street. Their presence is intensely public. Their narrative of their experience of interaction with the agents of the state is organized around values of self-respect and dignity and feelings of humiliation and injury. The encounters with the state destabilize their masculine constructs and necessitate a renegotiation of their masculinity.

In addressing the question of young men's activism and opposition to the state, I suggest that we need to examine how gender constructions mediate their relations with the state. The humiliation they experience in dealing with state agents threatens their dominance at home, exposing their powerlessness and bringing women in as mediators with the state. At the same time, changes in marriage arrangements and in women's employment challenge hegemonic masculinities. The young men experience social change in the family as threatening to their position of power and dominance and the terms that define their masculinity. Public discourse and practices of socialization into masculinity construct manhood in terms of guardianship of honor and responsibility for providing for the family. Yet the exigencies for lower-class women's work, documented in the late 1980s by Arlene MacLeod (1991), continue to unfold in the early 2000s. Women are household heads in the absence of husbands who have deserted them or become migrant workers. Further, ongoing changes to the cultural and ideological organization of space undermine the principles of a gendered separation of space. Yet, women continue to appear as the ultimate boundary of community in the young men's narratives. In the young men's accounts of women's transgressive conduct, as evidenced by their attire, their mobility, and their appropriation of public space, we find enactments of masculinity that seek to reinstitute an alternative construction of acceptable femininity, harking back to visions of female domesticity that are central to hegemonic masculinities.

My analysis of the intersection of youth activism, gender relations, and state power rests on a particular reading of the wider field of state–society interaction. In this reading, I propose that there has been a shift from welfarism and corporatism toward an articulation of security politics with neoliberal politics. The next chapter follows signs of this articulation focusing on ordinary citizens' encounters with the everyday state and the *dispositif* of security that frames the population of the new urban quarters.

Chapter 5

The Politics of Security: An Economy of Violence and Control

THIS CHAPTER IS FOCUSED on ordinary citizens' encounters with the everyday state in Bulaq al-Dakrur. My main argument is that there has been a marked and qualitative shift from the distributive state to the security state and that this development is part of a wider dynamic of state–society relations involving processes of engagement and disengagement on the part of both the state and societal forces. State disengagement, as we have seen in chapter 3, has taken the form of withdrawal from the provision of public social services, including the elimination of subsidies, masked privatization of schooling, contracting out, and privatization. Societal disengagement emerges in the increased levels of participation in informal economic activities and in the people's preference to eschew state authority when seeking to resolve issues of daily governance.

In one sense, it can be argued that the popular sector tries to keep the state out of its business. This preference is captured in Um Hasan's reflection on and evaluation of the early days of Bulaq's development: "Things were better when there was no government and the world was loose" (*lama ma kansh fi hukuma wi-l-dunnya kanit sayba*). Yet things are not that simple. Despite their desire for distance, quarter residents are engaged with the state in, for example, processes of regularization and acts of control and resistance. As such, in people's everyday encounters with the state, we find the dynamics of engagement. These encounters take place when state agents try to impose their vision of law and order in the market or when they oversee the application of various municipal regulations relating to the use of public utilities, hygiene, and so on. In such instances, we find attempts at imposing control and public authority. However, residents resist these attempts in small ways that nonetheless reveal systematic and sustained efforts at countering policies and regulations that may undermine individual or group interests. At the same time, the nature of interaction goes beyond the simple categories of domination and opposition. In examining quotidian interaction, we glimpse something of the conviviality that binds ruler and ruled, as discussed by Achille Mbembe (2001). We also observe the strategies of horror that reinstate the state as fetish. In negotiating interaction with the popular strata, the state pursues a range of strategies, including co-optation, infiltration of societal spaces, and incorporation of popular practices. At the same time, as this chapter demonstrates, policies of discipline and control have expanded and widened in scope.

The discussion is organized around three key issues: (1) the quotidian encounters between people and agents and agencies of the state that tell us about the effects of practices of rule in the everyday life of residents of lower-income urban neighborhoods; (2) the discursive constructions that are part of governmentality, or the narratives justifying practices of government taking as an example the reinvention of *baltaga* (thuggery) and the subversion of its use in public discourse; and (3) the practices of discipline and surveillance making up the *dispositif* of the politics of security.

Encountering the Everyday State

The patterning of relations between quarter residents and the state must be traced back to the quarter's origins and to its demographic expansion and residential and infrastructural development. I will sketch these only briefly here, focusing instead on actual patterns of interaction between residents and the state as they were conveyed to me in discussions and interviews and as I was able to discern them in my field observations of everyday happenings in Bulaq.

For the purposes of the present discussion, it is important to recall that Bulaq was built on agricultural land and that most construction in the quarter, including during recent phases, has transgressed some public regulation. Most housing, therefore, was not integrated into the public amenities system (water, electricity, and sewage). In time, proprietors and tenants engaged in processes of regularization and obtaining service. In the effect, they came into contact with various state authorities in the hope of gaining legal recognition, accessing the utility infrastructure system, or diffusing a potential conflict over the legality of their dwelling, construction, or economic activity.

Insights into Bulaq residents' relations with the state may be gained by focusing on their encounters with the municipal administration, the utilities police, the electricity authorities, the water authority, and the security police. Residents' accounts of these encounters may be characterized as narratives of oppression and resistance. The accounts highlight injustices on the part of the state and resistance and resentment on the part of the residents. They also tell of acts of transgression against the rules. These narratives bring into focus areas of interaction with the state and the nature of interaction. My discussion on welfare networks in chapter 3 noted that state disengagement from welfare provision and the residents' efforts at creating self-sufficiency in social and economic spheres point to a significant change in state–society relations. The social or moral contract defining these relations in the 1950s and '60s has weakened, if not dissolved. Students of Egyptian politics defined this contract as entailing state provision of goods and services in exchange for acquiescence and incorporation of the people. In other words, claims to political rights were forsaken for social rights. For residents of the new popular areas, that deal is inoperative. Access to state employment is limited, and many people have turned to the informal sector for jobs. Also, there are diminished opportunities for making profit by procuring and trading in subsidized public sector goods. Thus, the peddlers who traded in goods procured from state cooperatives have either been replaced by new peddlers or have become part of the nationwide networks of private commerce. Their contacts are not in state shops but in private markets, and their suppliers are not state co-ops but private wholesalers.

Similarly, public goods are being replaced by private services in health, education, and housing. In addition, the costs of infrastructure are now paid for directly by the citizens themselves. In some instances, access to social and basic goods (e.g., housing and utilities) is gained informally. The informality or illegality of their economic and social forms of organization is the pretext for the emergence of conflictual and antagonistic relations between citizens and state authorities. In what follows, I highlight some of the areas of conflict and the dynamics of interaction between the state and citizens.

The outdoor markets are important spaces where interaction occurs between representatives of state authority—namely the utilities police and the supply police—and community members. The particular salience of this interaction arises from its public nature and its recurrence on a regular basis. Given that space is a contested resource, its appropriation and claims to title over it are the subject of conflict with the representatives of the state. Many of the vendors, whether shop or stall keepers, display their wares in the street. This causes traffic disruptions and imposes terms of spatial organization that conflict with conventional notions of public order. The utilities police are deployed regularly to restore order. In response, shopkeepers and vendors remove their goods but are fined nonetheless for obstructing the road. The dynamic of interaction here brings out the entanglement of power and resistance as rulers and ruled engage in chases, evasions, and perhaps mutual ensnarement.

Interventions by the utilities police often involve the seizure of scales used by street vendors for weighing produce. The equipment is essential for conducting business, but police consider it a means of carrying out unlicensed vending. Hence, the scales come to stand for the contest over rights and rules—the vendor's right to a livelihood and the state's rules regarding licensing. Some vendors resist the seizure of their scales, risking or incurring physical punishment from police soldiers and officers. Tales of this type of interaction between residents and authorities are recounted repeatedly. They describe scenes of confrontation that elicit strong reactions on the part of the people. Abu Zayd, a university student who works in a family-owned variety store on Tir'at Zanayn Street, the location of the main market, gave me an account of one of these episodes of confrontation. He told of the utilities police arriving at the market in their vans and beginning to harass the merchants. One of the police soldiers ('askari) seized the scales of a young female vegetable vendor, approximately eighteen years of age. According to Abu Zayd, the woman is her family's sole breadwinner and earns about seven pounds per day. He wondered whether the actions of the utilities police would drive the woman to become "morally deviant" (mish tinhirif).[1] Along with other vendors, he watched as the young woman resisted the seizure and was beaten by the soldier. He viewed the action of the police as unjust and wanted to intervene on the woman's behalf but did not do so because of the likelihood that this would result in a physical fight between himself and a uniformed officer in the police van. Such a confrontation would lead to his imprisonment and would jeopardize his future. Abu Zayd was a law student in his third year of studies. It is worth pointing out that Abu Zayd himself had been warned by the utilities police about his use of street space to display his wares. The warning was accompanied by a veiled request from one agent for a cash payment. Subsequently, he arranged to meet with this agent in the coffee shop nearby where he slipped him a twenty-pound note.

The response of Abu Zayd and other vendors to the incident involving the young woman vendor betrays their fear of the authorities—a fear that one may consider as resulting from the repressive measures. But something else is at play in these encounters. In Abu Zayd's narrative, he indicated that the presence of a uniformed policeman in the van kept him from intervening. The uniform stood for the state. In the uniform we can see the workings of "the state effect" whereby distance and acquiescence are required from the citizen and not just fear. The abuse by the police does not explain the onlookers' response; rather, it is the symbolism of the state in full effect. We should think of the way we feel when approaching immigration and customs officers at border checkpoints and recall the dread and worry that these encounters often elicit. The structure of feeling elicited through this face-to-face encounter with "the state that is"—the state that comes down to earth—is not without its links to the reinstatement of the state as fetish and its abstraction and elevation above society.

In dealing with the effects of the confrontations with the representatives of state authority, vendors benefit from relations of solidarity. For instance, when goods and scales are seized, resources are pooled to replace the confiscated goods. Further, a hierarchy of power is at work: small vendors locate next to big ones for protection. They, in turn, provide support when fights break out among the vendors. Resistance strategies include spatial tactics of evasion and countermonitoring surveillance. Vendors position *nadurgis* (watchers or lookouts) at the entry points to the market. The *nadurgis* notify the vendors when utilities police approach the area. A game of hide and seek ensues whereby vendors withdraw their carts into the side alleys and the courtyards of people's homes. In a number of household interviews, residents expressed feelings of sympathy for the vendors and confirmed their involvement in helping them hide their goods. In his work on politics in the postcolony, Mbembe (2001) speaks of conviviality to characterize relations between rulers and ruled. I suggest that conviviality develops among the ruled in relation to power. Intimacy with power in the sense of knowing it closely and sensing it insinuate itself in one's daily business and surroundings creates the context for complicity among the ruled. In the face of raids, they position watchers; when they are notified, they arrange a retreat. The goings-on in the market extend beyond the vendors and implicate buyers, passersby, and onlookers, who are all residents of Bulaq and for whom these happenings are rituals of power to which they must respond and about which they have feelings. Raids by supply and hygiene police are not just pretexts for monitoring the proper running of some business. Rather, they provide occasions to punctuate the lives of citizens with the ritual of presence of the everyday state. They are also occasions in which ordinary citizens temporize with the state through evasions, compromises, complicity, conviviality, and cynicism.

Other encounters with state authorities center on the residents' efforts to gain access to public utilities such as water and electricity. These utilities are provided unevenly throughout the community with some neighborhoods and households receiving full or partial services and others none at all. The process of acquiring services such as water or electricity involves considerable negotiations and power strategies.

In their efforts to obtain basic public amenities, residents come into contact with particular local government departments. To get a water connection, a resident must apply to the water authority to do preliminary measurements. The fee for the water connection ranges from 500 to 1,500 pounds. Given that the residents do not know on what technical basis the estimate is made, they must rely on the service provider and either accept the fee or find a way of reducing it. More important, however, is getting approval for the connection. If the home is found to have been built with the wrong construction material—mud, for instance—a permit may not be issued. Bribes are often paid to secure the permits. The process for doing this is widely known. Indeed, applicants exchange information with each other regarding the "bribe fee" and who receives it, when to pay it, and what connection estimates have been agreed in the past. One afternoon, I was speaking with Um Hasan in the *hara*, when a group of women passed by. Um Hasan addressed one of these women, asking how her encounter with the water authority went. The woman responded that she paid a bribe of 100 pounds. Um Hasan, in response, said that she had paid only fifty pounds, but that the difference had to do with the fact that different materials and procedures were required for her connection. A few days later, I learned from Um Hasan that her con- nection was delayed because a piece of equipment, for which she had already paid, was missing. Um Hasan considered her options in light of her own sense of the workings of government. She said she could buy a new piece on the market, but in doing so would end up paying twice for the same item. Alternatively, she could wait for the water au- thorities to procure the piece in question—a wait that was indefinite. Um Hasan's savoir faire is evident here. Recall that she expressed pref- erence for the time when there was no government (*hukuma*), under- stood as an absence of rule and not of the actual government of the day. Encountering government necessitates knowledge of how to deal with it, and that knowledge is precisely what Um Hasan and the other women cultivate. They had learned which engineer to seek, to which secretary the money should be given, and what the amount of the cut should be. Um Hasan had also learned how to read government tac- tics such as delaying service. Her exchanges with the women on the way back from their day at the water authority office show intimacy with power, an intimacy that animates the conviviality among the women.

When I asked Um Hasan why it was she and not her husband or son who ran the errands and handled the various dealings required for getting the water connection, she explained that young men would not tolerate the abuse in government offices and departments—being pushed aside and spoken to badly. In contrast, women bear it in order to meet their needs. She said the *harim* were tough. The role assumed by women in this respect goes beyond that of service seekers or clients. As I have shown in the previous chapter, women have emerged as me- diators with state authorities. In taking on the responsibility of dealing with public authorities, women reckon that they are sparing their male family members a potentially confrontational situation with represen- tatives of the state. Womanhood is constructed as an asset and a shield to be deployed in the face of abusive authorities. Women's anticipa- tion of greater conflict with government if the encounter were to in- volve their men reveals the masculinist shape of state power. The men will not tolerate the abuse, not because they view themselves as citizens with rights, but because the encounter functions like a challenge, a dare that will require a riposte in the terms suggested by Pierre Bourdieu (1977). Women as intermediaries see the challenge differently. This is not to say that they do not feel humiliated by the condescending and demeaning attitudes of state officials. Rather, women's modes of dealing with the challenge are focused on getting the service; hence, they learn how to navigate through the system.

Access to public utilities is sometimes gained illegally through theft and through unauthorized connections to water, electricity, or sewage infrastructure and the like. Such infractions bring residents into conflict with the authorities. If discovered, such practices could lead to formal charges, fines, and possibly protracted court hearings. Residents' narratives and court and police records of infractions indicate that monitoring of the residential streets by the electricity and other utilities police has become pervasive. Municipality action, and ways of dealing with it, set the background for expressing resentment and anger toward state authorities. Hajj Sam'an, a 72-year-old proprietor of a small grocery shop in an inside *hara*, recounted to me his experience with the utilities police following an infraction on his part. He tapped into a public electricity box in the street to power a tool he was using to repair the door of his shop. The current in the regular electrical outlets was not strong enough even for the few minutes of work he had to do. As it happened, the municipality van passed by while the tool was connected to the street power source. The van stopped, and the agents in it charged hajj Sam'an with violation of the electricity code.[2] Later, he was visited by an officer of the utility police who summoned him to a hearing at the electricity authority. Hajj Sam'an had been charged with electricity theft and fined 260 pounds, equivalent to an entire month's pension. He admitted to the offense but saw grounds for leniency. He attempted to contest the decision, question its fairness, and ask whether it conformed to the principles of the justice system. However, during the hearing, the utilities officer humiliated him, and he felt compelled to leave. He paid the fine out of fear of ending up in court and incurring a heavier fine or a jail sentence. He knew he could not afford to mount a proper defense and believed the judge would take the officer's side. In commenting on the municipality rules and the role of the utilities police, he stated that "they make the people angry," and added that "terrorism comes from anger."

Surrounding hajj Sam'an's narrative was a commentary on government, the President, corruption, and the system of "Yes Sir" or

"*Tamam Ya Fandim.*" In his view, there was rupture between the state and the people. He believed that there were no government reports revealing how unhappy the people were. In his case, he expressed his anger in a sanitized form that would allow him some protection from the wrath of the police. After he paid the fine, he expressed his indignation at the whole affair by shouting out: "God is my succor, best helper and supporter" (*hizbyya Allah wa ni'm al-wakil*).[3] This expression of contestation is relatively safe as it invokes God and cannot be easily punished.

Unlike hajj Sam'an's apparent acquiescence to government intervention, the local rebel, hajj Sayyid, takes a position of outright rejection. At 70 years of age, hajj Sayyid's life trajectory is marked by confrontations with state authorities. As a youth, he was a runner for hashish dealers in Old Cairo. Hajj Sayyid refers to these days as *ayam al-shaqawa* (days of transgression) when he had run-ins with the authorities. Then, his position was one of defiance, refusing to work as an informant. In response to police pressure, he chose to exit and pursue work in Kuwait for many years. Upon return to Egypt, following the Gulf War in 1991, he opened a coffee shop. His apprenticeship with law breakers may have given him the competence in confronting the authorities. He recalls that in the 1960s, he and his brother put up a sign in their family-owned shop saying "we fight those who fight us" (*nu'adi man yu'adina*), a motto used by President Nasser at the time. In many ways, I find that hajj Sayyid's authoring of self bears similarities to the *futuwwa* Yusuf Abu Haggag's (1993) autobiographical narrative.

Hajj Sayyid's days of youthful transgression may be over, but his relations with authorities continue to be marked by conflict and confrontation. His coffee shop, for instance, has no permit. When the municipality authorities come to the shop and raise the matter of the permit, he tells them to "reopen the door" for permits so that he may acquire one (the municipality had suspended the issuance of coffee shop permits). He is usually rebuked by the municipality personnel, but he says he does not fear them. In fact, hajj Sayyid has had numerous clashes with the authorities. In one instance, he quarreled publicly with the head of the municipality over street lighting. The confrontation deteriorated to the level of insult. The point of such a public display, hajj Sayyid explained, was to show the discrepancy between the policies and the actions of the authorities. In his words, "[government officials] are cozy with rich people like the market proprietor, but fail to do their job and provide services." He refuses to pay taxes, saying "taxes should be paid by well-off people, not by people like me." His other infractions include building a wall without a permit at one of his homes. Also, he has a problem with the electricity authority over the installation of an electricity meter. He had requested that a meter be installed for the first floor of a building he owns. The authority refused, however, claiming that hajj Sayyid had removed the first-floor meter and installed it in on the second floor to legalize its status—the second floor had been built without a construction permit. Hajj Sayyid denies the charge. He believes that government has a responsibility to the people. This view guides his dealings with the authorities and is at the center of his dogged pursuit of social benefits such as his old age pension and public services.

The maneuvers of Um Hasan, hajj Sam'an, hajj Sayyid, and Abu Zayd underscore the intimate and immediate relations to power into which they are drawn. Their strategies for dealing with power practices express a range of feelings shared by the subjects of power: for instance, disbelief in its legitimacy and desire to dare authority—to take on the challenge and call the game into question. In the end, each acts in a manner informed by her/his knowledge and experience of power.

The encounters recounted are, in some sense, rituals of the everyday state. However, they are not of the type that brings subject-citizens to the heights of state majesty (i.e., not like the rituals of grandeur such as ceremonies, national celebrations, and inaugurations). Rather, they are rituals of state in the everyday life,[4] through which the subject-citizens come to form their view of the state and to develop feelings about and toward it. In Um Hasan's words, "it" is something they can do without. The unfairness and inconsistency of its rules and practices are noted by hajj Sam'an, hajj Sayyid, and Abu Zayd. As it comes down to the level of the people, the state, as a construct and image, takes a battering. Yet, I would suggest that through practices of discipline that induce fear, "it" recovers something of its hold. In their intimacy with power, the subject-citizens come to experience the state in the ways in which it does not exist for them and not just in the ways that it does. Hence, they articulate a kind of doubling of power that is both an affirmation and a negation captured in my informants' often-repeated phrase: "Here there is no state, here, the people live in a state other than the state" (*hina ma fish dawla, hina nas 'aysha fi dawla ghayr al-dawla*).

The Politics of Security

Encounters with the everyday state take place in the widened arena of security politics. In the preceding section, we looked at encounters relating to regulation in the utilities services sector. These are part of the government of the social carried out mostly by the police. The arena of security politics falls more squarely within the mandate of the police. In the 1990s, the politics of security expanded widely in the social field. The everyday politics of the governed was to be brought under control through the intervention of the security apparatus and through a process of mapping out subjects for the purposes of discipline and surveillance. I now turn to these developments.

Reinventing Baltaga: The Production of a National Security Crisis

Illustrative of the politics of discipline is Law 6 on thuggery passed in the National Assembly in 1998. The law is associated with a national campaign against street violence and disorderly conduct in popular quarters. In discussion in the National Assembly, Zakariya Azmi, then Secretary General of the ruling National Democratic Party, claimed that there were 130,000 thugs in Greater Cairo alone (*al-Jumhuriyya*, 26 February 1998). Other reports put the figure for the governorate of Cairo at 15,000 thugs (*al-Ahali*, 22 September 1999). Also, according to data from the Center for Social and Criminological Research, there were 5,000 cases of thuggery in 1998, of which 70 percent took place in informal housing communities (ibid.). Of those arrested on thuggery charges, the majority (60 percent) fell in the age category of 22 to 40 years. Most of these latter had low levels of literacy, with 70 percent of them illiterate.

The articles of the thuggery law detail the forms of behavior that are considered antisocial and threatening. They also specify the necessary punishments. Law 6 of 1998 provides the police with the power to arrest and detain citizens suspected of undermining public order through displays of aggression and physical strength, or through the intimation that they will cause harm to others. These powers widen the scope of legal provisions covering the maintenance of public order. Under these provisions, police action in popular quarters may include stopping, questioning, and searching young men on the streets. Like security raids and morality patrols (to be discussed later in this chapter), the law on thuggery aims at the discipline and control of young men and their bodies

in public space. It is not a coincidence that the citizen's body is at the center of what the legislation on thuggery constructs as a problem and seeks to regulate. The display of physical strength with an intimidating effect or with the intention to intimidate is thought of as the attribute of the "able bodied" or of "strong bodies," exemplified by the body of the young man. The contest is over the street and the presence of these bodies on the streets—an imagined sheer physical force that must be tamed.

In the late 1980s and early 1990s, the epithet *baltagi* (thug) was invoked by state officials and media to refer to Islamist leaders. The term was seen as particularly applicable to Sheikh Gabir in Imbaba. The act of *baltaga* (thuggery) denotes a range of activities considered illegal and destabilizing to a neighborhood; it is carried out by a social actor referred to as *baltagi*.[5] As the Egyptian state appeared to have contained the Islamist *baltagi* type, the violence and confrontation between its agents of law and order and the population in popular quarters has been recast in terms of "social *baltaga*." *Baltaga* is spatially inscribed: a *baltagi's* actions are territorially based and delimited by a neighborhood. The contest over space—between social actors, such as youths, vendors, peddlers, and drivers on the one hand and state agents, on the other—is reinscribed in the *futuwwa-baltagi* continuum and brings these members of the popular strata into conflict with representatives of the state. Once again, they are cast along the lines in which historically segments of the poor were cast as *harafish* and *ghawgha'* (rabble).

The elevation of issues of law and order in society to the level of a national security concern has been taken up by the media. In one representation of the challenges to public order by the *baltagiyya*, a journalist with the newspaper *al-Usbu'* contended that political terrorism by Islamists was replaced by social terrorism aimed at ordinary people. However, in this journalist's view, this type of terrorism threatens national security (*al-Usbu'*, 30 August 1998). It was claimed, also, that *baltagiyya* represented no less a danger than militant Islamists.

The transformation from Islamist terrorist to *baltagi* terrorist was further narrated in a report entitled "Imbaba: From Terrorism to Baltaga," published in an opposition-party newspaper. The report's author argued that the rule of Islamists in the quarter of Imbaba had been replaced by the rule of *baltagiyya*. The evidence given in support of this assessment emerged out of the journalist's reading of the social and spatial arrangements found in Imbaba. For example, the vendors are referred to as *baltagiyya* for having refused to remain within the

walled plot of land assigned to them by the municipality. The report puts forward the conventional views of law and order and the necessity of maintaining control of population. In this respect, it could be said to belong to the dominant narrative surrounding discipline and surveillance. The report is also noteworthy for its depiction of a situation similar to that of Bulaq with the difference that Imbaba was famed for its Islamist activism. What the reporter decries is that the spatial organization remains outside of state control despite the funds invested in paving streets and providing lighting. According to the reporter,

> [t]he governor has reorganized the area, removed the Friday market to Burqash, erected a market for peddlers after removing Higazi market. He also put new minivan stations instead of the haphazard stations. But, as usual, all these efforts were in vain. Imbaba reverted from the rule of Islamists to the rule of *baltagiyya*, with everyone doing whatever they wanted. The area has become a jungle where the strong takes his power with force. An example of this is an event that took place a few days ago in Kit Kat Square where a police utility force went to remove the carts of some vendors after they had left them for months and the street had become theirs. Worse, they defended this usurped right, while one of the *baltagi* vendors stood up to the police force which comprised three officers, a number of *amin shurta* and assistants and seven soldiers. He even threatened them with a knife that had his name inscribed on it, and broke the windows in the city council building in an unabashed challenge to the city council and the police. (*al-Wafd*, 12 February 1998)

The reporter goes on to note that the police officers left the situation as it was and let the vendors occupy the street and the square. The description of the market arrangements is also of interest:

> In the Hegazi market above the Munira underpass, there was a tragedy. The vendors destroyed the market walls that were erected by the municipality and went out to the Munira Street in a way that rendered the road accessible to one car at a time. Tens of vendors congregate in this area and have spread their merchandise on the sidewalk and a large part of the road, closing it to the pedestrians. Also, the peddlers and fruit vendors have occupied tens of streets in Ard al-Gam'iyya. As for the minivan drivers, it is another matter. They parked their cars in the middle of the road waiting until they are full with passengers. They drive in the opposite direction of the traffic in all streets, in particular in the Munira underpass. (ibid.)

To amplify the threat from *baltaga*, the media has carried stories detailing lurid events surrounding the lives and deaths of *baltagiyya*.

Sabri al-Gin's story is emblematic. Al-Gin means "genie" and evokes a supernatural force that could be malign or benign. In the press stories, however, the nickname appeared to suggest devilish skills. Newspaper accounts of *baltaga* have also traced its history, naming famous *baltagiyya* and their deeds, even sketching their characteristic attire. For the contemporary period, press reports drew up a sociological and psychological profile of the *baltagi*, calling on the expertise of social scientists and on the opinion of religious scholars. Additionally, the sensational features of the new *baltagiyya* have been emphasized, beginning with their odd nicknames and unconventional lifestyles.

In public discourse, especially in the mass media, the scope of *baltaga* has widened to include an increasing range of apparent or perceived transgressions against the law, public regulations, and social conventions. Peddlers, for instance, have come to be referred to as *baltagiyya*. In particular, peddlers working in public areas that are popular with Cairenes, such as the Corniche al-Nil and al-Muqattam, have been singled out. Both these sites are visited daily by thousands of Cairenes out on leisurely strolls and to enjoy the view and openness of the space. Peddlers go to these areas to sell drinks and snacks to the visitors. This practice has been construed by one commentator writing in a popular magazine as that of "stealing the Corniche" and "depriving poor people of their pleasure" (*Ruz al-Yusuf*, 30 August 2003). The focus of this objection is not on the use of the space for this type of commerce but rather on the fact that the peddlers are squatters of a sort. They are not subject to the control of public authorities or to regulations. The author of the article proposed that vendors in these areas be required to wear uniforms and come under the control of municipal authorities, and that the latter, consistent with their expressed desire to manage the vendors, provide uniform vending carts and standardize the space between various carts. The control and ordering of space is at the heart of the desire to regulate the peddlers. Their unregulated presence undermines official views of order and urban government. Invoking *baltaga* in reference to peddlers recalls a trope of social deviance and unruliness now used to characterize the challenge that peddlers and informal markets represent to public management.

The *baltaga* problem is presented as one of great dimensions. It is asserted that the *baltagiyya* control the Egyptian street (*al-Ahrar*, 30 August 2003). Indeed, an *al-Ahrar* article described it as "a ticking time bomb" (ibid.). The problem is generalized to wider segments of the

population such as children (al-Ahrar, 15 March 2003). However, baltaga is identified as a problem affecting informal housing communities and the new popular quarters, in particular. Ahmad El Magdoub, professor of criminal law at the National Centre for Sociological and Criminological Research, defined the baltagi in the following terms: "A thug, usually a young, unemployed, poor illiterate man. He lives in a shanty or slum area, but he usually works in middle- and upper-class districts where people need his services to replace the rule of law. Hiring bodyguards and security guards is basically a more sophisticated way of doing it." El-Magdoub's diagnosis is that thuggery expresses the frustration of the poor and their antagonism toward the rich. It is the weapon of the have-nots against the haves (Tadros 1999b).

The discourse on baltaga is articulated within a wider public discourse engaged in the production of a "moral panic" state of affairs.[6] The process of production seems to be perpetually in gear and drives a great deal of public discourse in Egypt. In the 1990s, the Egyptian public was confronted with increased evidence and growing signs of moral breakdown. For instance, in the mid-1990s, the "devil-worshippers" ('abadat al-shaytan) case provided gripping and shocking stories about the deviance of youths.[7] The fabricated nature of most of the reporting did not necessarily diminish the sense of danger that many families and parents felt. For many religious and devout citizens, the reported conduct of the youth was a sign of impending doom. More recently, the "Queen Boat" affair, involving the arrest of groups of men on charges of debauchery, focused the nation's attention on the moral threats facing Egypt and Egyptians.[8] Along with these sensational episodes, the citizens are sensitized to the new phenomenon of social breakdown. This is manifest in media reports on acts and incidents such as fratricide, patricide, "school girls using knives as weapons in conflicts among themselves," and "wives murdering their husbands."[9] The stories are recounted in conjunction with analyses by social scientists, religious scholars, and "experts" on the subject.

In the narrative of baltaga, we witness the working of a kind of invention noted by Nathan Brown (1990) in his account of processes of state building and the consolidation of the apparatus of order. In the late nineteenth century, the Egyptian state invented banditry as a national problem for the purpose of creating a centralized state security apparatus. Banditry, according to Brown, was the weapon of the

strong, not of the weak. This invention did not mean that the state fabricated the events that were invoked in the narrative. Rather, it was the manner of interpreting the events that was of the order of invention as well as the kind of emplotment given to these events. The logical orientation of the narrative was that of the necessity of establishing an extensive security apparatus. In the same manner, we find that by transforming *baltagiyya* into celebrities, by enumerating the range of *baltaga* acts, and by identifying episodes of social conflict as ones between state agents and *baltagiyya*, *baltaga* has been woven into the national security narrative. In the contemporary period, the consolidation of the police state takes the form of the expansion of the remit of agents of *al-amn al-'am* (public security) through security patrols (*dawriyyat amniyya*), enlarged security-campaign raids (*hamalat amniyya mukabara*) on popular quarters, and campaigns aimed at *mushtabah fihum* (suspects). The logic of these campaigns is to allow the agents of order to enter into all spaces. Thus, new cars have been designed for security campaigns. They are station wagons built narrow enough to enter into alleyways and to navigate the *hara*, with space in the back for the transport of suspects. Residents of Bulaq have labeled them "Atari" in reference to the video game. Further, a specific patrol, named *shurtat al-indhibat* or discipline police, has been deployed to carry out disciplinary tasks in neighborhoods.

But Who Is the Baltagi?

Critics of state policies and public corruption have seized upon the expanding narrative of *baltaga* in the media and the looseness of its definition in Law 6. In both government-controlled and opposition media, a wide range of activities has been described as *baltaga*, some involving the state and its agents. In a manner similar to the discourse on terrorism, where attempts to limit its scope to nonstate actors were unsuccessful, the Egyptian state has found itself accused of *baltaga*. In the debate on who is a *baltagi*, state agents are not spared. More importantly, residents of popular areas, including Bulaq, direct charges of *baltaga* at the state and its agents. The return of the drug dealers to the corners of Gam'iyya and Zanayn Streets was explained in terms of the reappropriation of surveillance tasks by the state. In Mahmud's terms, he and his neighbors—in particular his *tabligh wa da'wa* associates—had "cleaned" the area. However, it became "soiled" again by the return of drug dealers that followed police intrusion into the area.

The drug dealers are known to be informants for the police. Their protection is ensured by their patrons, the *amin al-shurta* (police personnel below officer rank). In other words, the *baltagi* works for the state. There is a reverse criminalization in this analysis. The state controls the market, the minivan station, and the street through the *baltagi*. Indeed, the residents' narratives show that the state has failed to protect them from the *baltagi*, as when the residents of one street collected signatures requesting protection from al-Malti, a known *baltagi*, but the police refused to intervene. Similarly, hajj Sultan's reign in the market is enforced by Rizq, a local *baltagi*, while the *carta* system (a fee system that informally regulates minivan traffic on particular lines) was controlled by Atiya al-Zuna and, after his death, by his associates. Kamal Zaydun and members of his family are also in the *carta* system and are suspected of being informants. All of these *baltagiyya* work or have worked for the state.

The incorporation of *baltagiyya* through the *carta* system and as police informants, or *murshid*, has projected the *baltagi* as an agent of the state. The *baltagi* maintains order in the minivan station and controls the drivers. However, there is ambiguity in the *baltagi's* role, as some of his functions could also be seen as those of the *futuwwa*. In one neighborhood of Bulaq, this ambiguity appears in reference to the local tough, Kamal Zaydun, who assumes a combined *futuwwa-baltagi* role. In his links to his *hara*, he acts as a *futuwwa* who intervenes in fights and is viewed as having good morals and ethics (*akhlaq hamida*), according to one of his neighbors' accounts. From the vantage point of the coffee shop on Tir'at al-Zumor Street, he also monitors women's conduct, a conventional *futuwwa* concern. However, the women think he is flexing his muscles in front of the *amin shurta* with whom he sits at the coffee shop. Finally, Taybun is thought to have ties with the Islamists while also informing on them. In these latter respects, he plays a *baltagi* role.

Discipline and Surveillance

Suspicion and Investigation (ishtibah wa tahari): *Policing "Suspicious Subjects"*

In addition to the introduction of the law on thuggery, the exercise of police powers of discipline and surveillance has expanded. These powers fall under the rubric of a category of operations and procedures known

as "suspicion and investigation" *(ishtibah wa tahari)*. They involve stop *(is-tiqaf)*, arrest *(dabt)*, and investigation *(tahari)* powers directed against people who are construed as "suspicious persons." The definition of *sus-picious* is loose and seems to apply to young men on the streets in popu-lar areas, particularly at night. The High Court of Appeal has recognized walking late at night (after midnight) as a cause of suspicion *(al-Wafd,* 10 July 1998). Investigation *(tahari)* by security forces falls within police pow-ers of arrest but has no clear basis in law. According to one leading jurist, the powers of investigation *(tahari)* were exercised by the British colonial administration in Egypt and have been retained since then. Meanwhile, the category of "suspect persons" is specified in the criminal code and appears in association with another category of persons, namely "va-grants" *(al-mutasharidin)*.[10] The category of "suspect persons" makes its first appearance in Law 98 of 1945, later modified by Law 157 of 1959, Law 110 of 1980, and Law 195 of 1983 (Marsum Biqanun Raqam 98). Ac-cording to this law, a *suspicious person* is someone who is above eighteen years of age and who was sentenced more than once for crimes specified under its Articles. The crimes that Law 98 specifies are the following: the assault on a person for money, threatening to do so, mediating in the re-turn of stolen goods, stopping public transportation, drug dealing or drug offering, forgery, prostitution, escape from prison, arms dealing, training others to commit crime, and hiding suspects. Also considered suspicious are persons who "for acceptable reasons have a reputation for habitually committing these crimes" (Law 98 of 1945). Thus, conviction is not the only cause of suspicion; a reputation for involvement in the criminal activities specified by the law could also render a person suspect.

I collected numerous accounts of the administration of *mahdar ishtibah wa tahari* from the young men I interviewed. These accounts highlight police use of this process to discipline young men. Ayman's ac-count of his personal experience of *mahdar tahari* reveals the disciplin-ing dimensions involved in police action. Ayman was arrested by a police officer right in front of his home. He was standing by his door when the police officer passed by. They exchanged looks (perhaps of an antago-nistic nature). The next day, the same officer came by, and, again, looks were exchanged. The officer then approached Ayman and began to ask him questions. Ayman showed him his identity card. Then the officer asked him to get into the police car. He was taken to the station and held there for three days and then brought before a public prosecutor and administered a *mahdar tahari*. The prosecutor took the officer's side.

The *mahdar* stated that the officer had found a paper containing drugs
in Ayman's possession. Ayman was released, but he has a police record
of some kind. In front of the prosecutor, Ayman denied the drug charge
and attributed it to police prejudice. In his assessment, he was arrested
because he dared to look back at the officer. He believed the officer construed his posture and demeanor outside his home as signs of defiance.

The lines of Ayman's narrative echo what I read in police and
court reports of similar cases. One police investigation report gave an
account of a nighttime police street patrol that was part of "a large
campaign to arrest suspects and outlaws and capture those disturbing
public order" (Giza Security Directorate, Bulaq al-Dakrur Police Station. Police Report 3862/97, 5 May 1997). The police officer who filed
the report was patrolling by car along with a force of *umana shurta*
(policemen below officer rank). While passing through Tir'at al-Zumor
Street, at the intersection of Hamfirst, he saw a man standing alone in
the area. The man reportedly threw a yellow paper wrapper on the
ground when the police approached. Upon chemical examination,
the wrapper was found to contain traces of narcotics. During the public prosecutor's interrogation, the accused denied the drug possession
charge against him (Public Prosecutor, Prosecutor Investigation Report Case 3862/97, 5 May 1997). He stated that at the time of his arrest he was sitting at the coffee shop with some friends. At one point,
he was addressed in a disrespectful manner by a man dressed in civilian clothes. He responded in kind to the man and found himself surrounded by a number of other men. He was then dragged into a
police van. According to the case report, the man's legal counsel
questioned the police account, noting that the arrest took place late
in the evening, allegedly in a place where the lighting was poor and
where it would have been difficult to distinguish a small paper wrapper being thrown to the ground by someone. Further, because the
wrapper was not found on the accused, it could not be assumed to belong to him. Also, the defense counsel raised the matter of why the
man was arrested before the contents of the wrapper had been as-
certained (ibid.).

The loose nature of the definition of suspicion can be discerned
from police reports and from strategies used by defense lawyers in their
responses to suspicion charges. In police reports relating to the administration of *mahdar ishtibah wa tahari*, we find the use of the procedure
being justified in such terms as "the person was walking in a crowded

street and was looking left and right" or "the individuals were leaning on the front of a car in a suspicious manner." In response, lawyers contend that the behavior in question does not warrant suspicion or amount to "acting suspiciously": People walking in crowded streets must look left and right to ensure that they do not bump into other pedestrians, and leaning on the front of a car is conduct common to thousands of citizens daily. Yet, the charge of suspicion or acting suspiciously places the onus of proof on the individual and not on the observing officer.

In a group meeting I had with some young men from Bulaq, the narratives of *ishtibah wa tahari* emerged as structuring elements of their experiences of encounter with the state. Each of the young men had at one point or another been arrested and taken into police custody for *tahari* (investigation into their record). Hisham began his account by saying: "appearance is important (*al-mazhar muhim*), any injury or scar on the face or on the hand would cause suspicion on the part of the officer." He added, "After three incidents of *tahari*, an officer can administer a case of *ishtibah* (suspicion). This is *bahdala* (something that unsettles or disturbs one's sense of honor and integrity) and one would only be released after paying bail." Hisham's own experience of *ishtibah wa tahari* shows the arbitrary nature of the procedure and its application. One evening, when he was standing in front of a car dealership in Saft al-Laban, a newer district of Bulaq, a fight broke out in the street. Soon after, the police arrived and officers began arresting young men. One police officer asked Hisham to get into the police van. Hisham noted that the officer checked out his clothes and appearance. On that day, he was well dressed. The officer inquired into the nature of his work, and Hisham responded that he was in private security. In his own assessment, it was his response and his assertive demeanor that irked the officer and led to his decision to arrest him. However, another officer interceded in his favor noting that Hisham had a "clean appearance" and "looked good" ("*shakluh kiwayyis*").

Other young men narrated their experience in custody and at the police station once arrested. One of them recounted how he found the situation at the station strange. He said that he was taken "underground, into a basement, to a place that does not see the sun." He continued: "Underground there are no humans. Upon arrival one is checked by the person responsible for detention—another detainee. The people who are below wait to hear the story of each newcomer. Listening to each story is a diversion (*tasliyya*), an entertainment, as there is no TV." In the narratives of former detainees, the descriptions

of detention rooms, usually located in the basements of police stations and other Interior Ministry buildings, are salient. They recall the absence of light, the pervasive suffocating smell, the tightness of space, and the overall terrible hygiene conditions (see also Human Rights reports for testimonies of the experience of such conditions).

In commenting on the experience of arrest, the men stated that anyone in popular areas can be arrested. They viewed the corruption of police officers as one of the reasons for the various campaigns aimed at the arrest of young men. One young man explained the arrests as a fund-raising strategy by a weak police (*shurta da'ifa*). By this, he was referring to the bribery that goes on when low-ranking officers are involved in arrests. Indeed, according to many, arrests are designed to create bribe situations. In contrast, it was pointed out that if a high-ranking officer was involved, there was no easy way out.

Policing the People

The control and discipline objectives of *mahdar ishtibah wa tahari* are supported by a wide range of practices and techniques allowing the kind of continuous supervision necessary for spatial domination. Such practices include the fabrication of drug trafficking and possession charges, detention without charge, the deployment of large numbers of informants, and the use of torture to extract confessions from prisoners and detainees. What we find, then, is that techniques of power have been deployed with a view to establishing a general system of police associated with the modern state (see Mitchell 1989). The practices of police surveillance and monitoring were laid down earlier on in the process of formation of the Egyptian state. However, state formation is a continuous project, subject to reenactment, reinvention, and revision. In this section, I present an overview of practices aimed at disciplining the population. It is by no means exhaustive, as practices of control and discipline multiply in an ever-expanding repertoire. In reflecting on the purposes of some of these practices, Mbembe's (2001) proposition on the postcolony holds true: "[t]o exercise authority is, above all, to tire the bodies under it, to disempower them not so much to increase their productivity as to ensure the maximum docility" (110).

Charges of drug possession have come to be viewed by quarter residents themselves as one instrument of control. A common belief within the neighborhood is that police officers keep drugs in their

offices to plant on anyone who refuses to cooperate with them or on those whom they view as undesirable or as troublemakers. This view about police practices was confirmed in a 1993 report by Mustafa al-Kashef, former deputy head of the Anti-Narcotics Unit. According to al-Kashef, each police station in Cairo was at the time concocting about five drug charges per day. With forty police stations in the city, the number of false cases could total as many as 200 per day, or approximately 73,000 per year. In al-Kashef's view, "that is 73,000 more people hating the government and the police every year" (quoted in Hammond 1998).

There are a number of interpretations as to why the police are fabricating drug charges. In bureaucratic terms, the police must fill a quota of arrests and charges for different types of crime. That is, the police must produce records for a specified number of crimes and felonies investigated and solved. The practice of fabrication may appear as a manifestation and proof of police corruption, inefficiency, and ineptness. However, this view does not take into account the disciplinary purposes of the practice. Youth on the street know they are subject to possession charges whether or not they have drugs on their person. They also know that "charged with possession" is a technique of establishing control and discipline. As we have seen, Ayman may have been charged because he dared to look an officer in the eyes. Similarly, in the police report quoted previously, the accused explained that he was charged because he answered back to an officer who was wearing civilian clothes. Finally, the threat of being charged is used to pressure individuals to cooperate with the police and act as informants. Citizens understand the use of this technique and have reasoned that police officers keep pieces of evidence in their desk drawers to use against innocent citizens (e.g., paper wrappers containing traces of narcotics).

Bulaq residents believe that officers also keep available in their desk drawers blank arrest forms presigned by the Minister of the Interior. The forms are meant for use in matters of state security under the Emergency Law, but there is a widely held belief that police use them indiscriminately. The powers to detain citizens without charge fall within the remit of the Emergency Law that was implemented in 1981 and has been renewed regularly ever since.[11] The residents' beliefs about arbitrary arrest and detention are confirmed by a report of the Egyptian Organization for Human Rights (EOHR), published in 2003. The report shows that citizens practicing their basic rights such

as freedom of expression or freedom of association have been taken into custody and detained. Under detention regulations, imprisonment does not issue from a court order, nor does it follow a court order of arrest. Rather, people are arrested at the police officers' discretion and can be detained for months or years. The report also confirms that administrative detention is used by the heads of police investigative units to punish citizens who refuse to work as police informants (EOHR 2003, 20). In such cases, officers submit reports to the security division for their particular units stating that a person (or persons) represents a danger to general public security. The report is then forwarded to the Interior Ministry, which issues an internment order (ibid.). According to the EOHR, the number of appeals made against detention orders reached 20,017 in the period between January and December 2002.

Emergency laws are being normalized. As the EOHR points out, this has taken the form of new laws integrated into the legal system, as, for example, Law 97 of 1992, known as "the law for combating terrorism." This law gives greater powers to the security apparatus and further limits the liberty of citizens. The definition of terrorism is loose and covers disparate acts. Further, the law widened the scope of crimes punishable by the death penalty (EOHR 2003, 9). Article Three gives the authorities the right to detain "individuals deemed dangerous to security and general order and suspects." Within these provisions, administrative detentions have been applied to an increasing number of citizens, including individuals deemed dangerous in a political sense as well as in a social sense—both are constructed as "dangerous to public security" (*khatar 'ala al-amn al-'am*). The expansion of the category of "dangerous subjects" to a wider segment of the population is designed to cover the nondocile bodies, those who refuse to cooperate. The categories of *baltagi* and terrorist, as well as the slip-sliding between them, are mapping devices for governing the population.

In their efforts to ensure maximum docility, the police implicate members of the population beyond those viewed or labeled as "suspect," "accused," and "dangerous." This wider population covers the family members, especially sisters, mothers, and wives, of suspects and detainees. The arrest of female relatives aims to force suspects to turn themselves in. One woman viewed this tactic as a manipulation of honor values: The son or brother of the woman will feel honor-bound to turn himself in to secure the release of his mother or sister since it

is widely believed that women who are taken into custody are violated by the police in some way. The practice of interning family members as hostages to secure arrests or confessions from suspects is noted in reports by the Egyptian Organization for Human Rights. The tactic has the effect of ensnaring a wider segment of the population in the implementation of disciplining practices. Family members and neighbors are pressured to inform on suspects or to notify police of their whereabouts. If they resist, they become targets of direct disciplinary actions themselves. The Nadim Center has documented the subjection of entire families by means of strategies of horror—beatings, the destruction of household belongings, and public humiliation—intended to punish recalcitrant subjects.

Reports by human rights organizations confirm that torture is becoming routine in police stations.[12] Instances of abuse provide pretexts for confrontation with the police and for attacks on police officers or stations. For example, in Belqas, following the death of a citizen who had been detained for interrogation, the people attacked the station and all other public buildings in the area. The action lasted several days and constituted something of a mini revolt. Police organizations have attempted to portray torture as an aberration in their practice of policing. However, an increasing body of evidence indicates that torture is used systematically to gain confessions from the accused, to intimidate potential witnesses, and to create a general atmosphere of fear.[13]

The expansion of state security and police practices of surveillance has entailed the recruitment of a large number of informants. According to one report, Egypt has become "a state of informants and watchers." The security apparatuses employ an estimated 250,000 informants. These include conventional informants collecting crime-related information, but also those who operate as undercover watchers in NGOs, political parties, government departments, and local communities. Three designations are currently in use to refer to different surveillance tasks: guide, informant, and watcher. Watchers are generally used in the surveillance of criminal activity and are recruited from among individuals who have criminal records. Guides (*murshid*) are recruited from within the civilian population to assist intelligence agencies and security police in their collection of information. In addition to guides who are informally recruited, the police have a body of official informants, known as *mukhbir*. They do not wear uniforms and are on the police payroll. It is interesting to note that citizens have developed counter-surveillance practices. As we have noted

previously, vendors use watchers in the market to monitor the arrival of supply and security police patrols, and youth use tactics of evasion, avoiding spaces where they are likely to be monitored, stopped, and questioned.

In Bulaq, the police use informants as well as local *baltagiyya* to collect information and maintain control. For instance, one local figure of the *futuwwa-baltagi* type, was incorporated into the police network of local informants. The individual in question plays multiple and somewhat contradictory roles in the community. On one hand, he intervenes to settle disputes and break up fights and, in this respect, is considered by some to be a strong and fair man of *futuwwa* stature. For example, Ashraf, a twenty-two-year old driver from the neighborhood of Madinat Amir, a poor section of Bulaq, recounted how the local *futuwwa-baltagi* intervened on his family's behalf to protect them from the aggression of some young men in the area. On the other hand, he is also thought of as a local police informant. This belief arises in part from the fact that he sits with police personnel (*umana' al-shurta*) in the coffee shop by the wood bridge on Tir'at al-Zumor Street. His police links are further evidenced by his appointment to the *carta* system, a position used by the police as inducement for local informers.

Refusal to cooperate with police can result in harassment and detention. Ra'fat, a tile layer, was arrested and interned without charge for sixteen months for refusing to act as an informant in the area. The police had offered him control of the *carta* (collection of the fee on the informal system of minivan traffic regulation). The line on Hamfirst Street is managed by the Giza governorate, and the drivers get receipts for their payments. The police appoint their informants to the position of collector. On Tir'at Zanayn, however, the *carta* system is informal and no receipts are given. It was first run by a local *futuwwa-baltagi*, a man known as al-Zuna, and then, after his death, by his associates. The police had given tacit consent to another *futuwwa-baltagi* to take control of that particular *carta* operation, but fights broke out between the contending parties and he was removed.

Spatialized Policing

Control of space, of its use, and of how it is ordered guide the spatialized practices of rule and articulate with the security objectives. The policies of enframing the population support the spatial interaction between citizens and the state. In its various campaigns of discipline, the

state in a sense descends to the people and the everyday, serving as a reminder and display of power. The surveillance of the population, particularly in popular neighborhoods, takes the form of a greater police presence in public, as well as specialized security campaigns targeting various sections of the population, such as youths and juveniles. Security campaigns are deployed under various provisions: utilities, supply, and discipline. During periods of unrest or increased supply shortages or when high-ranking officials are visiting an area, discipline campaigns (*hamalat indhibat*) are carried out to neutralize the population. Under utilities provisions, utilities officers can charge shopkeepers with obstruction for having signs of certain sizes and styles on their stores, placing chairs on the sidewalk in front of their stores or displaying goods on the street. Campaign officers issue fines, charge shopkeepers and craftsmen with road obstruction, and haul them into the police station. The idea, as explained to me by human rights activists, is to keep these segments of the population tied up and busy trying to clear themselves of the charges while the government official is in the area or while the demonstration is taking place.[14] During the March 2003 demonstrations against the American-led war on Iraq, it was reported that in a number of popular neighborhoods, shopkeepers, and coffee shop owners along with street vendors were charged under various utilities provisions. Not only were they kept busy, but also the arrests served as warnings to others not to get involved in the demonstrations. The various campaigns thus take the form of hide-and-seek games that the authorities initiate and encourage the population to play, having set the rules and the penalties for transgressing them.

Another tactic police use to establish their presence in an area and to raise their national profile is to carry out campaigns of execution of court orders (*tanfiz ahkam*). These orders authorize such things as the demolition of illegally built structures, the removal of a business, or arrest for financial fraud (passing bad checks, for instance). The Annual Reports of the Security Condition (*Taqrir al-Amn al ‘Am*) issued by the Ministry of Interior provide staggering figures on the number of orders executed by the police. Over a three-year period between 1998 and 2001, the police executed a total of 13 million orders (quoted in *Al-Ahrar*, 25-01, 2001). Of these, more than 4 million concerned felonies covered by a prison term, approximately 3.5 million concerned contraventions of public regulations, and more than 600,000 cases resulted in fines. The execution of orders is also carried out under campaigns of discipline

(*hamalat indhibat*). The figures for the number of orders executed annually confirm the intense public presence of the police. District courts in popular quarters process an estimated 2,000 orders per month on average, covering infractions relating to supply and electricity regulations, construction permits, road obstruction, and other charges.

Police campaigns are devised to monitor and control various segments of the population. Police records and reports of their expanding surveillance activities indicate intensified efforts at monitoring and policing adolescents and children. A police report of one of these campaigns states that "the campaign is carried out within the plan of the Juvenile Police concerning fighting crimes of juveniles." Further, the report states that "the police authority has issued directives to its personnel to undertake campaigns and raids of this nature in popular areas and districts of the city" (MI, Juvenile Police-Division of Social Security. Police Report of Investigation 58/1/2/3 M. 1 February 1999). One of the surveillance aims is to protect public morality through the monitoring of films screened in coffee shops. In these campaigns, young men may be forced out of coffee shops (sometimes being dragged out physically), dispersed from street gatherings, or simply arrested. For example, one police investigation report gives an account of a raid on a coffee shop carried out on the pretext that films contravening public morality regulations were being shown there. Following the raid, six young men were charged with "exposing themselves to immorality and deviance" (MI, Juvenile Police-Division of Social Security. Police Report of Investigation 58/1/2/3 M. 1 February 1999). Another report tells of a raid on an unlicensed video game business located in a private residence in one of Bulaq's alleyways (MI, Juvenile Police Division Police Report of Investigation 462/1/2 M. 27 November 1999). It took place after undercover police had been monitoring a group of youth in the street. The officers tailed the group to a home where video games were being played. The police registered that the business was unlicensed. They seized the video game machines and arrested the owner. According to the report, the police let the youths go because of their young age.

The management of population in space entails its mapping into categories of subjects. Thus, children, as one segment of the population, are constructed as subjects of surveillance and monitoring under the categories of "vulnerable to delinquency" (*mu 'arad lil inhiraf*) and "vulnerable to danger" (*mu 'arad lil khatar*).[15] The category "vulnerable to delinquency" is specified in Child Law 12 of 1996 and has its origins in

earlier laws such as Law 31 of 1974 (Human Rights Watch 2003, 39). It should be noted that the category "vulnerable to danger" was introduced in 1997 as part of the implementing regulations of Law 12 of 1996, giving police wider discretion in their operations targeting street children (ibid.). Children on the street, viewed from the standpoint of the police as "offering services of little value," are arrested for being "vulnerable to delinquency." This classification has a history and recalls the category of "juvenile vagrants" discussed by Ahmed Sami, an early-twentieth-century Egyptian social reformer (Sami 1923).[16] The reworked categories underwrite practices aimed at controlling the presence in public of children under the age of eighteen. The figures for children arrested under these categories provide evidence for the massive scale of the campaigns of clearing the streets of children. In 2001, the number of children arrested under the two categories reached over 11,000 and represented one-quarter of all arrests of children (Human Rights Watch 2003). In the same year, the number of children arrested under the category "vulnerable to danger" rose from zero to 185 (ibid.). Arrest campaigns aimed at children arise out of a logic of spatial control and population management. This logic is at work in the commentary of one policeman who explains that the purpose of arrest campaigns is to "demonstrate the government's presence. Because if we didn't have arrest campaigns, the streets would fill up quickly with kids selling tissues and wiping cars and begging."[17] The rationality of government here has its specificity as it operates on the basis of assumptions relating to the particular categories of subjects, in this instance, "delinquent children."

Police street patrols and security campaigns are associated with regular scenes of public confrontation. In Bulaq, police patrols concentrate on the main road junctions, particularly the minivan stations. They often end with policemen chasing drivers through the streets, thus contributing to increased tension. Arrested minivan drivers and drug suspects are put in police vans and driven to deserted areas where they are beaten up and either dumped or taken back to the police station for interrogation. One of my informants reported seeing young men tied to police cars and dragged in the street. Night patrols monitor the bridges, requesting the identity cards of the youths crossing into or leaving the quarter. This police practice is common in other popular areas where residents believe they cannot return home after 11:00 p.m. or midnight without being searched, roughed up, and humiliated. Raids tend to be carried out on the main thoroughfares rather than in the alleys. This explains, in part, why many alleyways

have their own coffee shops and are attracting neighborhood clientele. It should be recalled that alley life has its code of sociability that outsiders must respect in order to be admitted. This makes police entry into the alley an intrusion into a collectively guarded space.

En-countering the Police

Residents' accounts of relations with the police emphasize the latter's abuse of authority and use of violence and humiliation. At the same time, they express a desire to avoid dealing with the police even when there may be a need for their intervention as in the case of street fights and disputes between residents. As such, a great deal of conflict goes unreported and is settled internally whether peacefully or violently. The view among citizens is that the police are unwilling to intervene and prefer to let people settle their own affairs. My own observations confirm this view. One day, I was sitting in front of a shop on Tir'at Zanayn Street in the middle of the market. A fight broke out between one of the vendors and a few young men from the adjacent alley. I was told that this was a continuation of a fight that had started the day before. A group of policemen on patrol was positioned just around the corner, and everyone in the area could see them. A number of vendors noted that the police stayed away. They intervened the next day, however, when the fight resumed and a car parked in the area was damaged.

On the occasions when the residents sought police help, they found them reluctant to intervene. In one case, a group of neighbors approached the police seeking protection from al-Malti, a local thug who was in the habit of getting drunk and harassing passersby. The neighbors collected their identity cards and presented a complaint to the police. The officer in charge advised them to take care of al-Malti themselves. In response, the group requested that the officer put his advice in writing so that if they followed it, there would be no legal retribution. The policeman retorted that it was up to them to act. Indeed, he opined that if they failed to do so, it would mean that al-Malti had made them wear veils (*khalih yilabiskum turah*). In other words, their inaction made them more like women (i.e., their manliness was diminished).

Residents interpret the unwillingness of police to intervene as evidence of police implication in the illegal activities they are supposed to prevent. In their narratives, they allude to police involvement in protecting drug dealers and thugs. Policemen below officer rank are

believed to be part owners of unlicensed minivans. The involvement of the police in the drug trade appears not to be of the same scope found in Rio de Janeiro's favellas as described by Goldstein (2003). However, the structure of feelings that guides the residents' interaction with the police in Bulaq is strikingly similar to that of favella residents. In Rio favellas, the police do not provide protection against gang violence; rather, they are violent, corrupt, and terrorizing. In Bulaq, the experiences of arbitrary arrest, suspicion, and investigation and of false drug charges de-legitimize the police. If favella residents turn to their local gangs for protection, Bulaq residents turn to the institutions of elders, to *majalis 'urfiyya*, and to religious groups to avoid having to go to the police. In Imbaba, the Jama'a under Sheikh Gabir's leadership performed "security" tasks and responded to needs in a parallel manner to the gangs in the favellas (Goldstein 2003, 205–7). In a context where everyday violence is ritualized and where the law is de-legitimized, youth gangs, religious fraternities, thugs, and notables present alternatives to the arbitrary violence of the "formal" order. However, as demonstrated by the cases of the notables who mediate with the state and the thugs who act as its informants, the alternative institutions may well serve as links between rulers and ruled. This does not mean that incorporation and co-optation are inevitable outcomes. Rejection of the police is expressed when citizens like Ra'fat refuse to work as informants and when the latter are equated with thugs in the popular imaginary. This unwillingness to work as informants may be the reason that the police manipulate individuals with a criminal record to do the job of informing, while also rewarding them with permits for vending kiosks or with running the *carta* system.

Conclusion

My analysis of the data gathered on political life in Cairo's new urban quarters points to certain developments in state-society relations that should be explained in relation to the interplay between socioeconomic and political determinants at the macro level and sociospatial factors at the micro level. The developments in state–society and state–citizen relations should be analyzed in terms of arenas of interaction. These arenas appear to be increasingly circumscribed and centered on control, discipline, and regulation. Thus, state withdrawal from social and economic welfare arenas is accompanied by the state's

increased engagement in the security and order arenas. Determinants at the micro level interact with these macro-level changes. The expansion in informal economic, social, and governance activities is shaped by the sociospatial characteristics of the new quarters. Physical and symbolic characteristics have produced the effects of separation both from the rest of the city and in relation to government. Thus, while community residents maintain links with other districts and draw on their resources (schools and hospitals), localized activities in the economic, social, and governance spheres point to efforts aimed at achieving disengagement from the state. Much of the economic activity of the residents is conducted outside the scope of state regulation. Management of collective needs in areas of security and moral governance affirms a desire to eschew state authorities, particularly the police and the courts. Yet, Bulaq residents have cultivated an intimate knowledge of the everyday state. Indeed, much conviviality—in the market, in alleyways, and on visits to state offices—develops in relation to power and in the cultivation of knowledge about its workings. Intimacy and familiarity with power are expressed in the citizens' accumulation of knowledge about its workings. A logic of domesticity is exemplified, for instance, in the chases that ensue in the market.

Everyday-life politics takes on specific dimensions when looking at relations to government and the patterning of state–citizen interaction. Existing on the margins of the sphere of formal politics, if not outside it, the citizens' engagement with the state is viewed in terms of neglect in relation to their needs and of suppression aimed at controlling individual and collective public action. In this dynamic of interaction, contestation and control are spatial maneuvers. The everyday state's engagement in the area is most visible in the surveillance of streets through patrols, in security campaigns, and in monitoring people's use or abuse of public utilities. Intermediaries between the people and state authorities are chosen for their ability to secure "public order" and control. Thus, *futuwwa* and *baltagi* are put in charge of the minivan system, while community notables are incorporated into the structure of influence and power. In all of this, the purpose is to undermine the actualization of collective action.

Police and court documents, interview data, and personal observation support broad findings concerning state–community relations. Police campaigns aimed at rounding up suspects in matters of public order and security indicate a national policy that reflects the state's view of a need to control the territory. The politics of security acquires

primacy in the state's interaction with the residents. The citizens' experience of their encounters with the security state structures much of their feelings about government. They are conscious of the illegal nature of some of its power tactics—false drug accusations, for instance. They are intimately aware of the tactics of control deployed to beat them into submission. This awareness does not translate into a predetermined mode of action. Rather, in the relations between rulers and ruled, we see mutual ensnarement, evasions, and concealment, and, once in a while, we glimpse signs of contestation.

Postscript

Collective Action and the Everyday State

Notes on Contentious Action

Against the background of state disengagement from welfare provision and the intensified politics of security, what kind of state–society relations obtain in Egypt? Inaction, passivity, evasion, and fear are all features of encounters with the everyday state. Meanwhile, trickery appears as one modality of citizen interaction with the state. The questions that arise are: What of resistance? What can we make of instances of confrontation or of events in which we find popular contentious action? There is a need to examine these events closely and to scrutinize their features in the hope of developing a clear view of the nature of contentious action in Egypt.

By the mid-1990s, the state had contained militant Islamist activism. Political contention then appeared to take new forms. If 1997 was marked by the spectacular terrorist attacks in Luxor, 1998 was the year of citizen confrontation with the police. In that year, a number of mini-rebellions or popular uprisings took place in villages and towns around the country: Hamul, Belqas, al-Gurna, al-Fawakhriyya, and many other places. Since then, events of this type have become regular occurrences, signaling citizen dissatisfaction with and opposition to government. Additional episodes of unrest such as those of Mit Nema, Abu Sina, and Awlad Sayf occurred in the years to follow.[1]

Two key causes of popular outbursts and social unrest can be gleaned from a preliminary reading of these events. Deficiency of public services, or an absence of services altogether, appears to constitute one pretext of uprising. The abuse of citizens in police stations is another. In Mit Nema, Abu Sina, and Awlad Sayf, protests and clashes with the police followed the death of a citizen who was hit by a car

while crossing a public road. The absence of pedestrian crossings on expressways is one example of government neglect leading citizens to engage in contentious action. In Belqas and Hamul, popular protest took place in reaction to the death of a citizen while in police custody.

These events provide us with clues as to the nature of contentious action in Egypt today. On the whole, as instances of collective action, they are short lived. However, they are recurrent and fairly widespread. They reveal the absence of popular-level organization and the workings of spontaneous movements. They take place at moments of the breakdown of citizen fear, and they express challenge to the repressive authorities that had worked so methodically to instill that fear. In each of these incidents, citizens of the entire village descended into the streets and confronted the police. They attacked the symbols of government and stood in the line of fire. In Mit Nema, Abu Sina, and Awlad Sayf, citizens blockaded public roads and set public buses and police cars on fire. They pelted police with stones, stopped trains, and brought traffic to a standstill.

Undoubtedly, government reaction in these events is usually exaggerated. However, it also represents the security state's reading of citizen activism and of social phenomena in general. In response to the demonstrations and protests, central security forces are always mobilized, with armored cars, special units, and the crowd control equipment they feel is needed to overwhelm citizens. In each case, the authorities used a mixture of force and cajoling to try to end the standoff. Tear gas was used and rubber bullets fired into the crowd. At the same time, government representatives sought a negotiated end to the confrontation. In all of these events, calm was reestablished following public meetings between citizens and government representatives in which grievances were aired and demands were made. For instance, in the case of the pedestrian deaths, the citizens were promised funds for the construction of bridge crossings, and they were reassured that investigations would be conducted into any neglect that may have caused the accidents.

A similar repertoire of actions accompanied protests over deaths in police custody. However, they also have a certain specificity as they tend to have the police as the focus of their grievance and anger. In both Hamul and Belqas, citizens marched on the police station and demanded that the police take responsibility for their action. In both cases, the families of the deceased refused to accept the body of their

dead relative when the police attempted to deliver it to them. Instead, they brought the corpses back to the police stations with the support of their neighbors and the wider citizenry of their areas. In refusing to bury the bodies, the families and their supporters were demanding that the police take responsibility for their actions by having a coroner's examination and an independent inquiry into the death. In Hamul, they congregated in front of the local hospital awaiting the coroner's findings. When faced with the possibility of cover-up, citizens marched to the local assemblies and pelted government offices with stones, set one representative's car on fire, and occupied the city center. In the process, they clashed with central security forces. The battle continued through the night. In Belqas, the demonstrations lasted for an entire week with the loss of two citizens killed when police fired on protesters.

What do these episodes tell us? Are they the expression of random social violence, not to be viewed in terms of collective social action? Or can we find in them elements of popular action or, perhaps, the seeds of a social movement? There are a number of issues to consider. First, these events took place primarily in villages and small towns outside Cairo and other large cities. Therefore, it may be argued that rural conditions set the background for contestation. However, it is important to point out that the pretexts for these contentious actions may be found anywhere in Egypt, including urban areas. Arbitrary police actions and use of torture in detention are common occurrences in urban centers. Everyday encounters with the state in the urban setting bear the marks of repression and neglect on the part of the authorities and resentment on the part of the citizens. We may ask, then, why we find instances of spontaneous, smaller popular uprisings outside and not within Cairo? I am not suggesting that the specific conditions of small towns and villages are not important. I am merely pointing out that we find similar pretexts of action in the urban setting, where other factors come into play.

Urban areas and Cairo, in particular, have witnessed the greatest expansion of security politics, with some neighborhoods virtually besieged by the police who stand ready to intervene immediately. Popular neighborhoods are under intensive monitoring and surveillance, as we have seen with the multitude of daily campaigns carried out by the various police departments—supply, utilities, and electricity—within an overall policy of maintaining discipline on the street.

Villages and towns are less subject to this kind of monitoring. In all episodes of confrontation outside Cairo, central security forces had to be brought in from the outside. Thus, the question of territorial control remains a factor. Egyptian observers, who looked at these events closely, are of the view that traditional solidarities of family and clan are strong bases of mobilizing people against the authorities.

Now we should consider that there have been instances of collective mobilization, protests, and demonstrations around what is commonly referred to as "national issues." The widespread demonstrations of April 2002 against the Israeli Defense Forces' incursion into West Bank towns and cities and the March 2003 demonstrations against the American-led war on Iraq are examples. The 2002 demonstrations began on university campuses with the predictable police response of closing the gates of campuses and stopping the students from leaving the university. In Alexandria where students managed to get to the streets, the clashes were violent and at least one protester died. In 2003, the police and central security forces squeezed demonstrators in public squares into corners and prevented the spread of protests. These demonstrations were instances of mobilization around national, or more precisely nationalist, issues. However, they do express opposition to the regime.

The question that arises here relates to the apparent absence of contentious actions related to issues of daily concern to the citizens—issues that emerge out of their encounters with the everyday state. When I present my findings of encounters with the everyday state, I am always confronted with the question of whether this situation is revolutionary or whether there will be revolution in Egypt soon. In my work on the Islamist movement, I argued that the infrastructures of collective action lay in the everyday forms of organization, in the structures of everyday interaction. That is, they lay in neighborhood relations of exchange and solidarity, in spaces or sites of mutual aid such as the mosque, and in the market arrangements. The militant Islamists penetrated these spaces and arrangements and came to occupy governance roles as mediators in daily disputes and as referees in the conflicts of everyday life in communities. The militants succeeded to an extent, before being crushed by the heavy hand of the state. Here, the failure of the Islamists should not be explained solely in terms of police repression. The Islamists committed tactical errors as well. In particular, they set out to confront the authorities through attacks on

tourists, police officers, and politicians. They sought confrontations prior to securing a large popular base and without establishing social-movement organization. The trajectory of militant Islamist movements in Egypt, and in Tunisia and Algeria as well, show that the informal structures are not sufficient to support long-term opposition to the state. There is no doubt that social movement organization—coordinating activities, devising strategies, and harmonizing objectives—is essential for long-term mobilization (Ismail 2004, 394). Groups like al-Jama'a al-Islamiyya excluded the possibility of forging alliances with formal organizations or political parties that would sponsor an Islamist agenda. They foreclosed these choices both ideologically and tactically (ibid., 395).

Today, no organizations are working to invest themselves in the micro spaces of opposition with the purpose of bringing about a fundamental transformation in relations of power and the system of rule. Organs associated with the main opposition movement (the Muslim Brotherhood Organization), such as al-Gama'iyya al-Shar'iyya, operate on the basis of an elitist and conservative ideology that seeks, at best, to work within the system and that, at its core, aims to regulate morality rather than to facilitate empowerment and liberation.

What are the constraints on popular organization from below? A simple answer is fear and the culture of fear that continuous monitoring, surveillance, humiliation, and abuse have created. Linked to the culture of fear are the ambiguous and contradictory citizens' relations to the state. These relations, and the constructs of the state that support them, could be summed up in the idea that the state does not exist and that the state is everywhere. In my research in Bulaq and other parts of Cairo, I was told repeatedly that there was no state: "*hina ma fish dawla, hina nas 'aysha fi dawla ghayr al-dawla*" ("here there is no state, here people live in a state other than the state"). What is the state that does not exist, and what is this state that is other than the state? The constructs of the state that come out of these views capture much of the puzzle that social scientists dealing with the ever-elusive construct have attempted to work out.

"There is no state; we are not in a state. This is a group of thieves, a gang. The Interior Ministry protects the system, the regime. But what keeps us together is the country, our fear for the country. There is nation, but no state." This analysis, found in the words of one human rights activist, was also expressed to me by ordinary citizens. At the

same time, while the analysis asserts that there is no state, it also affirms that there is a state everywhere: in the police, in the water bill, in the electricity bill. In all these sites, there was penetration of the state and there was exploitation. In the construct of "the state that is everywhere," is recognition of the state effect discussed by Mitchell (1991). In it, we find the material constraints on action without necessarily posing an opposition between thought and action. The citizens are aware that the state is not legal and that it is repressive but weak. However, fear structures their relations to its agents and their practices.

In one sense, the state that is projected as absent, nowhere, and non-existent in people's discourse is the ideal-type state as conceived in the social sciences, with the abstraction of law and order, a set of clear rules, consistency, and legality. The state that is—the state that exists for the people and that they talk about as existing—is the state that is other than legal. But where is the legal state? Is it a state of the imagination? In what follows, I take one recent episode in the life of the state to reflect on its elusive character as both existing and not existing.

The State That Is Not and the State That Is

In February–March 2004, the Egyptian public was presented with an impressive display of state force. State security forces descended on an island in the Upper Egypt governorate of Assiut (previously a hotbed of Islamist activism) and laid siege to it. I want to use this event to probe into the complexities of the state construct that underpin citizens' relations to the state. I will begin, however, with some necessary background information.

The state laid siege to the island of Nikhayla to take out a drug lord/arms dealer who had been in operation there for some time.[2] The island was controlled by this drug lord and the Hanafi clan to which he belonged. It was considered off limits to state agents. The clan had erected a watchtower at the entrance of the island and had positioned armed guards around its periphery. The clan was thought of as the island's government, and it conducted its affairs there virtually without challenge. Only another strong clan, the Marzuqs, had refused to accept the dictates of the Hanafis and, as a result, were engaged in an ongoing feud with them. The pretext for the police siege was that the Hanafi leader, Ezzat Hanafi, had taken hostages to prevent police from apprehending him. He was wanted on charges of theft and rape,

among other things. Yet, this was not a simple operation aimed at apprehending an outlaw. Ezzat Hanafi headed a powerful clan involved in various illegal activities, including the cultivation of *bango* on some three hundred feddans of state-owned land. The clan had been engaged in this activity for over a decade. Ezzat, who had recently replaced his brother Hasan—murdered by the Marzuqs—as clan leader, had taken hostages on three separate occasions in the few months that preceded the siege. Significantly, the power of the Hanafis had gone unchecked for over a decade, during which time they built a drug and arms empire, according to some reports. This raises several key questions: What was the siege really about? Did the Hanafis' ability to operate for so long have anything to do with police corruption?

There is no doubt that some police officers were on the clan payroll and that the police turned a blind eye to its illegal activities. However, something more was going on. We get a glimpse of "the state that is not" in the public discourse interpreting the event. On one hand, the media, and off-the-record analyses, spoke of a police alliance with the Hanafis forged sometime in the late 1980s or early 1990s. The alliance was part of the police battle with the Islamists. According to this interpretation, the containment of the Islamists by the mid-1990s presented an opportunity for the state to go after the Hanafis. After all, the clan was no longer needed to fight the Islamists. This account validates the state in its Godlike image. It recognizes that some members of the police apparatus were corrupt but, in the final analysis, interprets the actions and strategy of the state in the Hanafi affair as being based on raison d'état—the security of the state was the reason for the alliance. This account is favored by police officers and the Ministry of the Interior.

Another interpretation that appears less plausible, but is telling nonetheless, is that the Ministry of the Interior received some of the proceeds of the drug trade and used the money to pay off the Islamists. The logic of this more imaginative explanation holds that the state had nothing else to offer the Islamists and that buying the activists off was the only means of containment. Both accounts of the state's dealings with the little empire of Nikhayla acknowledge state collusion with the criminals. In the second account, however, the state itself is a partner in the drug dealing, perhaps, itself, a drug lord. The boundaries of the legal/illegal state are blurred, and the state that is not is the state that is.

In considering the constraints on collective action, I suggest that we need to probe into the workings of the elusive state: the state that does not exist, but is everywhere, the state that is not and the state that is. Drawing on Slavoj Žižek's work on ideology, Yael Navaro-Yashin (2002), in reference to Turkey, demonstrates how cynicism rather than false consciousness frames the subject's view of the state. The citizen, as subject of the state, knows that the state is not all-powerful but acts as if it is. Long after recognizing the fakeness of the state, the subject continues to act as if he/she believes in its existence as such (Navaro-Yashin 2002, 161). In the subject's acting "as if," Žižek identifies the cynical agent—someone who, in the Lacanian psychoanalytic tradition, recognizes her illness but holds on to it.

In the same manner described by Navaro-Yashin, we find mundane cynicism and disbelief in the state as a legal order or even as a Godlike entity, despite its coercive powers. Yet, along with the disbelief, there is a holding on to the construct of the state. Is this the work of fantasy, as suggested by Navaro-Yashin? I want to suggest that fear, as much as cynicism, frames the structure of feeling toward the state. Further, it is through fear that the state is reinscribed where it has been eroded. Youth arrested in Bulaq spoke of "weak police," meaning police that are out to be bribed and can be easily bribed. Ayman was conscious that he was considered a dupe by the state, that its agents treated him as an unaware citizen. He contradicted this view and protested that he was aware of the thieving and deceitful nature of those in positions of power. For him, the state was a mafia, a gang. Equally telling is that, for many, the state did not want them conscious and was actively undermining their ability to think critically by enmeshing them in daily struggles for survival. In their awareness of the broken nature of the state, its existence as broken bits (*dawla mufakaka*, it was said), the subjects of the state have imagined a fantastical actor, an evil, monstrous entity whose sites of presence include the streets but are found also in the desk drawers of police officers, where drug-tainted paper wrappers are kept until they are planted on suspects and in the blank arrest forms signed in advance by the Minister of the Interior and waiting to have a name, any name, inscribed on them. In the underground, dark, and smelly detention cells and in many similar sites, the state recovers something of its unity, of its hidden Godlike presence.

Appendixes

A. The "Field" and "Home":
   The Politics of Location

B. Thematic Outline of Interview Frames

Appendix A

The "Field" and "Home": The Politics of Location

IN THIS STUDY of everyday-life politics in Bulaq, I have relied on methods and techniques of inquiry common to critical political ethnographies. The collection of primary data was based primarily on open-ended interviews with quarter residents and personal observations of everyday interactions and activities within the quarter during two separate periods of daily visits—one in 2000 lasting six months and one in 2001 lasting three months. I made subsequent periodic visits to Bulaq in 2003 and 2004. I conducted 115 interviews, 40 of which were carried out within the household setting, that is, in people's homes. Sixty of the interviews were workplace-based, conducted in the interviewees' shops, outdoor kiosks, or other places of work and business. Additional semi-structured interviews were carried out with individuals in positions of leadership in the quarter, such as the mosque preacher, the managers of mutual aid societies, and a local councilman.

Household and work-based interviews were conducted at two levels. A first level consisted of semi-closed questions designed to gather information on the social and economic background of the residents. At a second level, interviews were conducted in open-ended fashion with at least one member of the households that participated in the semi-closed interviews. Proprietors of small enterprises as well as workers in shops and other work establishments in the quarter were also participants in the open-ended interviews. An additional type of interview consisted of questions I posed during ad hoc group meetings. Three such meetings involved young men who had gathered at the youth club and at two of the workshops. A fourth was with women

peddlers from Manshiyyat Nasir, a popular quarter northeast of Cairo. All the women were involved in microcredit "small business" arrangements. A fourth category of interviews comprised discussions with activists in Bulaq and other parts of the city, using semi-closed questions. These interviewees were engaged in community-level work in such areas as charity, human rights, economic and social development, community affairs, and women's rights.

My quarter-based interviews were set up using the snowball method, with introductory meetings arranged with the help of key informants. This was the optimal method given the particular access constraints faced by researchers. Indeed, as scholars who have conducted fieldwork in Middle Eastern urban quarters attest, the researcher-subject relationship must be negotiated carefully (Altorki and El-Solh 1989). Access to quarter residents and spaces through personal contacts and referrals was an important first step. In fact, it was a personal contact, someone whose office was located in Bulaq, who facilitated my initial meeting with a butcher and his family in Old Bulaq—my veritable point-of-entry into the quarter. In a later phase of the research, I was fortunate to gain the trust and help of a local woman activist who became my main informant. She was known to many quarter residents, had connections to many of the community's support networks, and was able to arrange for introductions to individuals in households and workshops. My fieldwork also included visits to institutions that were important in the lives of the residents such as the Bulaq al-Dakrur hospital, a number of primary schools, private voluntary organizations, and zawiya (small mosques; prayerooms). These visits allowed me to gain further insights into community life, in general, and especially into social interactions at the institutional level.

The interviews are supplemented by a variety of other sources of information on everyday politics, governance practices, and state–citizens relations. For instance, I draw on court and police records as well as transcripts from municipal and criminal court cases involving Bulaq residents. In addition, I use print media reports on the new popular quarters for an analysis of the public discourse and popular representations of the quarters and quarter life. Beyond this, I trace developments in state laws and policies that have had a direct bearing on the lives of quarter residents, especially the law on thuggery passed in the Egyptian National Assembly in 1998.

During the initial phase of the fieldwork, I experienced some of the difficulties discussed by other researchers having to do with ties and obligations and with the sense that the social circle one has just entered is closing or closed. The help I received from Um Hisham, the butcher's sister, during the phase of entry into the field placed certain obligations on me. For example, I had to go back to her for additional introductions rather than rely on new contacts. Um Hisham also expected that I visit her first every time I went to the alley. She became protective of me and assumed the position of my guardian. I tried to explain to her the need to expand my contacts and that it was necessary that I accept introductions from other residents in the *hara*. Although I sensed that she would be hurt by this, I resolved nonetheless to expand my work beyond my first *hara* and Um Hisham's circle. Following a month of visits to this *hara* during which I conducted interviews, sat with the women, participated in their outdoor sociability activities, watched television soap operas with them, or listened to their narratives about local events and goings-on, I began to think that my circle of contacts was closing. This, in my view, meant that I was being exposed only to a certain range of quarter experiences and narratives about events. It became imperative, therefore, that I get a sense of the quotidian in other alleys and sub-districts of Bulaq. These concerns about the fieldwork led me to seek new informants and to bring my inquiry into other *hara-s* and neighborhoods of the quarter.

I tried to widen my area of investigation beyond the alleyways of Old Bulaq and Madinat Amir by gaining entry into the newer areas of Bulaq, in particular, the neighborhood of Nahya. With the help of a local voluntary association, I was fortunate to make contact with Manal, a young woman activist who did volunteer work in the social networks of a number of neighborhoods in Bulaq. Manal became my main informant and facilitated my introduction to many households, workers, and workshop proprietors. She was present at many of the meetings and at times interjected with questions and comments that expressed her own views of the social issues discussed or her critical assessment of the problems, ideas, and perspectives that emerged in discussion. She enjoyed the respect of quarter residents as well as their appreciation for her solidarity work and for her forthrightness. Although she did not conform to community expectations regarding gender relations, her engagement in social affairs seemed to have earned her the

right to be viewed in different terms—that is, as a social activist and a community figure. Manal was instrumental in my gaining access to youth fraternities, both religious and workshop based, which are key structural elements of young men's everyday lives.

As I moved from the first *hara* into other sections and alleyways of Bulaq, I became more at ease explaining to quarter residents both my purpose in the area and the subject of my research. This feeling of ease may have contributed to the fact that I did not encounter the questioning suspicion about my motives that I was met with upon initial entry into the area. However, in the poorer sections of Bulaq, as in Madinat Amir, residents rendered my explanation and exposé of the work in particular terms, namely in terms of their own needs and desires. For example, some residents responded to my presence in their neighborhood by trying to place me there as a social worker and by requesting my intervention to resolve such issues as housing problems or to help with a pressing financial need. My reaction to this construction of my role was influenced, among other things, by the socioeconomic conditions of the area. Although I did not want to reinforce any confusion about my role nor tie my research objectives to objectives of a different type, such as personal assistance, I could not ignore some of the requests and did feel compelled to provide help, both financial and in kind. For example, I purchased some needed household items for one family and I donated a sum of money to another. With families that were not necessarily in need of help, there were still expectations of exchange and gift-giving such as bringing a *ziyara* (an offering) to someone in the hospital. On at least two occasions, I was the recipient of a gift given not only in reciprocity but also as a confirmation of a special bond that had been established.

As mentioned previously, my initial "entry" into Bulaq al-Dakrur was arranged through a personal contact who introduced me to a local butcher whose shop is located in one of the quarter's main commercial streets. His was one of the older families of Bulaq, well known especially in Bulaq al-Qadima (Old Bulaq). It was the butcher's sister, Um Hisham, who arranged for my introduction to the residents of one of the alleyways in Old Bulaq. Um Hisham herself lived in this particular alleyway and, therefore, knew many of the residents. During my visits, I was admitted into the *hara* women's social circle and began to learn of their practices of sociability. This admission was not straightforward, however, and I experienced difficulties and constraints. De-

spite the fact that I was introduced to the *hara* residents through Um Hisham, whose family was well known and who was herself trusted, my interest in the community and the residents' everyday-life practices was the object of suspicion. During the first week of my visits to the *hara*, I discussed my research with a group of women that Um Hisham had arranged for me to meet. I was conscious that if I expressed interest in political issues, I might raise alarm. Thus, I used what may be called a false subject, but a subject still at the heart of my research concerns. I explained that the research aimed to look at changes in everyday life in the *hara* and at what has survived of the old practices of sociability and norms of interaction that were documented in historical as well as contemporary studies of old popular quarters of the city. One of the women who joined us in the discussion, Um Samia, commented that she did not see much good in looking at the past when the present needed so much attention. Thus, my attempt to describe the study in less political terms, by framing the research as a comparison of past and present practices, was not necessarily a helpful strategy.

Other details relevant to my research status were also complicating factors. I indicated to my informants that the study was part of my research interests, and its purpose was to help me learn about social relations and everyday life in popular quarters. I told them of my position as an academic and that I had research leave to undertake the study. This, however, was a cause of complication because in the minds of many residents, research was something done by students enrolled for a degree. My circumstances simply did not fit the usual pattern. The fact that I was affiliated with a foreign university raised additional concern. This had to do with whether the findings would be used in a manner that would make Egypt look bad. The issue of local and foreign researchers sullying the country's reputation was raised repeatedly in the press and was a tool used by the government to discredit critical researchers. At the time I was conducting my research, Saad Eddine Ibrahim, Professor of Sociology at the American University in Cairo, had been arrested on charges of receiving foreign funds without permission and working to undermine the government. The media reports focused on the issue of foreign funding and presented a generally simplistic and negative image of researchers affiliated with foreign institutions. The debate about the objectives of such research was framed in nationalist terms (i.e., whether or not the work promoted or served the interests of Egypt and demonstrated loyalty to the country).

Local official figures who worked in the municipality and the district council and with whom I discussed my research, expressed their suspicion of all studies with foreign affiliation. They were tactful enough to exclude me from this category, but were undoubtedly guarded towards me nonetheless. One municipality figure named a foreign NGO worker as a spy working for the CIA. He said she asked very dangerous questions. When I asked him to give an example, he noted that she asked questions about income and household expenses. He went on to say that this particular worker was expelled from the country. I later learned that the NGO worker in question was still in Egypt and continuing her project. My presence in the quarter, as well as my research, was the subject of concern among a number of NGO workers. Although I was initially helped by a social worker affiliated with an NGO active in the area, I found that the workers associated with two other social programs that were either foreign funded or had government support, perceived that my research had the potential of undermining their work, attracting government attention, or drawing resources away from them. I tried to dispel these concerns on a number of occasions, explaining that I was not connected to any NGO program and that I had no links to foreign-funded programs with which they may be in competition. The attention given to my presence in the area by these NGO workers seemed to dissipate as my network of contacts widened, and, in particular, as the research shifted its focus onto workshops and away from women and households, the primary "target clients" of the NGO programs.

As noted, in the alley where I began my work, residents raised concerns about my research and presence in the neighborhood. They framed my presence in relation to the state. That is, I was seen as either working on behalf of government or as an outsider commissioned by a foreign country to work against the Egyptian state. Both possibilities were viewed as equally negative. As this study demonstrates, residents, on the whole, wanted to stay away from government. They preferred to have nothing to do with it and wanted it to just stay out of their lives. In time, I learned that after debating the question among themselves, a number of the residents had concluded that there was nothing to fear. For example, Muhammad, a twenty-year-old worker in the tourist sector, responded to his neighbors' concerns by pointing out that their lives contained no "state secrets" and that there was nothing that they needed to hide. I cannot say that all the suspi-

cions that surrounded my initial entry to the *hara* were dispelled, but gradually I gained admission into many homes and many people confided personal and intimate information to me. I think a number of factors contributed to my gaining their trust. A key one was the rapport I established with the owner of a coffee shop located at the intersection of one of the alleys and a main thoroughfare. My visits to this coffee shop and my discussions with the owner were visible to his clients, mostly quarter residents. He was a man who was well liked, and his support for my research was conveyed to people in the *hara*. I also entered into relations of sociability that were seen to conform to norms of propriety. For instance, I attended mourning gatherings organized by women on the occasion of a family member's death. I also visited ailing residents at the hospital or in their homes and participated in social festivities linked to weddings or holiday feasts.

I view the initial reaction to my intervention in Bulaq as tied to my personal location in social and political terms. Concerns relating to my intervention in the quarter were put to me in questions by Um Hasan, who, into the third week of my visits, asked: "Haven't you got enough information yet? What is there that requires so much attention?" Furthermore, during the early visits, other questions expressed doubts about the benefits of the study and the objectives that it could serve. To begin with, my being an Egyptian whose social background was identifiably different from that of the residents added to their sense of the incongruity of my interest. Um Samia and, later, many others in different contexts said people from better-off areas of the city like Muhandissin and Zamalek were not interested in the everyday life of people like themselves.

Um Hasan's questions and Um Samia's remarks go to the very heart of issues having to do with my position both as a researcher and as an "insider"/"outsider." The matter of my status as an insider or an outsider—both, by all accounts, problematic categories—is one that needs some attention. In some respects, I was an insider, being Egyptian-born and having grown up in Cairo. However, other considerations would place me as an outsider, in particular, my having spent most of my adult life outside of Egypt and my working in a Western academic institution. Yet, this manner of identification and categorization is unsatisfactory, as it does not capture the dynamics of my presence in Bulaq or the nature of my relations with the people I interviewed or with the informants to whom I became close. Similarly, I also find that I am

unable to situate myself in relation to categories of "the field" and "home." Bulaq is in Greater Cairo, which, in some sense, is home. However, I have been "home" elsewhere and have long resisted categorization that would reduce my identity to a single place and origin and that, by extension, makes assumptions of immanence. During the period of my research, I came to recognize that, more than at any other time, the long period of my living outside Egypt had left an imprint on my person and was both projected and perceived in terms of difference relating to outward appearance and to aspects of personal conduct in social situations. At the same time, my informants and I sought and found signs of community and elements of common ground in concerns, interests, and commitments. I clearly do not see my work in Bulaq as entailing anything that would approximate a "spatial travel into otherness"—the kind of experience that ideas of "the field" conventionally evoke (Gupta and Ferguson 1997).

Beyond the questions of personal location that biographical details may provide, there remains the issue of social and historical location. My choice of research subject arose out of my interest in socially and politically transformative movements. My choice of Bulaq was determined by the research questions that problematized the politics of everyday life in the new popular quarters. In my previous work on the Islamist movement, I conceived of Islamist activism as a protest movement whose transformative potential could be found in everyday forms of sociospatial organization in popular urban settings. My research into the everyday life of a single new popular quarter (i.e., Bulaq) aims to elaborate on this view but also to discover the hoped-for forces of change. Needless to say, the complexities of social settings often defy the hopes and desires of researchers. In reflecting on the social and political location of my intervention in Bulaq—that is, in tracing the elements of my situated intervention (to use Gupta and Ferguson's term)—I see myself as attempting to explore the micro level of politics in order to counter dominant abstractions on the authoritarianism and exceptionalism of Arab politics. I also see this intervention as tackling issues surrounding struggles against oppressive rule—issues that the latest academic trends dealing with democratization, liberalization, and civil society push out of their narratives on politics in "exceptional" settings. The intellectual energies devoted to the study of elections, civil associations, and NGOs as "instruments" of democratization contribute to a neglect of the politics of the governed

as manifested in their everyday interaction with state authorities and in their efforts to develop alternative modes of social organization. My interest in the politics of the governed arises out of my personal conviction that any academic engagement that aims to understand transformative processes and their likely spaces of unfolding must necessarily begin in those spaces.

Appendix B

Thematic Outline of Interview Frames

Dimensions of inquiry and analysis:

❏ Respondents' social biography
❏ Interaction within the quarter
❏ Interaction beyond the quarter
❏ Space and action
❏ Relations of power

Interviews with a particular individual consisted of one or more meetings. They were conducted with a single respondent on a one-to-one basis or with small groups of family members, friends, or colleagues in households or workplaces. Interviews were structured in two tiers: the first-tier questions were covered during the initial meeting and possibly completed in subsequent meetings. The information gathered at this level pertained to educational levels (see Table B1) and labor force

Table B1. Education levels

Levels of schooling	Women	Men	Total
No schooling or some primary schooling	13	9	22
Primary schooling completed	6	16	22
Preparatory school	9	15	24
Secondary schooling (including vocational training)	9	11	20
Postsecondary	3	9	12
Total	40	60	100

status and occupation (see Table B2), household size and composition, and the regional origins of the household heads. The second-tier questions were open-ended and covered at times in a single meeting and sometimes in follow-up meetings with a given respondent.

The themes covered in each level of interviewing were as follows:

1. Tier one interviews, first component

   Respondent's social biography

   ❑ Regional/geographical origins

   ❑ Socioeconomic background (individual, familial)

   ❑ Occupational skills, training

   ❑ Work-force status, experience

   ❑ Arrival in the quarter: circumstances of arrival, relationship to residents, formalities of establishment/settlement

2. Tier one interviews, second component and tier two interviews

   Interaction within the quarter:

   ❑ Spheres of sociability: pretexts, spaces, modalities of social interaction

   ❑ Political dimensions of interaction: engagement in organizational or governance activities, interaction with internal authority (mosque preacher, community leadership), and modes of social and political organization within the community

   ❑ Normative outlook (norms regulating life in the quarter): ideas of neighborliness, solidarity, and exchange and norms of propriety relating to gender relations as expressed in the narratives and discourses of the respondents

   Interaction beyond the quarter:

   ❑ Spheres of interaction: pretexts, purposes, modalities of interaction with the wider urban environment and with state authorities (bureaucracy in areas of employment, education, social services, religious observance, and national and local elections)

   ❑ Normative outlook: perceptions of life in other quarters of the city and meanings attached to interactions with other quarters and areas of the city

Table B2. Occupation

Principal occupation	Women	Men	Total
Peddler	8		8
Domestic worker	6		6
Construction trades			
Tile layer		3	3
House painter		2	2
Contractor		1	1
Carpenter		2	2
Auto mechanic		5	5
Motorcycle repair		1	1
Bicycle repair		1	1
Appliance repair		1	1
Manufacturer (leather)		1	1
Factory worker	1	1	2
Home-based producer	2		2
Shopkeeper (textiles, light household goods, groceries)	2	7	9
Entertainer		2	2
Coffee shop owner		1	1
Vegetable vendor	1	1	2
Driver		5	5
Plumber		1	1
Print shop worker		1	1
Barber		1	1
Professional	1	4	5
Worker (public sector)		1	1
Government employee	2	1	3
Business owner		5	5
Housewife	10		10
Retiree		1	1
Student	6	10	16
Unemployed	1	1	2
Total	40	60	100

Space and action:

❏ The physical organization of the quarter: conceptions of space in physical and symbolic terms, demarcation of community boundaries, and conceptions of private and public space

❏ Spatial location of the main sites of community interaction: market, mosque, clinic, coffee shops, and communal institutions

❏ Nature of interactions in these sites: types of encounters, purpose of the encounters or exchanges

❏ Spatial determinants of interactions: effects of spatial modes of organization on daily interactions (constraints, opportunities) and space and community autonomy (engagement/disengagement dynamic)

❏ Space and social control

Relations of power:

❏ Identification and recognition of "internal" authority: internal sources of community authority and legitimacy of this authority

❏ Identification and recognition of "external" authority: state presence within the community, perceptions of the state, limits of state authority

Notes

Introduction

1. For an overview of the sites of "informal" housing in Cairo and throughout Egypt, see al-Wali (1993).
2. This perspective on urban development in countries of the global South has been elaborated in scholarship on Latin American cities (De Soto 1989; Portes, Castells, and Benton 1989).
3. The critique of the literature on subalterns and resistance raises deeper questions with regard to ideas of subject positions developed in post-structuralist writings. For example, O'Hanlon and Washbrook (1992, 152–55) question how the subject, conceived as an effect of power or as discursively constituted, can rise to assume the position of an agent in struggle. In marked difference with the idea of the dispersed subject, their inquiry appears to revive the Marxist concern with the construction of anchored identities that can contest overarching relations of domination at the heart of capitalism. For a response from the view of subaltern studies' insistence on the decentering of the subject, see Prakash 1992. Coronil (1997, 16) provides a thoughtful approach to reconciling the view of the multiplicity of subaltern subject positions and the necessity of recognizing that a common ground may bring this multiplicity together.
4. See Pasquino (1991) for a genealogy of the apparatus of police as an effort of regulation whose field of intervention was the entire society. See also Foucault (2003b).
5. The relevance of Foucault's work to the countries of the global South has been insightfully argued by Arturo Escobar (1984–85). See Brass (2000) for an articulation of the relevance of Foucault's work to the wider field of politics and for a review of political studies inspired by Foucault's methods. Timothy Mitchell's (1989) study of colonial practices of governmentality is a noteworthy example of Foucauldian analyses applied to non-Western settings.
6. An excellent illustration of this point is given in Charles Hirschkind's (2001) study of Egyptian youth's cultivation of embodied piety through disciplined listening to religious audiocassettes.

7. Alan Hunt (1996) raises a similar critique of the division between premodern and modern in accounts of governmentalities in Europe.

8. Hindess (2000) notes that colonial governmentality had to cede some of its liberal principles as it adopted paternalistic attitudes toward the "natives" who were seen to exist at a lower stage of civilizational development. For an exploration of these attitudes in British colonial governmentality, see Kalpagam (2002).

9. Indeed, in the original sense of *police*, the "happiness" and welfare of the population were key objectives along with increasing state force. See Pasquino (1991) and Foucault (2003b).

10. Abrams (1988) argues that the construct of the state serves to mask the reality of political practice. As such, he found its usage to be a condition of ignorance rather than of knowledge. However, he goes on to suggest that what social scientists should examine is the state–system and the state idea. The former refers to "a palpable nexus of practice and institutional structure centred in government and more or less extensive, unified and dominant in any given society." The latter refers to how the state as an idea is "projected, purveyed and variously believed in different societies at different times" (Abrams, 82).

11. In his study of the construction of the Venezuelan state, Coronil (1997, 4–5) speaks of the processes of producing the appearance of the state as "transcendent unifying agent of the nation." Through the control of oil resources and their use in extravagant projects, the projection of an image of invincibility promoted by a kind of baroque theatre, and the extension of regulations and control over the economy, areas of culture, etc., the state effect came into being. Coronil underlines the work of magic involved in this production. By fostering spectacular developmental projects and fantasies of progress, the state cast a spell over its audience of citizen-subjects.

12. Ali's (2002) examination of the dynamics of implementing programs of population control in Egypt illustrates this point.

13. Soja (1989), and scholars who draw on him, such as Keith and Pile (1993), use the term *spatiality* to convey the idea of the sociality of space. Soja's critical interpretative approach emphasizes spatiality as "simultaneously . . . a social product (an outcome) and a shaping force (or medium) in social life. . ." (Soja 1989, 7).

14. Keith and Pile (1993, 17) note that the erasure of markings of spatiality from accounts of social life arises out of the will to homogenize experiences lived at the local level. The result of this erasure is what they aptly call "silenced spatiality" in the broad narratives of the universal.

15. For a discussion of the spatial dimension of urban collective action in Middle East cities, see the essays in Brown (1989), in particular those of Burke III and Seddon. Hajj Ali (1994) provides a good exploration of the reappropriation of Algiers' city spaces by the FIS during the period of showdown with the Algerian authorities. Also see Lowy (1979) for repertoires of urban action in the Tunisian context.

16. This point ties in with my argument that our analysis of Islamism should focus on its potential to be transformative and to alter relations of domination, rather than on the issues of its failure or success (Ismail 2003, chapter 6).

17. For comparison with modes of Islamist investment in the Algerian and Tunisian contexts, see Ismail (2003) chapter 5. On the Tunisian experience, see Vasile (1997).

1. Reconfiguring Cairo

1. For an overview of state responses to the Islamist presence in Imbaba, see Ismail (1996). On the Islamist implantation in new popular quarters, see Ismail (2000).

2. Over a long and sustained period of reporting on the "informal" quarters, the media, newspapers in particular, have contributed to the production of a public discourse criminalizing the inhabitants of these quarters and their modes of living. For an overview of local interventions by academics and government officials, see al-Sawi (1996).

3. On squatter settlements in Cairo, see DeBoulet 1990. For a comparative examination of the politics of squatter settlements in the Middle East and Latin America, see AlSayyad (1993).

4. The Six-of-October subdistrict of Bulaq should not be confused with the city of Six-of-October located in a new housing development to the southwest of Cairo.

5. Some families from Upper Egypt formed cooperatives and bought plots of vacant land collectively. They then either resold the land or built housing on it which they inhabited, rented, or sold.

6. According to 1996 census data, the majority of buildings in the area are privately owned and used for residential purposes.

7. In 2004, during a return visit to Bulaq, I found that *al-Kubri al-Khashab* was closed and its entrance blocked by a large iron gate, locked with a thick link chain and padlock. It had been replaced by a new overpass bridge erected nearby.

8. Privately owned microbuses are the main form of communal transportation within Bulaq. Most are unlicensed and driven by young men who themselves do not have valid licenses. The buses provide internal connections between the various parts of Bulaq al-Dakrur,

such as Saft al-Laban, Mi'timdidyya, and Nahya. There are short runs between the main intersections and designated areas of social services. For example, a microbus line runs from the Tir'at al-Zumor exchange to Bulaq al-Dakrur hospital. Other lines connect to adjacent areas and to other bus line depots. Thus, there are connections to Faysal, a newly constructed area next to Bulaq. Other lines go to a Giza bus depot where commuters may connect to other destinations as, for instance, a microbus to the southern Cairo suburb of Helwan. There does not appear to be any commuter bus service between Bulaq and the rest of Cairo. Indeed, given the narrowness of the streets inside Bulaq and the degree of congestion on the quarter's main streets, Cairo's regular public buses could not circulate easily in most of Bulaq. Moreover, exit/entry points on the quarter's main artery, Tir'at al-Zumor Street, are blocked by microbus stations and by dense market areas.

9. There are five routes for vehicular traffic into and out of Bulaq. Only three, however, connect the quarter to the rest of the city. Of these latter, the two principal routes are the overpass connecting Gami'at al-Duwwal al-'Arabiyya Street in Muhandissin to both Nahya Street and Ard al-Liwa in Bulaq and, further south, Tharwat bridge, extending from Cairo University Street, in Giza, to Tir'at al-Zumor Street. The third is an underpass route connecting Tir'at al-Zumor Street to the northern part of Giza.

10. The irrigation authority is chiefly responsible for the maintenance of the canal since it falls within its purview of administering irrigation infrastructure. It removes the refuse from within the canal and puts it on the side to dry. The refuse then becomes the governorate's responsibility. At this stage, the cleaning process moves into the hands of contractors hired by the governorate. There is usually a period of delay between the first step, involving the irrigation authority, and the second step managed by the governorate. According to the residents' accounts, the delay lengthens the amount of time the contractors take to bring in their equipment and undertake the cleaning, thus increasing the charges levied on the governorate.

11. Interviews revealed that unemployed women with no education tended to stay in Bulaq and rarely go outside the quarter.

12. For a political-economy reading of transformations of Cairo, see Dona Stewart (1999). Her account is hampered, however, by the close links (parallels) she draws between changes in political regimes and urban change.

2. Internal Governance

1. *Majalis 'urfiyya* have a long history in rural Egypt, where they were set up to deal with feuds that pitted clans against one another. There are cases of highly publicized *majalis 'urfiyya* in which state representatives served as members. See Botiveau (1987–88) and BenNefissa (1999).

2. In his study of the police in nineteenth-century Egypt, Khaled Fahmy (1999) discusses cases of people from lower-class neighborhoods calling on the police in instances of disputes between family members.

3. See the reports published on Imbaba in *al-Mussawar 3558*, 18 December 1992.

4. For an examination of the informalization of the labor market, see the essays in Assaad (2002a), in particular those by Assaad and by Moktar and Wahba. On informal businesses, see al-Mahdi, also in Assaad.

5. State rituals of grandeur are discussed by Navaro-Yashin (2002). For an examination of the construction of spectacular projects as an expression of state power, see Coronil (1997).

6. This contrasts with the kind of rituals of power discussed by Anagnost (1997, 116) in which the subject's returned gaze is a confirmation of power.

3. Neoliberalism and the Relocation of Welfare

1. Data on coverage by contributory insurance schemes indicate that 15.5 million people had insurance in 1992–93. In addition, 5.8 million people were pensioners or beneficiaries related to pensioners. Based on the figures for the insured sector, it emerges that a considerable proportion of the population does not have insured earnings. This can be explained, in part, by reference to the transformation of the labor market whereby growing segments of the population work in the informal private sector, which, by definition, is not subject to insurance. A growing percentage of the working population is engaged in irregular economic activities, such as daily or temporary work.

2. The first law of social security was Law 116 of 1950.

3. The text of the law uses the term *bint*, which translates as "girl" in English. Here *bint* (girl) signifies not only marital status (i.e., being unmarried) but also that the woman has remained a virgin.

4. These figures along with the ones cited in this paragraph are provided by the Central Agency for Public Mobilization and Statistics (CAPMAS), 1998.

5. I have also examined the work of the al-Gam'iyya al-Khayriyya, another charitable organization registered with the Ministry of Social Affairs. I found its charitable activities and modes of operation to be similar to those of the al-Gam'iyya al-Shar'iyya.

6. The precise nature of al-Gam'iyya's political affiliation in the present is subject to debate. It is thought that earlier on, Hasan al-Banna, the founder of the Muslim Brotherhood Organization had sought a merger with al-Gam'iyya but its founders resisted his efforts. Following that, a split in the al-Gam'iyya took place and the group of Ansar al-Sunna al-Muhammadiyya was founded. The latter is considered to be more conservative and closer in thought to the *Wahabi* ideology. Despite claims of independence, the al-Gam'iyya al-Shar'iyya continues to have affiliations with the Brotherhood and receives funding from it (*Ruz al-Yusuf* no. 3419, 20 December 1993, 26–28). However, it should be noted that certain branches of the al-Gam'iyya are dominated by board members who are active in the ruling National Democratic Party.

7. The work of the al-Gam'iyya is extensive, reaching a large number of households. For example, one Bulaq branch of the al-Gam'iyya claimed to have handled approximately 400 cases during a single year. Most of these cases involved widows and orphaned children.

8. Based on its experience, the al-Gam'iyya al-Shar'iyya has estimated that an income of 150 to 200 pounds per month is insufficient to meet family needs. The al-Gam'iyya al-Khayriyya defined poor and low-income households as those with a total monthly income below 300 pounds. According to one of the al-Gam'iyya al-Khayriyya board members of a Bulaq branch, the branch supports 100 households per month.

9. According to one report, the project of sponsorship of orphans began in 1988 and was initiated by a doctor in a hospital in Matariyya. His membership on the Board of Executives of the al-Gam'iyya Shar 'iyya was rejected by the security authorities that advise the Ministry of Social Affairs. However, he took charge of the sponsorship project informally. The project has a pyramidal structure with branches in the quarter, district, city, and governorate. The papers of sponsorship carry the stamp of the al-Gam'iyya central organization. In 1990, the project of orphan sponsorship had 255 branches in seventeen governorates and sponsored a total of 55,000 children. Its spending in 1990 was 4.5 million pounds. (*Ruz–al-Yusuf* no. 3419, 20 December 1993, 26–28). By 1996, the orphan sponsorship program had a budget of more than 84 million pounds and supported 230,000 children.

10. For example, I was told that the Bulaq branch of al-Gam'iyya al-Khayriyya has received donations from such sources as a group of army generals who make their donations in person at the local mosque, a doctor active in the al-Gam'iyya al-Shar'iyya, a merchant from Muski, and a *hajja* described as having a mosque in Faysal and another in Muhandissin. Additionally, a group of three individuals made a one-time donation of 10,000 pounds. The donations come under the rubric of *zakat mal* (alms paid on capital savings) and *zakat fitr* (alms paid to make up for being unable to do the fast). These funds are not registered with the Ministry of Social Affairs, however. Rather, they are distributed directly to people on a list of low-income households.

11. For a review of Islamic legal traditions on *zakat*, see Mattson (2003).

12. Charities drawing on the western register became involved in western style philanthropic activities. For instance, a food bank was organized for the first time in Egypt in 2001 by a benevolent society named al-Risala (the mission). Al-Risala is modeled after the American food bank experience started by Hnagel in Phoenix, Arizona. Like the American model, al-Risala collects food from supermarkets and restaurants for distribution to those in need. The founder of al-Risala, like Husam Badrawi, merges the two registers of Islamic tradition and western modernity: "If the food bank idea could be applied in the West, we thought, then it could be implemented in Egypt where religious values of charity prevail"(Shahine 2001).

13. For a probing examination of the politics of Islamist women's activism in charitable organizations, see Hafez (2003).

14. See Koptiuch (1999) on the construction and integration of "informality" into the discourse of international aid organizations. For a review of earlier shifts in the discourse of development articulated by the World Bank, see Finnemore (1997). For a critical reading of the concept of social capital as it was adopted by international development actors, see Fine (2001). It may be argued that these discursive shifts are integral to the universalizing drive of the liberal project in the contemporary period. For an insightful reading of the mobilizing force of this project, see Young (1995).

15. Along with the propagation of the family as an enterprise, and informal employment as a business, the category of "female-headed households" has functioned as a metonym for the poorest of the poor and has become an arch sign deployed by a multitude of actors in the development field. In Egypt, the category is flagged in the discourse of Mrs. Suzanne Mubarak, the wife of the President. It is also invoked by community development organizations, women's NGOs and state officials. The inclusion of women heads of households in the category of beneficiaries of microcredit is a recent development in the

operation of foreign aid programs in Egypt. In a study of programs of poverty alleviation dating to 1997, Nadia Farah (1997) found that women constituted a very small percentage of all recipients of small loans from the main lending organization, namely USAID. There has been a significant change in this respect. USAID reports that, to date, it has funded a total of 220,000 people through its small and medium enterprises program. Of these, women represent one-third of all recipients. The UNDP's intervention beginning in 2003 aims to expand the number of beneficiaries and widen women's share.

16. This view was expressed to me by Iman Bibars, Executive Director of ADEW, in a discussion meeting in Cairo, April 2004.

17. It is instructive to compare the workings of microcredit and its disciplinary techniques with the technologies of power deployed in the family planning program initiated by the Egyptian government and sponsored by foreign donors. In a critical study of these programs, Ali argues that the family planning program, in seeking to convert women's ideas of their bodies and fertility, are engaging in the construction of "the modern individual,"—a subject with rights and responsibilities who is entrusted to control her sexuality and reproduction in line with a collective good (Ali 2002, 13–14)

18. Stephen Gill (1995) notes the disciplinary techniques at the macro level that are deployed in the surveillance work of international organizations and private agencies feeding into the policies of "global supervisors," namely the IMF and the World Bank. The micro-level disciplinary techniques discussed here undoubtedly link up with macro-level "disciplinary neoliberalism."

19. A 2001 International Labor Organization study on Egypt found levels of education to be a factor in observed patterns of poverty, with the most severe forms of poverty being associated with individuals with no schooling (El-Ehwany and El-Laithy "Poverty, Employment Policy Making in Egypt," cited in Human Rights Watch 2003, 11).

4. Youth, Gender, and the State in Cairo

1. I conducted most of the field research over an extended period of work in Cairo in 2000 and 2001 and over shorter periods in 2003 and 2004. I interviewed forty-five young men and women.

2. The role of the state in shaping gender relations has been examined from a different angle focused on policies aimed at transforming the position of women in the labor force and in the wider project of modernization. Mervat Hatem (1992) examined the implication of the state in gender interaction, terming some of its policies as "state feminism."

3. The recent edited volume by Meijer (2000) is an exception in this regard.

4. This issue goes beyond youth to include other societal groupings. Historically, neighborhood residents undertook the monitoring of their coresidents' moral conduct in matters of sexuality
   (see Rafeq 1990).
5. This strategy is discussed in Mahmood (2001).
6. It is interesting to note the parallels between these practices and
   the Islamic youth subculture in Turkey examined by Ayse Saktanber (2002).
7. See Ghoussoub (2000) for a discussion on the construction of
   women's sexuality in terms that highlight the sense of threat and
   challenge felt by men in Egypt.
8. In her analysis of Egyptian novels treating the construction of manhood, Magda al-Nowaihi (1999) highlights how manhood-forming
   processes are tied to the organization and gendering of space. Notions of acceptable femininity and appropriate female space enter
   into conceptions of masculinity. In one of the novels she examines,
   Ayyam al-Insan al-Sab'a, the male protagonist who rebels against traditional practices associates gendered space with backwardness.
9. See Roy (2003, 115–26) for an insightful exploration of how poor
   men in Calcutta construct their masculinity in a manner designed
   to regain positions of dominance in the family and to allow them
   to appropriate terms of hegemonic masculinity under conditions
   of subordination.
10. By this I mean that the social construction of the body continues to
    be upheld and invoked. As explained by Bourdieu (2001, 24), this
    construction institutes the body as "*socially differentiated* from the
    opposite gender" (i.e., as a female or a nonmale habitus).
11. Tourists from Arab Gulf countries contract temporary marriages of
    sorts with Egyptian women from low-income neighborhoods. In
    both Imbaba and Bulaq al-Dakrur, many young women have en-
    tered into these kinds of temporary marriages. *Fatwa* (religious
    edict) legitimizing such marriages within Sunni Islamic traditions
    unearthed classical rulings on the marriages of male travelers. In
    some cases, young women treated this form of marriage as a means
    of raising the capital necessary for a second permanent marriage to
    a young Egyptian man. It remains the case, however, that poor fam-
    ilies have sought to improve their financial situation by marrying
    off daughters to male tourists from the Arab Gulf.
12. Samia's marriage came up in conversation with my informant.
13. In one case, a young man opted to marry the mother of a woman
    who was his prospective bride. During a visit to negotiate a dowry
    and other financial matters with the family of the prospective bride,
    the man's friend suggested that he marry the mother, who was a
    widow, instead. This alternative arrangement, it was thought, would
    reduce marriage expenses significantly. Subsequently, the young

man married the mother using an *'urfi* contract (customary marriage) that allowed him flexibility in terminating the marriage without any obligations. Indeed, following a dispute with the woman, he tore up the contract and the marriage came to an end. The state has tried to ban *'urfi* marriages, but has thus far been unsuccessful.

14. These narratives recall Yusuf Idris's scripts of subalterns in the city.

5. The Politics of Security

1. The fear that Abu Zayd's remark conveys is that the young woman would become a prostitute. He is invoking a category of persons, "*munharif*," that state agencies of reform and normalization deploy in dealing with various segments of the population. As will be discussed later in this chapter, the discipline and control of children is organized under the category of "*mu'arad lil inhiraf*," or "vulnerable to delinquency." *Inhiraf* translates as deviance or delinquency.

2. In 1997, the number of cases of electrical theft reached 148,900 with fines totaling 41.2 million Egyptian pounds. (Quoted in *al-Ahali*, "The Annual Security Report 1997," 21 November 1998). There are indications that the electricity police operate on the same lines as the security police. One important indicator of this is the appointment in 1998 of a high-ranking officer (*liwa*) to the position of head of the General Directorate of the Electricity Police. The officer in question was part of the leadership cadre in the state security apparatus (*al-Ahali*, 29 July 1998.)

3. The classical Arabic formulation of this Quranic pronouncement is "*hasbiyya Allah wa ni'm al-wakil.*" The enunciation of hajj Sam'an turned "*hasbiyya Allah*," meaning "God suffices for me," into "*hizbyya Allah*," meaning "God is my party." This enunciation is likely to carry the inflection of a particular regional dialect. However, the same inflection leaves the meaning open for the listener. I thank Yasir Suleiman for drawing my attention to the linguistic nuances in the formulation. I also thank Zuleikha Abu Risha for drawing my attention to the play of dialect in the enunciation.

4. Anagnost (1997), in her study of Chinese peasants, looks at other types of rituals of state in everyday life. Her examination of the production of subjectivities through ceremonies celebrating ideal citizenry illuminates how power produces a self-referential reality that is necessary for its own validation.

5. See El-Messiri (1977) on the *futuwwa-balatagi* continuum.

6. The concept of "moral panic" was developed by Stanley Cohen (1980) and in Stuart Hall et al., (1979). Observers and scholars of Egypt have noted that various episodes of moral panic inducement have been authorized by the Egyptian state. See the Human Rights Watch report entitled "In a Time of Torture" on the creation of

moral panic in reference to homosexuality (HRW 2004): http://www.hrw.org/reports/2004/egypt0304/4.htm   (accessed 21 July 2004).

7. The "satanic cult" episode unfolded when a group of youth from upper-middle-class families attended punk rock parties that were raided by the police. The media reported that the youth were part of a cult of Satan worshippers. Following police investigation, no charges were laid and the youth were released.

8. The "Queen Boat" case refers to the arrest of a group of men in a nightclub located on a boat that once belonged to Queen Nariman, hence the name "Queen Boat." The arrests were part of a wide-ranging police campaign against gay men in Egypt. The campaign included the surveillance of areas known to be cruising spots for gay men, entrapment of men through Internet chat rooms, and the use of informants. See Human Rights Watch, "In a Time of Torture." It should be noted that in both police records and media reports, this campaign of arrest invoked the idea of the satanic cult (ibid.).

9. These are the titles of stories reported in the crime pages of national newspapers. There were also reports investigating whether Egyptians were aggressive by nature.

10. According to Ahmad Sami (1923), the category *vagrants* appears in a law enacted in 1908 and known as the Law of Vagrancy. However, the Hisham Mubarak Center traces the 1945 Law to Laws 15 of 1909 and 17 of 1909, which remained unpassed. Ener (1999, 327) traces the origins of the vagrants law to the middle of the nineteenth century when Qanun al-Muntakhabat was passed.

11. Article 3(1) of the Emergency Law empowers the President (and, by extension, his representatives) to restrict individual movement, freedom of association, residence, and circulation. The same article empowers the police to arrest and detain suspects or subjects deemed dangerous to public security and order. These powers, along with the right to search homes, are to be exercised without restriction by the articles of the law of criminal procedures (*Law of Criminal Procedures*, 171).

12. See, for example, the report by al-Nadim Center for Treatment and Psychological Rehabilitation of Victims of Violence, *al-Ta'dhib fi Misr, Haqa'iq wa Shihadat* (*Torture in Egypt: Facts and Testimonies*), Cairo: al-Nadim Center, 2002. Newspapers, particularly those of opposition parties, contain numerous stories of police abuse and torture and of citizen deaths while in police custody. A semi-official newspaper, *al-Jumhuriyya*, also carried a report in 2003 on the problem of police abuses, entitled "Who Do They Shoot? Crimes of Police Officers Have Gone Too Far."

13. Amnesty International has documented Egypt's record of purchasing instruments of torture. These include electroshock equipment

and stun guns (see report on instruments of torture). In an interview with one police officer, I was told that at times the use of torture was the only way to present a solid case to the prosecutor and that torture is used when officers are certain that the accused is guilty. This account from a young officer is problematic for assuming guilt prior to presenting a case to court. However, it should not be read as just confirming that torture is a practice on the job, but that it is a policy with the official sanction of the Ministry of the Interior.

14. Interviews with Mr. Hafez Abu Si 'da, Head of the Egyptian Organization for Human Rights (EOHR); with Mr. Gasser Abd al-Raziq, a lawyer with EOHR; and with Mr. Baha' Taher, a lawyer with the Hisham Mubarak Centre, April and May 2004.

15. I am using the terminology employed by the Human Rights Watch report on the condition of street children to translate the categories specified by Egypt's Child Law. See "Charged with Being Children," *Human Rights Watch*, vol. 15, no. 1 (E), February 2003. As noted in the report, *inhiraf* can connote deviance and aberrance, connotations implied in the uses of the term *delinquency*.

16. "Juvenile vagrants" were identified in the 1913 Annual Report of the Judicial Advisor as youngsters who are homeless orphans and ". . . who wander about the streets cleaning boots, selling periodicals, daily papers and lottery cards, etc. They generally swarm the more important quarters in the big cities like Cairo and Alexandria, jumping into Tram Cars and causing great inconvenience to passengers. . . . They are the first to find their way into, and to participate in, disturbances. It is from this class that young robbers and thieves are recruited" (quoted in Sami 1923, 251). Sami adds other activities to the list of those that identify juveniles as vagrants, including the collection of cigarette butts. The same activity appears in the 1996 definition of "vulnerable to delinquency." See *Human Rights Watch*, "Charged with Being Children," 39.

17. Quoted in *Human Rights Watch*, "Charged with Being Children," 41. The statement was made in a Human Rights Watch interview with an *amin shurta* in the Bulaq al-Dakrur Police Station.

Postscript

1. My account of these events is based on newspaper reports for the period covered and on documentary material collected by the Egyptian Organization for Human Rights.

2. This account relies on newspaper reports of the siege, conversations with journalists, and an interview with a police officer who participated in the siege.

Bibliography

Abaza, Mona. 2004. "Brave New Mall." *Al-Ahram Weekly* 708, 16–22 September.

Abrams, Philip. 1988. "Notes on the Difficulty of Studying the State (1977)." *Journal of Historical Sociology* 1, 1: 58–89.

Abu Haggag, Yusuf. 1993. "Memoires of a Street Tough," trans. Everett K. Rowson. In *Everyday Life in the Muslim Middle East,* ed. Donna Lee Bowen and Evelyn A. Early, 38–46. Bloomington: Indiana University Press.

Abu-Lughod, Janet. 1965. "Tale of Two Cities: The Origins of Modern Cairo." *Comparative Studies in Society and History* 7: 429–57.

———. 1969. *Cairo: 1001 Years of the City Victorious.* Princeton, NJ: Princeton University Press.

———. 1987. "The Islamic City—Historic Myth, Islamic Essence, and Contemporary Relevance." *International Journal of Middle East Studies* 19: 155–76.

Abu-Lughod, Lila. 1990. "The Romance of Resistance: Tracing Transformations of Power through Bedouin Resistance." *American Ethnologist* 17, 1: 41–55.

Ali, Kamran Asdar. 2002. *Planning the Family in Egypt: New Bodies, New Selves.* Austin: University of Texas Press.

AlSayyad, Nezar. 1993. "Squatting, Culture, and Development: A Comparative Analysis of Informal Settlements in Latin American and the Middle East." *Journal of Developing Societies* 9 (July–October): 139–53.

Altorki, Soraya, and Camillia Fawzi El-Solh, eds. 1989. *Arab Women in the Field: Studying Your Own Society.* Cairo: The American University in Cairo Press.

Anagnost, Ann. 1997. *National Past-Times: Narrative, Representation, and Power in Modern China.* Durham, NC: Duke University Press.

Assaad, Ragui. 2002a. "The Transformation of the Egyptian Labor Market: 1988–98." In *The Egyptian Labor Market in an Era of Reform,* ed. Ragui Assaad, 3–64. Cairo: The American University in Cairo Press.

———, ed. 2002. *The Egyptian Labor Market in an Era of Reform.* Cairo: The American University in Cairo Press.

Assaad, Ragui, and Malak Rouchdy. 1999. Poverty and Poverty Alleviation Strategies in Egypt. *Cairo Papers in Social Science* 22, 1.

Aswani, 'Ala al-. 2003. *'Imarat Ya'qubyan.* Cairo: Maktabat Madbuli.

Ayubi, Nazih. 1995. *Overstating the Arab State.* London: I.B. Tauris.

Baron, Beth. 2003. "Islam, Philanthropy, and Political Culture in Interwar Egypt: The Activism of Labiba Ahmad." In *Poverty and Charity in Middle*

Eastern Contexts, ed. Michael Bonner, Mine Ener, and Amy Singer, 239–54. New York: State University of New York Press.

Barry, Andrew, Thomas Osborne, and Nikolas Rose, eds. 1996. *Foucault and Political Reason: Liberalism, Neo-Liberalism, and Rationalities of Rule.* Chicago: The University of Chicago Press.

Bayat, Asef. 1998. *Street Politics: Poor People's Movements in Iran.* Cairo: The American University in Cairo Press.

Belliot, Marcel. 1993. "Le Grand Caire: Dix ans après." *Cahiers de l'I.A.U.R.I.F.* 104–105: 166–82.

BenNefissa, Sarah. 1999. "The Haqq al-'Arab: Conflict Resolution and Distinctive Features of Legal Pluralism in Contemporary Egypt." In *Legal Pluralism in the Arab World,* ed. Beaudoin Dupret, Maurits Berger, and Laila al-Zwaini, 145–57. The Hague: Kluwer Law International.

———. 2002. "Cityonneté Morale en Égypte: Une association entre État et Frères musulman." In *Associations et pouvoirs dans le monde arabe,* ed. Sarah BenNefissa and Sari Hanafi. Paris: Editions du CNRS.

Bibars, Iman. 2001. *Victims and Heroines: Women, Welfare, and the Egyptian State.* London: Zed Press.

Bonner, Michael, Mine Ener, and Amy Singer, eds. 2003. *Poverty and Charity in Middle Eastern Contexts.* New York: State University of New York Press.

Botiveau, Bernard. 1987–88. "Faits de Vengeance et Concurrence de Systèmes de Droits." *Peuples Mediterraneens* 41–42: 153–66.

Bourdieu, Pierre. 1977. *Outline of a Theory of Practice.* Cambridge: Cambridge University Press.

———. 2001. *Masculine Domination,* trans. Richard Rice. Stanford: California University Press.

Brass, Paul. 2000. "Foucault Steals Political Science." *Annual Review of Political Science* 3: 305–30.

Brigg, Morgan. 2001. "Empowering NGOs: The Microcredit Movement through Foucault's Notion of Dispositif." *Alternatives* 26, 3: 233–58.

Brown, Kenneth, ed. 1989. *État, ville et movements sociaux au Maghreb et au Moyen Orient.* Paris: L'Harmmattan.

Brown, Nathan. 1990. "Brigands and State Building: The Invention of Banditry in Modern Egypt." *Comparative Studies in Society and History* 32: 258–81.

Burchell, Graham, Colin Gordon, and Peter Miller, eds. 1991. *The Foucault Effect: Studies in Governmentality.* Chicago: The University of Chicago Press.

Burke III, Edmund. 1989. "Towards a History of Urban Collective Action in the Middle East: Continuities and Change 1750–1980." In *État, ville et movements sociaux au Maghreb et au Moyen Orient,* ed. Kenneth Brown, 42–56. Paris: L'Harmmattan.

Castells, Manuel. 2002. "The Culture of Cities in the Information Age, 1999." In *The Castells Reader in Cities and Social Theory,* ed. Ida Susser, 367–89. Oxford, UK: Blackwell.

Central Agency for Public Mobilization and Statistics (CAPMAS). March 1998. *Ihsa' al-Khadamat al-Ijtima'iyya* [Statistics of Social Services]. Reference no. 1996/12321–71.

———. Markaz Nuzum al-Ma'lumat al-Jiyughrafiyya [Center for Geographical Information]. Qism Bulaq al-Dakrur. Map of Bulaq al-Dakrur.

Chatterjee, Partha. 2004. *The Politics of the Governed: Reflections on Popular Politics in Most of the World*. New York: Columbia University Press.

Cohen, Stanley. 1980. *Folk Devils and Moral Panic: The Creation of Mods and Rockers*. 2nd ed. New York: St. Martin's Press.

Connell, R. W. 1995. *Masculinities*. Berkeley: University of California Press.

Coronil, Fernando. 1997. *The Magical State: Nature, Money, and Modernity in Venezuela*. Chicago: The University of Chicago Press.

Dali, Marwa Ahmed, el-. 2000. *Private Philanthropy in Egypt: Institutionalized Private Philanthropy as a Mechanism for Sustainable Community Development*. Unpublished MA Thesis, American University in Cairo.

Davis, Hannah. 1992. "Taking up Space in Tlemcen: The Islamist Occupation of Urban Algiers: Interview with Rabia Bekkar." *Middle East Report* 179: 14–15.

Dean, Mitchell. 1992. "A Genealogy of the Government of Poverty." *Economy and Society* 21, 3: 215–251.

———. 1994. *Critical and Effective Histories: Foucault's Methods and Historical Sociology*. London: Routledge.

DeBoulet, Agnès. 1990. "État, squatters et maitrise de l'espace. *Égypte*." *Monde Arabe* 1: 79–96.

de Certeau, Michel. 1984. *The Practice of Everyday Life*, trans. Steven Rendall. Berkeley and Los Angeles: University of California Press.

Denis, Eric. 1998. "La Nahda *'umraniya* figure de la libéralisation: la déclinaison locale, au Caire, d'un nouveau mode d'habiter des élites métropolitaines." Mimeo.

Denis, Eric, and and François Moriconi-Ebrard. 1995. "Le Caire face au desert." *Urbanisme* 284: 21–7.

De Soto, Hernando. 1989. *The Other Path: The Economic Answer to Terrorism*. New York: Basic Books.

Donzelot, Jacques. 1979. *The Policing of Families*, trans. Robert Hurley. New York: Pantheon.

Doorman, Bill. 2002. "Authoritarianism and Sustainability in Cairo: What Failed Urban Development Projects Tell Us about Egyptian Politics." In *Planning Cities: Sustainability and Growth in the Developing World*, ed. Roger Zetter and Rodney White, 146–66. Rugby, Warwickshire: ITDG Publishing

Egyptian Organization for Human Rights. 2003. *Al 'Itiqal al-Siyasi, Siyasa al-Bab al-Mughlaq, wa al-'Itiqal al-Jina'i: Siyasat al-Bab al-Dawar* [Political detention, the policy of closed doors, criminal detention, the policy of revolving door]. A report on the phenomenon of arbitrary detention under the emergency laws. Cairo: EOHR.

Elyachar, Julia. 2001. "Finance internationale, micro-credit et religion de la so-
ciété civile en Égypte." *Critique Internationale* 13.

Ener, Mine. 1999. "Prohibitions on Begging and Loitering in Nineteenth Century Egypt." *Die Welt des Islams* 39, 3: 319–39.

———. 2003. *Managing Egypt's Poor and the Politics of Benevolence 1800–1952.*
New York: Princeton University Press.

Escobar, Arturo. 1984–85. "Discourse and Power in Development: Michel Foucault and the Relevance of his Work to the Third World." *Alternatives* 10:
377–400.

Fahmy, Khaled. 1999. "The Police and the People in Nineteenth-Century
Egypt." *Die Welt des Islams* 39, 3: 340–77.

Farah, Nadia Ramsis. 1997. *Poverty Alleviation with a Focus on Women Headed
Households and Micro Credit Programs.* New York: UNICEF.

Fine, Ben. 2001. *Social Capital versus Social Theory: Political Economy and Social
Science at the Turn of the Millennium.* London: Routledge.

Finnemore, Martha. 1997. "Redefining Development at the World Bank." In
*International Development and the Social Sciences: Essays on the History and Pol-
itics of Knowledge,* ed. Frederick Cooper and Randall Packard, 203–27.
Berkeley: University of California Press.

Foucault, Michel. 1995. *Discipline and Punish,* 2nd Vintage Books ed., *trans.*
Alan Sheridan. New York: Vintage Books.

———. 1991. "Governmentality." In *The Foucault Effect: Studies in Governmentality,* ed. Graham Burchell, Colin Gordon, and Peter Miller, 87–104.
Chicago: The University of Chicago Press.

———. 2003a. "The Subject and Power." In *The Essential Foucault: Selections
from Essential Works of Foucault, 1954–1984,* ed. Paul Rabinow and Nikolas
Rose, 126–44. New York: The New Press.

———. 2003b. "'Omnes Et Singulatim': Toward a Critique of Political Reason." In *The Essential Foucault: Selections from Essential Works of Foucault,
1954–1984,* ed. Paul Rabinow and Nikolas Rose, 180–201. New York: The
New Press.

Ghannam, Farha. 2002. *Remaking the Modern: Space, Relocation, and the Politics
of Identity.* Berkeley and Los Angeles: University of California Press.

Ghoussoub, Mai. 2000. "Chewing Gum, Insatiable Women, and Foreign Ene-
mies: Male Fears and the Arab Media." In *Imagined Masculinities: Male
Identity and Culture in the Modern Middle East,* ed. Mai Ghoussoub and
Emma Sinclair-Webb, 227–35. London: Saqi Books.

Gill, Stephen. 1995. "Globalisation, Market Civilisation, and Disciplinary Neoliberalism." *Millennium* 24, 3: 399–423.

Goldstein, Donna M. 2003. *Laughter Out of Place: Race, Class, Violence, and Sexuality in a Rio Shantytown.* Berkeley: University of California Press.

Gupta, Akhil. 1995. "Blurred Boundaries: The Discourse of Corruption, the
Culture of Politics, and the Imagined State." *American Ethnologist* 22,
2: 375–402.

———. 2001. "Governing Population: The Integrated Child Development
Services Program in India." In *States of Imagination: Ethnographic Explo-*

rations of the Postcolonial State, ed. Thomas Blom Hansen and Finn Stepputat, 65–96. Durham, NC: Duke University Press.

Gupta, Akhil, and James Ferguson. 1997. "Discipline and Practice: 'The Field' as Site, Method, and Location in Anthropology." In *Anthropological Locations: Boundaries and Grounds of a Field Science,* ed. Akhil Gupta and James Ferguson, 1–46. Berkeley: University of California Press.

Haenni, Patrick. 1997. "Gérer les normes exterieurs: Le penchant occidental de la bienfaisance islamique en Égypte." *Égypte, Monde Arabe,* 30–31, 2&3: 275–91.

Hafez, Shirin. 2003. "The Terms of Empowerment: Islamic Women Activists in Egypt." *Cairo Papers in Social Science* 24, 4.

Haj Ali, Smail. 1994. "L'Islamisme dans la ville: Espace urbain et contre centralité." *Maghreb-Machrek,* 64–97.

Hall, Stuart, Cats Crither, Tony Jefferson, John Clarke, and Brian Roberts. 1979. *Policing the Crisis: Mugging, the State and Law and Order.* New York: Holmes and Meier Publishers.

Hammond, Andrew. 1998. "Reining in the Police." *Cairo Times* vol. 2, issue 1. http://www.cairotimes.com/cairotim...tent/issues/hurights/reininb1.html.

Hammouda, Dahlia. 1998. "Mobilising Charity." *Al-Ahram Weekly* 408, 17–23 December.

Hansen, Thomas Blom, and Finn Stepputat, eds. 2001. *States of Imagination: Ethnographic Explorations of the Postcolonial State.* Durham, NC: Duke University Press.

Hatem, Mervat. 1992. "Economic and Political Liberalization in Egypt and the Demise of State Feminism." *International Journal of Middle East Studies* 24: 231–51.

Hindess, Barry. 1997. "Politics and Governmentality." *Economy and Society* 26, 2: 257–72.

———. 2000. "Divide and Govern." In *Governing Modern Societies,* ed. Richard V. Ericson and Nico Stehr, 118–40. Toronto: Univeristy of Toronto Press.

———. 2001. "The Liberal Government of Unfreedom." *Alternatives* 26, 2: 93–111.

———. "Liberalism—What's in a Name?." In *Global Governmentality: Governing International Spaces,* ed. Wendy Larner and William Walters, 23–39. London: Routledge.

Hirschkind, Charles. 2001. "The Ethics of Listening: Cassette-Sermon Audition in Contemporary Egypt." *American Ethnologist* 28, 3: 623–49.

Hoodfar, Homa. 1997. *Between Marriage and the Market: Intimate Politics and Survival in Cairo.* Berkeley and Los Angeles: University of California Press.

Hourani, Albert. 1981. "Ottoman Reform and the Politics of the Notables." In *The Emergence of the Modern Middle East,* 36–66. London: Macmillan Press.

Human Rights Watch. 2003. "Charged with Being Children: Egyptian Police Abuse of Children of Need of Protection." *Human Rights Watch* 15, 1(E). February.

Human Rights Watch. 2004. *In a Time of Torture: The Assault on Justice in Egypt's Crackdown on Homosexual Conduct.* http://hrw.org/reports/2004/egypt0304/4.htm.

Hunt, Alan. 1996. "Governing the City: Liberalism and Early Modern Modes of Governance." In *Foucault and Political Reason: Liberalism, Neo-Liberalism, and Rationalities of Government,* ed. Andrew Barry, Thomas Osborne, and Nikolas Rose, 167–88. Chicago: The University of Chicago Press.

Ismail, Salwa. 1996. "The Politics of Space in Urban Cairo: Informal Communities and the State." *Arab Studies Journal* 4 (Fall): 119–32.

———. 1998. "Confronting the Other: Identity, Culture, Politics, and Conservative Islamism in Egypt." *International Journal of Middle East Studies* 30, 2: 199–225. Reprinted in *Rethinking Islamist Politics: Culture, the State, and Islamism.* London: I.B. Tauris, 2003.

———. 2000. "The Popular Movement Dimensions of Contemporary Militant Islamism: Socio-spatial Determinants in the Cairo Urban Setting." *Comparative Studies in Society and History* 42, 2: 363–93. Reprinted in *Rethinking Islamist Politics: Culture, the State and Islamism.* London: I.B. Tauris, 2003.

———. 2003. *Rethinking Islamist Politics: Culture, the State, and Islamism.* London: I.B. Tauris.

———. 2004. "Islamist Movements as Social Movements: Contestation and Identity Frames." *Historical Reflections* 30, 3: 385–402.

Joseph, Gilbert M., and Daniel Nugent, eds. 1994. *Everyday Forms of State Formation: Revolution and the Negotiation of Rule in Modern Mexico.* Durham, NC: Duke University Press.

Kalpagam, U. 2002. "Colonial Governmentality and the Public Sphere in India." *Journal of Historical Sociology* 15, 1: 35–58.

Kandiyoti, Deniz. 1994. "The Paradoxes of Masculinity: Some Thoughts on Segregated Societies." In *Dislocating Masculinity: Comparative Ethnologies,* ed. Andrea Cornwall and Nancy Lindisfarne, 197–213. London: Routledge.

Kadi, Galila el. 1990. "Trente Ans de Planification Urbaine au Caire." *Revue Tiers Monde* 31, 121, (January–March): 185–207.

———. 1995. "Le Caire à la recherche d'un centre." *Annales de Geographie,* 16: 37–72.

Keith, Michael, and Steve Pile. 1993. "Introduction: The Politics of Place." *In Place and the Politics of Identity,* ed. Michael Keith and Steve Pile, 1–21. London: Routledge.

Kharoufi, Mostafa. 1991. "The Informal Dimension of Urban Activity in Egypt: Some Recent Work." In *Informal Sector in Egypt,* ed. Nicholas Hopkins. *Cairo Papers in the Social Sciences*: 8–20.

Kholy, Heba Aziz el. 2002. *Defiance and Compliance: Negotiating Gender in Low-Income Cairo.* New York and Oxford: Berghan Books.

Koptiuch, Kristin. 1999. *A Poetics of Political Economy in Egypt.* Minneapolis: University of Minnesota Press.

Korayem, Karima. 2001. "How Do the Poor Cope with Increased Employment Inadequacy in Egypt." Paper presented to The Second Mediterranean Social and Political Research Meeting, Florence, March 21–25.

Labib, Albert, and Tiziana Battain. 1991. "Le Caire-mégalopole perçue par ses habitants." *Égypte/Monde Arabe* 5, 1: 19–31.

Lefebvre, Henri. 2001. *The Production of Space,* trans. Donald Nicholson-Smith. Oxford, UK: Blackwell.

Low, Setha M., and Denise Laurence-Zuniga. 2003. "Locating Culture." In *The Anthropology of Space and Place: Locating Culture,* ed. Seth M. Low and Denise Laurence-Zuniga, 1–47. Oxford, UK: Blackwell.

Lowy, Paul. 1979. "Espace ideologique et quadriallage policier: le 26 Janvier 1978 à Tunis." *Hérodote* 13: 103–14.

MacLeod, Arlene Elow. 1991. *Accommodating Protest: Working Women, the New Veiling, and Change in Cairo.* New York: Columbia University Press.

Mahdi, Alia el. 2002. "The Labor Absorption Capacity of the Informal Sector in Egypt." In *The Egyptian Labor Market in an Era of Reform,* ed. Ragui Assaad, 99–130. Cairo: The American University in Cairo Press.

Mahmood, Saba. 2001. "Rehearsed Spontaneity and the Conventionality of Ritual: Disciplines of Salat." *American Ethnologist* 28, 4: 827–53.

Mann, Michael. 1986. "The Autonomous Power of the State: Its Origins, Mechanisms, and Results." In *States in History,* ed. John A. Hall, 109–36. Oxford and New York: Basil Blackwell.

Markaz Qadaya al-Mar'a al-Masriyya. 2000. *Al-Taharur min al-Faqr* [Liberation from Poverty]. Cairo: Markaz Qadaya al-Mar'a al-Misriyya.

Marsum Biqanun Raqam 98 L-sana 1945 Khas bil-Mutashardin wa al-Mushtabah fihum [Law 98 of the Year 1945 Concerning Vagrants and Suspects]. Cairo: Al-Hay'a al-'Ama l-shi'un al-Matabi' al-Amiriyya, 1987.

Martinez, Luis. 2000. *The Algerian Civil War 1990–1998,* trans. Jonathan Derrik. London: Hurst and Company.

Mattson, Ingrid. 2003. "Status-Based Definitions of Need in Early Islamic Zakat and Maintenance Law." In *Poverty and Charity in Middle Eastern Contexts,* ed. Bonner, Michael, Mine Ener, and Amy Singer, 31–51. New York: State University of New York Press.

Mbembe, Achille. 1992. "Prosaics of Servitude and Authoritarian Civilities." *Public Culture* 5, 1: 123–45.

———. 2001. *On the Postcolony.* Berkeley: University of California Press.

McCarthy, John D. 1996. "Constraints and Opportunities in Adopting, Adapting, and Inventing." In *Comparative Perspectives on Social Movements,* ed. Doug McAdam, John D. McCarthy, and Mayer N. Zald, 141–51. Cambridge: Cambridge University Press.

Meijer, Roel, ed. 2000. *Alienation or Integration of Arab Youth: Between Family, State, and Street.* Richmond, Surrey: Curzon Press.

Messiri, Sawsan el. 1977. "The Changing Role of the *Futuwwa* in the Social Structure of Cairo." In *Patrons and Clients in Mediterranean Societies,* ed. Ernest Gellner and John Waterbury, 239–53. London: Duckworth.

———. 1978. *Ibn al-Balad: A Concept of Egyptian Identity.* Leiden, Holland: E. J. Brill.

Messiri Nadim, Nawal al-. 1987. "Family Relationships in a 'Harah' in Cairo." In *Arab Society: Social Sciences Perspectives,* ed. Nicholas S. Hopkins and Saad Eddin Ibrahim, 212–22. Cairo: American University in Cairo Press.

————. 1979. "The Concept of the Hara: A Historical and Sociological Study of Al-Sukkariyya." *Annales Islamologiques,* 15: 313–48.

Migdal, Joel S. 2001. *State in Society: Studying How States and Societies Constitute One Another.* Cambridge: Cambridge University Press.

Mitchell, Timothy. 1989. *Colonising Egypt.* Cairo: The American University in Cairo Press.

————. 1990. "Everyday Metaphors of Power." *Theory and Society* 19: 545–77.

————. 1991. "The Limits of the State: Beyond Statist Approaches and Their Critics." *American Political Science Review* 85, 1: 77–96

————. 2002. "Dreamland." In *Rule of Experts: Egypt, Techno-Politics, Modernity,* 272–303. Berkeley: University of California Press.

Moktar, May, and Jackline Wahba. 2002. "Informalization of Labor in Egypt." In *The Egyptian Labor Market in an Era of Reform,* ed. Ragui Assaad, 131–57. Cairo: The American University in Cairo Press.

Al-Nadim Center for the Treatment and Psychological Rehabilitation of Victims of Violence. 2002. *al-Ta'dhib fi Misr, Haqa'iq wa shihadat* [Torture in Egypt: Facts and Testimonies]. Cairo: al-Nadim Center.

National Cooperative Business Association et al. 2003. Egypt Small and Emerging Business Development Organizations Project (SEBDO). Bashayer El Kheir: An Impact Tracking Study. Final Report Submitted to the United States Agency for International Development (USAID).

Navaro-Yashin, Yael. 2002. *Faces of the State: Secularism and Pubic Life in Turkey.* Princeton, NJ: Princeton University Press.

Nowaihi, Magda M. al-. 1999. "Constructions of Masculinity in Two Egyptian Novels." In *Intimate Selving in Arab Families: Gender, Self and Identity,* ed. Suad Joseph, 235–63. Syracuse, NY: Syracuse University Press.

O'Hanlon, Rosalind, and David Washbrook. 1992. "After Orientalism; Culture, Criticism, and Politics in the Third World." *Comparative Studies in Society and History* 34, 1: 141–67.

Ortner, Sherry B. 1995. "Resistance and the Problem of Ethnographic Refusal." *Comparative Studies in Society and History* 37, 1: 173–93.

Osborne, Thomas. 1996. "Security and Vitality: Drains, Liberalism, and Power in the Nineteenth Century." In *Foucault and Political Reason: Liberalism, Neo-Liberalism, and Rationalities of Rule,* ed. Andrew Barry, Thomas Osborne, and Nikolas Rose, 99–121. Chicago: The University of Chicago Press.

Pasquino, Pascale. 1991. "Theatrium Politicum: The Genealogy of Capital—Police and the State of Prosperity." In *The Foucault Effect: Studies in Governmentality,* ed. Graham Burchell, Colin Gordon, and Peter Miller, 105–18. Chicago: The University of Chicago Press.

Peletz, Michael G. 2002. *Islamic Modern: Religious Courts and Cultural Politics in Malaysia.* Princeton, NJ: Princeton University Press.

Peteet, Julie. 2000. "Male Gender and Rituals of Resistance in the Palestinian Intifada: A Cultural Politics of Violence." In *Imagined Masculinities: Male Identity and Culture in the Modern Middle East,* ed. Mai Ghoussoub and Emma Sinclair-Webb, 103–26. London: Saqi Books.

Portes, Alejandro, Manuel Castells, and L. Benton, eds. 1989. *The Informal Economy: Studies in Advanced and Less-Developed Countries.* Baltimore: Johns Hopkins.

Prakash, Gyan. 1992. "Can the 'Subaltern' Ride? A Reply to O'Hanlon and Washbrook." *Comparative Studies in Society and History* 34, 1: 168–84.

Posusney, Marsha Pripstein. 1997. *Labor and the State in Egypt.* New York: Columbia University Press.

Qanun al-Ijra'at al-Jina'iya [Law of Criminal Procedures]. *Al-Muhamah.* Supplement Issues 5&6 May and June 1988. Cairo.

Rabinow, Paul, and Nikolas Rose, eds. 2003. *The Essential Foucault: Selections from Essential Works of Foucault, 1954–1984.* New York: The New Press.

Rady, Faiza. 1999. "Banking for the Poor." *Al-Ahram Weekly* 443, 19–25 August.

Rafeq, Abd al-Karim. 1990. "Public Morality in Eighteenth Century Damascus." *Revue d'Études de Monde Musulman et de la Méditerranée* 55–56: 18–196.

Raymond, André. 1968. "Quartiers et mouvements populaires au Caire au XVIIIème." In *Political and Social Change in Modern Egypt*, ed. P.M. Holt, 104–16. London: Oxford University Press.

———. 1994. "Le Caire traditionnel: Une ville administrée par ses communautés?" *Maghreb-Machrek* (1er trimestre): 9–16.

Rose, Nikolas. 1996. "Governing Advanced Liberal Democracies." In *Foucault and Political Reason: Liberalism, Neo-Liberalism, and Rationalities of Rule*, ed. Andrew Barry, Thomas Osborne, and Nikolas Rose, 37–64. Chicago: The University of Chicago Press.

Rose, Nikolas, and Peter Miller. 1992. "Political Power beyond the State: Problematics of Government." *British Journal of Sociology* 43, 2: 173–205.

Roy, Ananya. 2003. *City Requiem, Calcutta: Gender and the Politics of Poverty.* Minneapolis: University of Minnesota Press.

Sabra, Adam. 2001. *Poverty and Charity in Medieval Islam.* Cambridge: Cambridge University Press.

Saktanber, Ayse. 2002. "We Pray Like You Have Fun: New Islamic Youth in Turkey between Intellectualism and Popular Culture." In *Fragments of Culture: The Everyday of Modern Turkey*, ed. Deniz Kandiyoti and Ayse Saktanber, 254–76. New Brunswick, NJ: Rutgers University Press.

Sami, Ahmed. 1923. "Juvenile Vagrants and Delinquents." *L'Égypte Contemporaine* 14 (January): 250–72.

Sawi, Ali al-, ed. 1996. *Qadaya al-Tanmiya: al-Ashwa'iyat wa Namadhiz al-Tanmiya* [Issues of Development: Haphazard Communities and Models of Development]. Cairo: Cairo University, Center for the Study of Developing Countries.

Sayer, Derek. 1994. "Everyday Forms of State Formation: Some Dissident Remarks on 'Hegemony.'" In *Everyday Forms of State Formation: Revolution and the Negotiation of Rule in Modern Mexico*, ed. Gilbert M. Joseph and Daniel Nugent, 366–77. Durham, NC: Duke University Press.

Scott, James. 1990. *Domination and the Arts of Resistance: Hidden Transcripts.* New Haven, CT: Yale University Press.

Seddon, David. 1989. "Popular Protest and Political Opposition in Tunisia, Morocco and Sudan." In *État, ville et movements sociaux au Maghreb et au Moyen Orient*, ed. Kenneth Brown, 179–97. Paris: L'Harmmattan.

Shahine, Gihan. 2001. "Good Will Hunting." *Al-Ahram Weekly* 563, 6–12 December.

Sibley, David. 1995. *Geographies of Exclusion: Society and Difference in the West*. London and New York: Routledge.

Singerman, Diane. 1995. *Avenues of Participation: Family, Politics, and Networks in Urban Quarters of Cairo*. Princeton, NJ: Princeton University Press.

Siyam, Imad. 2001. "Al-Harka al-Islamiyya wa al-Gam'iyyat al-Ahliyya fi Misr" [The Islamist Movement and Civil Associations in Egypt]. In *Al-Gam'iyyat al-Ahliyya al-Islamiyya fi Misr* [Islamic Civil Associations in Egypt], ed. 'Abd al-Ghaffar Shukr, 73–150. Cairo: Markaz al-Buhuth al-Arabiyya.

Slymovics, Susan. 1995. "Hassiba Ben Bouali, 'If You Could See Our Algeria': Women and Public Space in Algeria." *Middle East Report* (January–February): 8–13.

Soja, Edward. 1989. *Postmodern Geographies: The Reassertion of Space in Critical Social Theory*. London: Verso.

Sonbol, Amira el-Azhari. 2000. *The New Mamluks: Egyptian Society and Modern Feudalism*. Syracuse, NY: Syracuse University Press.

Stauth, George. 1991. "Gamaliyya: Informal Economy and Social Life in a Popular Quarter of Cairo." In Informal Sector in Egypt, ed. Nicholas Hopkins, 78–103. *Cairo Papers in the Social Sciences*.

Stewart, Dona J. 1999. "Changing Cairo: The Political Economy of Urban Form." *International Journal of Urban and Regional Research* 23, 1: 128–46.

Susser, Ida. 2002. *The Castells Reader in Cities and Social Theory*. Oxford, UK: Blackwell.

Tadros, Mariz Fikry. 1999a. *Micro Credit for Women: Does It Work?* Unpublished MA thesis, American University in Cairo.

———. 1999b. "A Question of Security." *Al-Ahram Weekly* 448, 23–29 December.

Taussig, Michael. 1992. "Malfecium: State Fetishism." In *The Nervous System*. New York: Routledge.

Tekce, Belgin, Linda Oldham, and Frederic Shorter. 1996. *A Place to Live: Families and Child Health in a Cairo Neighborhood*. Cairo: American University in Cairo Press.

Tripp, Aili Mari. 1997. *Changing the Rules: The Politics of Liberalization and the Urban Informal Economy in Tanzania*. Berkeley: University of California Press.

United Nations Development Program (UNDP). 2003. MicroStart Egypt, Assessment Report. http://www.uncdf.org/english/countries/egypt/microfinance/egyptdb.pdf.

Vasile, Elizabeth. 1997. "Devotion as Distinction, Piety as Power: Religious Revival and the Transformation of Space in the Illegal Settlements of Tunis." In *Population, Poverty, and Politics in Middle Eastern Cities*, ed. Michael Bonine, 113–40. Gainesville: University of Florida Press.

Wali, Mamduh al-. 1993. *Sukkan al-Ishash wa al-'Ashwa'iyat: Al-Kharita al-Iskan-niya lil Muhafazat* [The Inhabitants of Huts and Haphazard Communities: A Housing Map of the Governorates]. Cairo: Engineers Syndicate.

Williams, Caroline. 2002. "Transforming the Old: Cairo's New Medieval City." *Middle East Journal* 56, 3: 457–75.

Young, Tom. 1995. "'A Project to be Realised': Global Liberalism and Contemporary Africa." *Millennium* 24, 3: 527–46.

Žižek, Slavoj. 1989. *The Sublime Object of Ideology*. London: Zed Books.

Arabic Newspapers and Weeklies

al-Ahali
Al-Ahram
al-Ahrar
al-Akhbar
al-Anba' al-Dawliyya
al-'Arabi
al-Jumhuriyya
al-Midan
al-Mussawar
Ruz al-Yusuf
Sawt al-Umma
al-Usb'
al-Wafd

Legal and Government Documents

Ministry of the Interior (MI), Juvenile Police Department. Police Report 462/1/2 M. 27 November 1999.

Ministry of the Interior (MI), Juvenile Police Department. Police Report 58/1/2/3 M. 26 January 1999.

Ministry of Interior (MI), Juvenile Police. Division of Social Security. Police Report of Investigation 58/1/2/3 M. 01 February 1999.

Giza Security Directorate, Bulaq al-Dakrur Police Station. Police Report 3862/97. 5 May 1997.

Public Prosecutor. Prosecutor Report Case 3862/97. 5 May 1997.

Hisham Mubarak Center for Law. *Muzakarat b-difa'*? Presented to the Public Prosecution Office in the criminal case 2658 of the year 2000.

Hisham Mubarak Center for Law. Appeal Case 509 on 17 June 2003 Against the Public Prosecution Office.

Index

Abrams, Philip, 186n.10
Abu Haggag, Yusuf, 137
Abu-Lughod, Lila, 33
Abu Risha, Zuleikha, 194n.3
Abu Sina, citizen confrontation with police in, 161, 162
al-'Adawiyya (clan), 57–58
ADEW (Association for Development of Egyptian Women), 88
adolescents, monitoring and policing, 155–56
agricultural land, expansion of urban areas onto, 6, 31
Akhbar al-Yum, charity campaign of, 80
al-Ahrar (newspaper), 142
al-Akhbar newspaper, charity campaign of, 80
Alam, Tariq, 80
Algeria
    ties of rising notability to Islamists in, 52–53
    youth-police relations in, 123
Algiers
    reappropriation of city spaces by FIS in, 187n.15
    territorial identity of gangs in, 99
Ali, Hajj, 187n.15
Ali, Kamran Asdar, 186n.12, 192n.17
Amin, Mustafa, 80
Amnesty International, 195n.13
Anagnost, Ann, 56–57, 194n.4
Annual Report of Judicial Advisor (1913), 196n.16
Annual Reports of Security Condition (Ministry of Interior), 154

Ansar al-Sunna al-Muhammadiyya (religious association), xxxviii, 103–5, 106, 190n.6
Arab Gulf, marriage with male tourists from, 118, 193n.11
arbitration, Islamist activists engaged in, xl, 56
arbitration councils (*majalis tahkim*), 36, 37, 38
architectural renaissance (*nahda 'umraniyya*), 31
area (*mantiqa*), 19
arrest
    of children, 156
    of female relatives, tactic of, 151–52
    quota of, fabrication of drug charges to fill, 150
    under utilities provisions, to reduce involvement in demonstrations, 154
    young men's experience of, 121–22, 123, 146–49
artisanal quarters, setting up of new, 5
al-'Ashra (Street Ten), 12
'ashwa'iyyat (haphazard), 1
    citizens' initiative in development of, 1
    in representation of space, 4–5
Association of Iskan al-Mustaqbal, 80–81
al-Aswani, 'Ala, 54
authority
    factors contributing to establishment of personal, 37, 38–39

209

SALWA ISMAIL is Senior Lecturer in Middle East politics at the University of Exeter. She is the author of *Rethinking Islamist Politics: Culture, the State, and Islamism.*